THE CREATIVE MYSTIQUE

How to Manage It, Nurture It, and Make It Pay

THE CREATIVE MYSTIQUE

How to Manage It, Nurture It, and Make It Pay

JOHN M. KEIL

Executive Vice President,
Executive Creative Director
Dancer Fitzgerald Sample
New York, New York

JOHN WILEY & SONS

New York • Chichester • Brisbane •
Toronto • Singapore

RONALD SERIES ON
MARKETING MANAGEMENT

Series Editor: FREDERICK E. WEBSTER, Jr.
The Amos Tuck School of Business Administration
Dartmouth College

Library of Congress Cataloging in Publication Data:
Keil, John M.
The creative mystique.

(Ronald series on marketing management)
Includes index.
1. Creative ability in business. I. Title.
II. Series.
HD53.K45   1985   650.1   84-27059

ISBN 0-471-87961-4

Printed in the United States of America
10 9 8 7 6 5 4 3 2 1

TO BO

Acknowledgments

As an opening note to this book, I'd like to absolve anyone and everyone I've worked with or for by saying that the opinions (rash or wise) are mine unless otherwise noted and do not reflect the policies of Dancer Fitzgerald Sample Holdings, Inc., or any of its clients, or any other companies or organizations. The facts have been checked and, to the best of my knowledge, are correct, although in some of the reminiscences things may get a bit hazy.

I'd also like to thank some of the people who have been invaluable in helping with this book. A doff of the chapeau to Dr. Frederick E. Webster, Jr., E. B. Olsen Professor of Marketing at The Amos Tuck School of Business Administration at Dartmouth College, for his prodding to get the thing moving and his sage advice while doing it; to Steven Kippur, the original editor, and John Mahaney, who picked up when Steve moved on to other projects, for their suggestions, nudgings, and guidance; to Stuart B. Upson, Chairman of the Board of Dancer Fitzgerald Sample Holdings, Inc., for his policy reading (and proofreading) of every word and for his wisdom and encouragement; and to Barbara Ziegler for her role as typist, advisor, and cheerleader. And to all of the creative cohorts and account people and clients and friends and foes with whom I've worked over the years who have stuffed me with the material that you'll soon digest and relish. Finally, to my family, who have been patient and encouraging and have had to listen too many times to "Hey Bo, how does this sound?" They never complained. They often helped. (The section on living with a creative person in the last chapter was stimulated by and mainly provided by my wife, Barbara.) And so away we go and over the top and on with the show.

J. M. K.

Contents

INTRODUCTION

What's so unusual about being creative?

Everything. The way creative people live, think, work, interrelate, produce. Each one seems to do it differently from each other. And collectively they approach the challenges of their callings differently from people who don't consider themselves creative. It's a mystique that seems to surround every facet of the creative process. But if we were to take all of the creative souls in the world and put them together, there might be certain general characteristics and habits that we could classify as usual. At least among them.

Because the creative side of the brain works differently from the other (we are told that the right side whips along darting in and out of moods and thoughts and rivers of consciousness, while the straight-down-the-middle, orderly left side tries to organize things) everything about it is unusual. And if the creative side is dominant, the left side usually throws up its hand, sighs, and mutters resignedly, "I tried, Lord knows I tried." Well, in life there are the doers and the directors, and in the world of creativity the directors are the left side. They are the ones who try to organize the doers and make their lives productive and worthwhile. To be successful they had better know something about what the doers are doing, including how they do it. Not so difficult when one is talking about the partners of a law firm dealing with bright young attorneys. There are certain rules, instincts, and procedures gathered from years of training and experience that they can pass on to their successors. The same is true of engineers and, in a way, sales executives. It's because in all of these fields of endeavor the left side of the brain is probably dominant. That's not to say that the creative right side isn't working away. It's just that order and practicality and analytic qualities and common sense are in the driver's seat.

But when it comes to dealing with the creative process we're talking about the unusual. Hello Mr. Right-Side. Unfortunately, among the directors charged with overseeing the creative doers, there seems to be a plethora of people who are constantly mystified as to how and what and why the creative doers do what they do. The creative mystique is very real to them.

And that's what this book is about.

How to take some of the mystery out of dealing with the unusual—the creative process. I hope you'll find some practical advice, guidelines, and thoughts on how to get better results no matter what kind of creativity you're involved with. Because my area of expertise is the advertising agency business, many of the more pertinent examples will be from this field. But that doesn't mean that the material isn't applicable elsewhere. I think you'll see that it is. At least the majority of it.

Take the chapter on making presentations, for example, the princi-

ples, methods, procedures, and philosophies apply to just about anything or anytime you want to convey an idea or message, whether you're
a lawyer presenting a case to the jury, or a psychologist introducing a
new theory of patient care to a symposium of doctors, or a teacher opening a fall semester on Shakespeare. And the section on how the creative
mind works may give insights into how to get better results no matter
what the endeavor. I'll suggest ways of developing objectives and strategies, which have to be the starting point of creative activities, whether
it's writing a novel (Has anyone ever written a successsful novel by just
sitting down and working it out as the words appear on the computer
screen or typing paper?), a popular song (Is it a love song or a blues or a
story set to music? Even June-moon-cartoon has to have some idea as to
where it's going.), or an advertising campaign (preparing advertising
without knowing the purpose of the advertising is an unconscionable
waste). One of the most frustrating things is to have to say: "Great solution. I wish it had something to do with the problem."

I'll use experience and expertise to talk about recruiting, getting
along with, evaluating, and, when necessary, terminating those creative
people who may be too usual to succeed in an arena that demands the
unusual. We'll explore ways to judge creative efforts, including some
guidelines to follow when important decisions have to be made as to
what's good and what's not so good. I'll look at the increasingly important and often misused role that research is playing in the creative
world. And through it all, I'll touch on the qualities that seem to bolster
creative leadership, whether you're heading a team of architects, or
producing television commercials, or running a stable of promotional
writers for a department store, or presiding over a company whose reason for existence is developing new ideas.

While creative solutions are more often than not the result of careful
planning, long hours, hard work, and lots of mind probing, every so often an insight, the result of looking at a problem or situation in a new
way, results in unbelievable success. And having that ability to step
away from the usual and take an entirely different look at something is a
quality to develop, nurture, and cherish no matter what field you're in
or how dominant the left side of your brain is. Look what it did for a
little company called Mannington Mills.

THE CASE OF THE UNEXPECTED KISS

Mannington Mills, Inc. is a very successful manufacturer of hard surfaced floor coverings located in southern New Jersey. In the 1920s it was
a small company whose forte was printed, felt-base floor coverings in
which a series of flatbed presses printed tough enamel prints on a felt
backing to make flamboyantly colorful patterns at a modest price. Late
one night the president of the company, a hard driving, imaginative
Scotsman named Neil Campbell, stopped by the printing operation to
look at a new, experimental design he was interested in. Some test runs
had been done that afternoon. The foreman, who was then shutting
down the operation, showed Campbell the results. The CEO wanted to
see the first run of the afternoon. "No good," said the foreman. "I threw
it away." He gestured to some discarded sections of floor covering.
Campbell picked up one of the discards, which was lying face down
against the blank back side of another discard. To his amazement he had
in front of him not one but two samples of the new pattern. The foreman
had thrown the rejected piece down before it was dry. It had kissed the
blank backing and accidentally transferred the pattern almost perfectly,
not unlike the principle of offset printing. "Two for the price of one,"
Campbell thought.

The next day, Campbell set up test runs, thickening the original
paints, and then, at the end of the assembly line, kissing the finished
design with a blank role of felt backing, thus transferring half of the paint
thickness in a perfect duplicate of the original.

The "kiss" process was patented by Mannington Mills, establishing
them as a leader in low-cost floor covering because this "light bulb" or
application of instant creativity allowed them to undersell their competitors. "Ah ha," you say, "that's not creativity, that's opportunism." True.
But how many of us would have looked at the discarded pattern and
said: "What a mess. Look, it got paint all over that other backing. We've
got to do something about getting faster drying paints." I contend that
creativity is more than a process or approach. It's also a state of mind
that's always alert and ready to turn any kind of stimulus into an idea.
It's the ability to look at things differently. Suggestions as to how to attain this state of mind will be covered later.

THE MOVABLE BRIDGE GAME

To me, one of the nicest examples of creativity fulfilling a need concerns my favorite uncle, Boyd Mullan. In the mid-1920s, in the era of slickers, knickers, and Model Ts, Boyd was attending Colgate University in upstate Hamilton, New York. Because his home was in Rochester, about 150 miles of hilly, high crowned, two-laned roads away, transportation was a challenge: no superhighways, no airplanes, and only the O. & W. Railroad connecting indecisively with the New York Central at Utica. So Boyd purchased a Ford Model T phaeton. To help pay for it, he would charge up to four passengers for rides to and from Colgate. However, he discovered that competition was steep. A good number of Rochesterians traveling to Colgate and other nearby colleges had the same idea. And so Boyd's right side went to work. He looked at the situation differently. "What could I offer that's more than transportation?" was his challenge. He removed the body of the phaeton (to those in their puberty, Henry Ford's early pride had a body like a large bathtub, with or without a soft roof. Boyd's was without) and replaced it with the tall wooden body of a milk wagon. He removed the racks for the milk bottles and put in a bridge table, four folding chairs, and a floor lamp operating from a small portable generator. Thus was born the Rochester-Colgate Movable Bridge Game. For four years, it was a tradition on U.S. 5, 20, and assorted side roads. People cheered when they rolled through hamlets and villages en route.

I like to think that this kind of creativity was somehow inherent in Boyd's success as a lawyer and eventual president of the New York State Bar Association. Of course, the fact that he was a droll after-dinner speaker didn't hurt. But that, too, is creativity fulfilling a need.

These two examples show creative solutions to problems by people who stepped away from the usual, looked at things from a different point of view. And they did it almost instinctively because they seem to have, if not a dominant, at least a swollen, right side of the brain. Most of the book, however, will be directed to the conscious use of creativity in problem solving: the challenges that creative people wrestle with, conquer or are frustrated by and get paid for solving day after day. In doing this I'll explore such subjects as the back burner and how to stoke it, getting on board the train of thought, when it's right to lie, an outline to set up the search for facts, the selling ballet and its part in a presentation, how research testing can help—and inhibit. I'll use examples and anecdotes to illustrate points and to break any potential turgidity. Realizing that all subjects may not be as interesting to all readers as they are to the author is a first step in creative awareness.

THE ADVERTISING AGENCY

At this point, and because much of what you will read has to do with relationships between advertising agencies and clients, it might be wise to explain, for the uninitiated, just how an advertising agency is structured and operates. Those readers who are familiar with the business might wish to skim this section and come back to intense perusal at the last section, "Who Needs It?"

Advertising agencies come in a variety of sizes and shapes, but because their principal role in life is the creating of advertising for their clients, the heart of any agency—no matter what its size or structure— must be the creative department. The creative people are copywriters, art directors, and television and print production specialists. They are supported by other specialists in the areas of sound, music, casting, typography, and so on. Most agencies organize their creative departments in the classic pyramid style with the workers at the base. Smaller agencies may have a creative director as the sole creative boss. But as the agencies grow in size, so, obviously, do the supervisors, creative group heads (many agencies divide the pyramid into a series of self-sufficient groups), and creative directors. Each of these groups has the capability of developing advertising campaigns from the concept stage to the finished product. Outside sources are hired by the agencies to actually produce the finished commercials or print advertisements, but they do so under the close direction and supervision of the agency creative people.

Creative Support

Obviously, there are a number of other specialists used in the process of preparing and placing advertising. Research people do everything from

probing the consumer psyche for attitudes, habits, and opinions to exploring new ways to pretest advertising campaigns. Much of what they
do is designed to help the creative people. The media department's
function is to handle everything concerned with the placing of the advertising. They have specialists in newspaper, magazine, television, cable, radio, and out-of-home (billboards, posters, car cards, and so forth).
Their principal relationship with creative people comes when they recommend specific media availabilities (a television special, narrow-
targeted publications, a five-page print spectacular, consecutively located outdoor boards), which call for appropriately tailored creative
approaches. In addition, many agencies have their own promotion departments, which usually use their own creative cadre to develop pro-
motions for client products and services.

If we were to place these key services around the rim of a wheel, the
hub of the wheel would be the account handling department. These
people are the principal contacts with the client and the nerve center of
the agency. They must guide and coordinate the effort of the other departments. In today's sophisticated business world they are often as
adept in the field of marketing as their client counterparts.

The account handling chain of command starts with an assistant account executive at the base and climbs through account executive, account supervisor, and account director, to management director at the
top. These titles and the number of people involved in the account handling process vary according to the size of the account and the agency.
Most agencies have account executives and their assistants assigned exclusively to a single account or brand. Account supervisors may have a
number of account executives reporting to them and thus be responsible
for more than one brand. The responsibilities continue to grow with
each title. Similarly both the management supervisor and the management director may have a number of account supervisors reporting to
them.

Loyalty—But to Whom?

One of the problems that every account person has to face is the schizo-
phrenic nature of the job. With the client they represent the agency,
but back at the agency, they represent the client, and their future de-

pends on how well they do both jobs. In the old days we used to hear of "hip pocket" accounts where, through a close relationship with the client, an account person could personally control the activities of the account. The danger, of course, was that the account person would lose objectivity and tend to represent the client both at the agency and when with the client. Because the client ultimately pays the bills (and indirectly the account person's salary) the temptation to "do what the client wants" was strong indeed. Most of these account–client relationships were based on individual contacts, usually between the account person and one member of the client organization (an old college roommate, a neighbor, and so forth) who was in a high enough position to control advertising policy. Luckily, by and large, those days have passed—mainly because the agency–client relationships are so large and complex that no one or two people can exercise undue influence or control.

A focus of this book is the relationship between the business person and the creative person. In the advertising agency business this means the account handling department and the creative people. One of the conflicts that arises in this relationship comes from deciding who has the final say. Who decides whether the creative effort is correct or not. Who says "OK, this is what we'll recommend to the client." Obviously, the best way is through teamwork, a meeting of the minds, a group consensus. But life doesn't work that way. With all of the influences bearing on the decision-making process, there are often wide differences of opinion. Various ways of solving this problem will be discussed later in the book. It's an important part of managing the creative process.

One of the key points to remember, however, is that an advertising agency's principal function is not researching the motivations for selecting one brand of toilet paper over another, or what the marketing strategy behind the introduction of yet another crispy, crunchy cereal should be, or whether to use sky writing or Burma Shave boards. (For those who don't remember, Burma Shave was a shaving cream a few decades ago whose principal advertising medium was a series of consecutive roadside signs that touted the product in rhyme, that is, "Man with face/smooth as glass/welcomes girl/who'll make a pass. Burma Shave.") The principal function of an advertising agency is making advertising, and, as such, the creative function has to be an agency's most important business. That's why skillfully managing the creative process is so important.

WHO NEEDS IT?

If you're an individual entrepreneur who depends on creative thinking to continue being an individual entrepreneur, or a manager who will be dealing with ideas designed to move products or services or philosophies, or anyone concerned with new ways to stimulate, direct, encourage, judge, and sell ideas, then read on. There may be something here that will help you look better, feel better, and sleep better by taking the mystery out of the creative mystique.

INSIGHTS INTO THE HABITS AND WORKINGS OF THE CREATIVE MIND

Everyone is creative. It's just a matter of quality and quantity that makes the difference. Don't believe me? You say you've never had a creative thought or idea in your life? OK. How about the time you were driving along at dusk and a kid on a bike came swinging out of a side street. You saw him in time, but it would have been better if he'd had something to illuminate him from the side. "Why don't they paint fluorescent stripes on the sides of the tires?," you mumbled. You had just been stimulated into a creative idea. Perhaps it wasn't fluorescent bike tires, but I'll bet, if you prod the nooks of your mind, you'll find a number of things you wish you'd invented. Or an idea for a political cartoon you wish you'd sent in to the local paper. Or a song title. Or a new computer use. Or a mystery story twist. Or a special barbecue sauce.

They're all examples of the creative mind at work. But, as I said, the big difference is in quality and quantity. You may be inspired once every six months or so. People whose business it is to create, discipline themselves to turn out good ideas—and lots of them—day after day. If they don't, they don't last long.

SOME CREATIVE MYTHS

So, before trying to manage the creative process, it would probably be wise to examine what kind of people need managing and, at the same time, to dispel some popular myths.

MYTH: *Creative people are sophisticated and worldly. They're cultured, well-read, and snobbish.*

FACT: *Creative people are usually curious, and this curiosity leads to knowledge in many different areas. The injudicious dissemination of this knowledge at cocktail parties or other social gatherings can impart a patina of sophistication. Of course, because key centers for advertising, publishing, broadcasting, the performing arts, and other creative fields are cities with prominent cultural attractions, the creative mind in New York, Atlanta, Chicago, or London has a better chance of coming in contact with new trends and ideas from around the world than the mind that flourishes in Altoona, Albany, or Pound, Virginia. (And I don't mean to disparage these three communities.) Creativity comes from within. But the myth of sophistication comes from big city association.*

MYTH: *Creative people are more intelligent than others.*

FACT: *Not any more than, say, a doctor is more intelligent than an engineer, or a lawyer than an economics professor. If they are successful, they know what they're doing in their own chosen field. In fact, we all know specialists who thrive in their particular areas but are ludicrously inept when away from them. There's the geneticist who has never heard of John Updike or the nineteenth century literature scholar who has trouble remembering the vice president's name. But because creative people's fields of endeavor often cover a wide range of subjects and, as mentioned before, because of their innate curiosity, they often give the impression of knowing more about a lot of things than the specialist who, in fact, may be much more intelligent. The generalist always seems to come out looking smarter. But a specialist with creative overtones, who is thus both a specialist and generalist, tends toward Renaissance personhood. And that is something to be admired.*

MYTH: *Creative people are disorganized.*

FACT: *Not if they want to make their living by being creative. Oh, some are neater than others, but don't confuse neatness with organization. One of the secrets of being a successful creative person is being able to organize one's thoughts. Without this organization, ideas come and go on a variety of subjects in a kind of free-flow manner, wondering where they can be used most effectively. Usually these kind of people see their ideas drift off into the night, novel thoughts looking for a problem to solve or forum to participate in. These are the kind of people who sigh and say, "Gee, I had a good idea once. I wonder what happened to it." Of course these creative thoughts that flit in and out of our minds can often be enjoyed, if never used. Once, when I was a young copywriter in a small New York advertising agency, a cohort turned to me and said, "We've got to get the Victoria Theatre account."*

ME: *Why?*

COHORT: *They've just closed it to enlarge the seating capacity.*

ME: *So?*

COHORT: *And I have the headline for the reopening.*

ME: *And it is . . . .*

COHORT: *Business was so good we had to throw another loge on the foyer.*

An idea looking for a problem. We both stood up, shook hands, and went downstairs to Longchamps for a drink. But it was close to lunch anyway.

MYTH: *Creative people are witty, seldom boring.*

FACT: *Ah, how we wish this were true. Unfortunately, there seem to be as many creative bores as other kinds. And, doubly unfortunately, because they're creative, they can usually come up with a great diversity of ways to be boring on a wide range of subjects. Again, one of the problems is their knowing a little bit about a lot and constantly inserting their expertise into whatever topic might be at hand.*

MYTH: *Creative people are more involved with liquor and drugs than others.*

FACT: *I don't know, but I don't think so (and that statement, dear reader, is an interesting interpretation of "fact"). Alcoholism may seem to be more prominent now, but I think it's because it has come out of the closet and more people are seeking help. Look at the number of clinics and treatment centers that are available now compared to the late 1960s. As you know, many forward-looking corporations have established their own in-house programs to help their employees. In the advertising business, long looked upon as the cutting edge of Sodom and Gomorrah, Madison Avenue Magazine, in a recent article, opined that creative people are no more or no less involved with drugs than the rest of society. My own observation is that, at least with alcohol, consumption is much less than it was*

in the past. Twenty or so years ago the two or three mar-
tini lunch was commonplace. In the three different
agencies in which I worked, there was at least one person
with whom one was warned not to talk after 2:30 P.M. be-
cause he didn't make sense. And there was another who
had the morning shakes so bad that we kept layouts out of
his hands for fear of terminal ripping. But happily for ev-
eryone, those days seem to be lost in the alcholic haze of
the past. Competition is too intense, the workload too de-
manding to allow for nodding off in the middle of the aft-
ernoon. Those who once fervently pursued Bacchus are
either gone or are denizens of Alcoholics Anonymous.

MYTH: *Drugs and alcohol stimulate creative thinking.*

FACT: *Most authorities agree drugs and alcohol can give a feel-*
ing of euphoria and false confidence. The creative stimu-
lation that results is somewhat like the ideas that come to
us in a dream. They seem earth shattering at the time, but
they evaporate like clouds of mist when we awaken. Or, if
remembered at all, they become pedestrian at best,
unintelligible most of the time. As far as creative stimula-
tion through drugs is concerned, I'd like to quote a former
teacher at New York's Parsons School of Design who told
his classes that they were the lucky ones because they
were able to get their "highs" through creative accom-
plishment. There's nothing like stepping back from a
painting (or a story or musical composition or whatever
project) and seeing that the ideas you'd conceived and for-
mulated had come to life just as you'd planned. It is in-
deed a creative high—and we revel in it.

SOME CREATIVE CHARACTERISTICS

Having put a few popular myths to bed, can we generalize as to what
characteristics creative people do have? I think so. First of all, obviously, they have to have ideas and be able to execute them. And with
those two qualities, a person can attain a modicum of success—perhaps
even be somewhat happy.

But the good—and successful—creative people that I've known (I know very few bad successful ones) have a few other things that help bolster their creative talents.

They Can Take Criticism

They're thick-skinned. They don't throw their hands in the air and heavy-foot it in the other direction at the first hint of anything but uproarious applause for their work. And they can take ludicrous and unjust criticism, too. They know when to sit and listen—and when (and how) to fight. They use logic—along with emotion—to win a point.

They Can Take Pressure

In most businesses, and especially in the advertising business, we are slaves to the clock and calendar. Unfortunately, circumstances constantly change the schedule, more often than not, robbing us of time. The good creative people adjust and get the job done. They know how to do it with their backs against the hot pipes. They don't freeze or clutch or become creatively impatient—or impotent.

They Can Work Wherever They Have To

Even though they may think that ideal conditions are needed for the muse to be nudged into life, they can work, under unusual conditions, in strange places. I've seen an art director and copywriter, after working hard all day long on a crash program for Frigidaire, finally come up with the answer over a late dinner at the Pen & Pencil on 46th Street New York. The rough layout and storyboard idea were sketched on the tablecloth. When the check was paid, they bought the tablecloth, took it back to the agency, and translated their sketches and scribblings into a new campaign for refrigerators.

The idea for the public service campaign "Take a Bite Out of Crime" came into being during a boring wait for a plane to be repaired in the middle of the night in the Kansas City airport. The pros do it where and however they have to, because they know it has to be done.

They Can Work on More Than One Thing at a Time

This is true of all leaders in all fields, but in the creative area, it may be more difficult because the muse has to be switched—often in midstream. Here is where the author, artist, musician, computer programmer, or accountant, isolated in a studio, office at home, or away from an organization, has an advantage. They can have hours of uninterrupted time to concentrate on the project at hand. But our subject is creativity as it relates to the business world, usually in an office environment. And interruption, in this milieu, is a frequent fact of life.

As an example, one morning I cleared my desk and calendar and set aside three hours to concentrate on a particularly difficult creative problem on a gasoline account. I was familiar with the problem, and I had some general thoughts for a solution but nothing serious. By the end of the morning, the "interruption log" went something like this:

	Interruption Time
5 Incoming phone calls	25 min.
2 Approvals of layouts	10 min.
1 Argument with account supervisor over sales meeting with producer	10 min.
1 Quick conference with producer over approval of TV commercial costs	10 min.
Total interruption time	60 min.

And so the time allocated to be quietly creative had shrunk from three to two hours. "Poor management," you say. "You should absolutely shut yourself off and delegate the interruptions to others." Possibly. But, unfortunately, another of the functions of creative leadership and/or understanding is being available when needed. At least a semiopen door policy is desirable. The secret, of course, is to be able to pick up your train of thought immediately after the interruption without having to spend time getting back into it. It's really a "switch on, switch off" technique, which will be discussed later.

Being able to compartmentalize the mind to work on more than one project at once is not a prerequisite to creativity—but it can be a big, and in the field of advertising, rewarding, help.

THE BACK BURNER

Back to my busy morning. While I concentrated on the basic problems of the moment (phone calls, creative decisions, and so forth) for one hour, the subconscious kept probing and dissecting various solutions to the big problem. So when the morning ended, I had a solution. The simmering on the back burner of the mind had helped. But to simmer, something's got to be put into the pot. And knowing what that something is—and when to let it simmer—is a creative instinct born of experience

Sometimes the birth seems accidental. A young copywriter spends an afternoon trying to develop a retail ad that will help introduce a daring new line of swimwear. She analyzes the audience, the competitive situation, the strategic approach, the current trends, the imagery of the company name—but nothing happens. She paces and thinks and experiments with several approaches. Nil. She struggles with an idea that highlights, tastefully and with a touch of humor, the sensuous daring of the product. "Barely there" and "What's nude, pussycat" are two rejections.

It's five o'clock and her cohorts give sympathetic smiles and leave. She stays and begins to experience the loneliness of the long-distance copywriter. At nine o'clock, hungry and frustrated, she leaves for a late dinner with a friend, a young lawyer. Somewhere between strawberries and cappuccino it happens. He is describing a discussion with his boss over the ethics of press coverage of a certain case. "The problem is sensationalism. I feel the press should censor itself. If every newspaper followed *The Times* slogan, 'All the news that's fit to print,' we'd be a lot better off."

Suddenly, she starts to write on the side of the menu. His comment had started something. The word "nude" has been lurking in the shadows of her subconscious. She grins and holds up the menu so that he can read "All the nude that's fit to squint." A new advertising campaign has begun to begin.

But the back burner would not have produced if our copywriter had not laid the groundwork. All of the ingredients—strategies, product information, competitive pressures—were stewing in the creative pot, steaming and bubbling, waiting for the stimulus that would trigger a solution. Now, to a lesser degree, this same thing can happen to any of us in a normal morning of interruptions. To help the "switch on, switch off" technique, alluded to earlier, I use the "last thought" method. As the phone rings, or the art director bounds through the door, I quickly write three or four key words of the thought I am concentrating on. Then, when the interruption is over and "switch on" time arrives, the key words can pull me right back to where I was without having to go through the start-up procedure. In addition, these key words just might be food for the back burner, which will be working in its own subconscious way throughout the interruption.

ORDERLY RELIEF

Obviously the back burner principle does not work if we keep the problem in the front of the brain all the time. It must be sublimated so that the subconscious can massage and sooth it. The problem can really become a problem if we don't know how to make it go away for awhile. One way, of course, is to consciously replace it with another problem or creative challenge. The danger here is that the creative juices may begin to run dry on any problem. Relief, however, can be sought in a completely different area. An author friend does it by turning to balance his books, getting his expense account in order, working with figures— forcing the mind to take an orderly approach. It can't wander as he concentrates on the columns of figures. And the back burner starts simmering. An architect moves into a mesmerized area of boredom as she jogs for miles. The pain of the first 20 minutes or so keeps her mind occupied. But gradually as she hits her stride, the back burner hits its stride and ideas begin to push through into the conscious. Reading in an unrelated field, studying, practicing block-chording on the piano, concentrating on a topspin backhand—whatever the orderly relief, it must, in itself, be demanding enough to keep the conscious occupied so that the subconscious can go to work. This ability to know when and how to use the back burner is an important creative characteristic—and discipline.

THE TRAIN THAT'S SELDOM LATE

Somewhere between the front and back burner is a way station through which runs the train of thought. Most good creative people know when to get aboard. You let the mind wander through the thoughts tumbling one on another in a kind of rolling progression, except that you've built in guidelines so that the train of thought now works over, in, and around the challenge that's been simmering on the back burner. Ah, but be careful. These thoughts are like mercury. They can pass through the fingers of your mind in an instant. A good idea is to carry pen and pad at all times to jot them down before they slide away forever.

Often it takes more than one person to get the train of thought rolling. This outside stimulation can range all the way from two people bandying thoughts back and forth to a more formalized idea stimulation session. In the latter, strategy and guidelines are submitted to the selected team (usually 8 to 10 people) a week or so in advance of the session. Each participant is expected to bring three to four starter ideas on 3 × 5 cards to the meeting. The basic ideas are read, and then the card is put in a basket in the middle of the table. And this is where the train of thought picks up steam. After each idea, there is a discussion. Additions to the idea are put forth. New ideas may be born. The only rule is that no thought, concept, or idea can be derided. Everything is accepted—and as the train gathers speed, the additional thoughts are also put on the 3 × 5 cards and put in the basket. In the end, the ideas are gathered and analyzed by the trained moderators who are hoping some of them will be a stimulus to new and different creative approaches. At times these train-of-thought sessions are held without the creative people directly responsible so that eventually they may receive completely objective, noninvolved insights into the problem.

FOCUSED GROUP INTERVIEWS

To keep the train of thought chugging along, the focused group interview is often used. While these are applicable to everything from reactions to new product development to attitudes on life styles, they can also be used to get consumer feelings of creative ideas or approaches. In this technique, trained moderators act as group leaders as typical consumers are exposed to different ideas. The moderator is present to guide and stimulate reactions. And by guide we don't mean to lead people into types of answers but rather to control some of their reactions. One of the big problems in focused groups is the know-it-all who can dominate the entire session, thus rendering the exercise useless. It's up to the moderator to keep this person under control while eliciting thoughts from the rest of the group. This idea stimulation and critique from the consumers—the people we're trying to reach—often can be the key to unleashing new approaches. A few years ago we were running a series of focused groups on attitudes toward various automobile companies in conjunction with new campaign development for our client, Toyota. As we asked those that owned Toyotas what it is they liked (or disliked) about their cars, we got answers like: "My wife loves that car. And she's never had that kind of feeling about cars before. She says that every time she gets in it, she feels good." Or: "I'm amazed at how low the maintenance is. Not going to the garage every other month is OK by me. It's a great feeling to know you don't have to spend an arm and a leg on your car." Or: "The best feeling of all is knowing you've got a car you can depend on."

The word "feeling" kept surfacing in these comments. And out of them came the genesis of an idea—the "Oh What a Feeling" theme —an idea that, over a period of years and in conjunction with the Toyota "jump," became one of America's best known advertising slogans.

AMBITION—SPELLED R-E-W-A-R-D

In managing the creative mind, it would be nice if all we had to worry about was the pure creative development. But, unfortunately, creative people are people, with all of the intertwining habits and slight psychoses everyone else has. And through it all flows the river of ambition, which means that for the work generated, the generator demands recognition and reward. Discovering what that recognition is for each creative person is another key to successfully managing the creative process.

Usually this recognition calls for more than money. For some it's also a title—a higher rung on the ladder to corporate success. For others it can be publicity—recognition from peers and the general public of a creative accomplishment. This publicity can be more than just ego stroking. It can mean new job opportunities.

The recognition given to the author of a talked-about compaign also alerts personnel agencies and directors. Competing advertising agencies will often offer prime salaries to known "stars"—a reality that must be dealt with by the agency housing the incumbent. For everyone, recognition should always mean a pat on the back, a well chosen "thank you," a feeling that you understand what's gone into the birth of a creative idea.

Good creative managers know exactly what ambitions all their creative people have. And they use these individual ambitions to help motivate the various creative machinations. One of the main problems in managing the creative process arises when creative persons' ambitions don't coincide with their talents. A brilliant writer, for example, might function best alone in a quiet room. When working with other people he becomes filled with doubts and insecurities. Yet, for some reason, he pictures himself as a dynamic leader of people, an articulate inspirer of thought and idea, when, in actuality, he becomes tongue-tied trying to order dinner in a restaurant.

It's up to the creative manager to find ways to convince creative people where their creative talents lie and what their limitations are. Sometimes it takes a lot of convincing.

An effective method of pointing out certain limitations is to assume that the creative person in question be given the new responsibilities she requests. Then describe a future day to the erstwhile creative leader and have her compare it with what she did yesterday. And make it real. The future day:

At 9:00 you'll be in conference room B for a meeting with account people and the client to develop alternate strategies for the advertising of a new disposable diaper. That should last through the rest of the morning. Lunch will be a meeting with research where they'll present the latest day-after recall results on the beer commercial your people developed. After the meeting you'll listen patiently to a number of approaches from your copywriters and art directors on how to advertise a new analgesic, with special attention to the legal ramifications and restrictions this type of advertising entails. This should take up to 5:00. After that you can spend time on your own idea for a campaign for a new children's cereal.

Now the comparison. The creative person looks at her feet and starts to describe her day yesterday.

At 9:00 I had an idea on the quality campaign for the car account. But it needed some more work. I took a walk over to the dealer near the river and just looked at those cars for awhile. Then I came back by the U.N. Gardens and smelled the roses and thought about the campaign. Halfway through the morning I was back in my office with the door closed—and I wrote the advertising. At noon the art director and I went to P.J.'s and talked it over. He did a rough storyboard in the afternoon, while I went over to the studio and worked with the music people on a demo for a song for the disposable diaper. Came back and presented the car idea to you—and you loved it. At 5:00 I went home feeling pretty good.

You look at her and simply ask which kind of day she'd rather be involved in. Most of the time she'll realize that she'd rather be thinking and creating and doing than listening and organizing and directing.

But sometimes even this doesn't work. And you may reach the point where you'll have to let your creative people prove to themselves where their talents lie. They have to have a chance to fail. This, however, should be the last resort because after they've had the opportunity and come up wanting—then what? It's often hard to bring them back to their old role. One way to handle this is to make sure at the very beginning that they understand the rules if they do fail. Sometimes this understanding will appeal to their sense of reason, and they'll give up the quest for a role they can't or shouldn't handle before they start. And sometimes it will trigger the fear that there'll be nothing to come back to if they fail because their old job will have to have been filled.

They must be convinced, however, that if they're good as a pure creative person, they'll be rewarded for what they produce just as much as if they had a particular title or leadership responsibility. Many creative individualists want the chance at management leadership because they're convinced that it's the only way to financial security. If the people running your company feel this is so, tactfully try to convince them otherwise or you'll be eliminating a whole special source of creativity. The people that can only create—but can't manage—will go elsewhere.

WHY AND HOW YOU SHOULD KNOW EVERYTHING THERE IS TO KNOW ABOUT YOUR CREATIVE COHORTS

Seems basic, but many managers manage without knowing what they're managing, because they don't go to the trouble of finding out what makes the creative person tick. And the ticking is a result of many things: talents, mood, instinct, experience, pressure, fear, knowledge, confidence, inspiration. All of these can be influenced by a variety of factors. Mood can be a result of personal relationships. If, for example, a personality clash sets off a negative mood with a creative cohort, face it and try and solve it, keeping in mind that your sole objective is to see that good work is produced by the creative people. And you should be willing to do anything that's legal to provide whatever atmosphere is needed to attain this end. The following is a classic example of what *not* to do (actually overheard in an executive art director's office in an advertising agency).

ACCOUNT SUPERVISOR: Hey, Red, how's the layout coming?

EXECUTIVE ART DIRECTOR: (warily as he bends over the drawing board) Ummm . . .OK.

ACCOUNT SUPERVISOR: Let's take a look.

EXECUTIVE ART DIRECTOR: (covering the layout with body English) Not yet, man, I'll show it to you in about 15 minutes. Got an idea here.

ACCOUNT SUPERVISOR: (catching a glimpse of the rough layout being sketched) Hey, that's not what we talked about.

EXECUTIVE ART DIRECTOR: Argh.

ACCOUNT SUPERVISOR: I mean I thought we were going to do something kind of straight. Big picture of the girl with headline underneath. And what's all that white space?

EXECUTIVE ART DIRECTOR: Look. I know what we talked about. And we can always do that. But, I've got an idea here that may be better. Lemme just finish the rough, and then we can discuss it.

ACCOUNT SUPERVISOR: Can't you just do it the way we said. Just wrist it, Redso, we don't have time to be creative.

EXECUTIVE ART DIRECTOR: (slamming down pencil) (Kind reader, even in this day of unfettered linguistic liberalism, I cannot bring myself to quote what the art director told the account supervisor to do.)

Critique.   The obvious is that the account supervisor should have bowed to the executive art director's request for 15 more minutes before discussing the new layout. The not so obvious is that the account supervisor should not have bothered the executive art director in the first place. Most creative people hate to be disturbed in the middle of creation. If the idea's not good, they don't want it exposed and derided. When completed, they want to step back and look at it, discuss it with their cohorts, and arrive at a recommendation. They may decide themselves that it's not right. But if it is good, they don't want to lose it through hasty, over-the-shoulder judgment.

In addition, the account supervisor entered the office with a preconceived idea of what the layout should be. Perhaps he had discussed it with the executive art director, but he forgot he was dealing with creativity. And creativity must have the right to explore. If there was a specific reason not to experiment or replace (and sometimes there is), he should not have wasted the time and talents of an Executive Art Director. There are lesser people on the creative ladder who, when needed, execute the usual.

Epilogue. The sad and actual result was that these two very good people (the account supervisor is quite talented, in his own right) were never able to work together again, and the agency and ultimately the client lost a potential for magic. This was a classic case of mismanaging the creative process.

FEAR—THUS IMPOTENCE

Fear is brought about by many stimuli, but the root of all fears for the creative person is the fear of failure. Therefore, it's most important—in most cases—that the creative manager do as much as possible to boost creative ego and keep this fear from breaking through. I say "in most cases" because with some people the fear of failure acts as the prod to get things moving. But this seldom has to be stated or even hinted at. It's deep within every creative person's psyche. Most of the time all that has to be said is, "Hey, let's get this done, because that's what we're getting paid for." Obviously, the operative word is "pay." But the fear of failure can also render creative people impotent. And this is especially true of the new kid on the block. In the following true case history, some names and situations have been changed to protect the innocent—and the guilty.

Some years ago a very well thought of and highly recommended creative director arrived at a large advertising agency to head up a creative group working, among other things, on a new after shave lotion. The strategy was to impress the potential customer with the soothing, cooling properties of the product. Happily, he went right to work and came up with a number of creative approaches to the problem. His favorite was an attention-getting device that dramatized the cooling properties of the product. A little snow swirling around the bottle. In a television commercial, when the medicine chest door is opened, there would be the sound of wind and the snow would blow out. If the bottle was left on the side of the sink, a tiny drift would built up around the base. In the store display, where there are lots of bottles, the clerk would put on his galoshes at the toiletries section and wade through the snow to get the product for a customer. The creative director even suggested naming the product "Kilimanjaro." ("Like the refreshing touch of mountain snow.")

The idea was discussed with various members of the account team, and they agreed it had great possibilities. No one else was doing anything like it. So the creative director proceeded to refine and expand the idea into magazine and newspaper layouts, outdoor boards, point-of-sale pieces, and promotional items. Finally, the day came to present his campaign (along with a number of others from different creative directors) to the agency's management director on the account. Unfortunately, this gentleman had strong ideas of what he felt men's toiletry advertising should be. He believed that product advantages should be presented in a straightforward manner. And he insisted on this approach even when, as in the case of the after shave, there was no real product advantage. He was so convinced that his way was the only way that he closed his mind to all other approaches. He let the new creative director know in a rather blunt fashion what he thought of image advertising for men's toiletries in general and the "snow" campaign in particular. He ended with something like, "I believe you should do some studying as to what motivates men to buy after shave lotion. I'm afraid you're lacking not only in this important knowledge, but perhaps in certain insights on this type of account." Rough words to a new and eager creative director.

The Result.   The loss of what might have been an interesting, new advertising approach. But more important, the complete shattering of the confidence of the new creative director. From that point on he stopped trying to be creative and concentrated on what he thought the management wanted. As a result, his direction and leadership began to wallow uncertainly. In meeting with the management director, his heretofore forceful presentation style became tentative and unsure. In short, his effectiveness as a creative director kept diminishing until he finally resigned.

Critique.   At the least, a more tactful handling of the criticism by the management director could have saved a relationship and a potential creative contributor to the agency. At best, the management director could have encouraged the development of the idea, along with other ideas he might have felt more kindly toward. Then the two or three best ideas (including "Kilimanjaro") could be qualitatively tested for consumer reaction. If it failed, at least the creative director would have felt that his idea had been given a fair trial.

Or ideally, the management director could have said: "This is not my cup of tea, and I don't believe that it's the way to sell men's toiletries, but I have faith in your creative instincts and therefore believe we should push ahead. But let's also look at some other campaigns a bit less imagey." In this way, the management director would have presented his point of view, demonstrated his faith in the creative director, and given the creative director the impetus to explore other areas without ruining his morale.

Epilogue.   The crushed creative director left the agency business for a year and took to converting a New England farm into a small ski resort. Disaster. He returned to New York and got a job as a copywriter with another large agency—just to get back in the business. It was a second start and it worked. He is currently the executive creative director of one of the world's largest agencies, a tribute to his talents and stamina. But it could have been much easier and much more profitable for the original agency if the management director had practiced the art of management a bit more judiciously.

HOW TO FIND OUT WHAT YOU SHOULD KNOW

And so it behooves everyone involved in managing the creative process to find out everything they can about the creative people they'll be working with. Be as aware as possible of the moods, foibles, habits, talents, and temperament of the people who can make you a hero. Here are some tips that have helped me.

1.   Talk to those who've worked with your creative cohort before. Find out what his working habits are. Idea people often have time clocks that vary from the normal business person's. Some work well first thing in the morning and are burned out by mid-afternoon. Others are late starters, and so forth. Incidentally, this is a most important and a very delicate subject. Obviously, it's convenient if a person can regiment creativity to working hours. And some can. But if they can't, don't hamper their productivity by forcing them. Find out as much as you can about home life, personality, background. Is he a frustrated playwright or author? What was her college major? Married? Divorced? Children? Temperamental? Aggressive or retiring? And perhaps most importantly, what are his creative accomplishments? What type of approaches does she take? Humor? Hard sell? Demonstration? Music? Off beat? Is she a specialist with certain types of writing? A poet or novelist might be fascinating in writing an annual report. This kind of unique casting might turn out to be a brilliant piece of creative management. But you've got to know the individual before you can try it.

2.   Have lunch with your cohort. Sounds obvious, but the obvious is often overlooked. Lunch is usually more relaxed and congenial than the meeting in your office. Look for a common ground on which to start your relationship. But be aware of the fact that some creative people feel there is no such thing. In the course of the lunch, ask what you can do to help them. Even if they say "the best thing you can do is keep your hands off my work," you'll have made an impression. If you run into this kind of a wall, be patient. Explain that your job is to make it easier for them to do their job. If they need information or directional help or even a noncritical sounding board, offer it. They'll come around because the majority of creative people need someone to be their ombudsman on the management side. And a good manager of the creative process is there when needed.

3.   Personal problems seem to have an inordinate influence on creative output. Perhaps it's because there's so much emotion tied up in both the personal and business life of creative people. Perhaps it's be-

cause part of the creative process seems to be staring at the ceiling, typewriter, or drawing board thinking—and if a personal problem is in the offing it will manage to insert itself into the thought process. It's at this point that the creative manager can sometimes be a listening post, letting the creative person clear her mind by talking it out. But be careful. Most of us are not trained psychiatrists. If advice is asked for, be wary; use your head and common sense. Don't become a part of the personal as well as the business problem. And be aware of the creative person who uses the tensions of private life as a constant excuse for not coming up with what they should be coming up with. A good creative manager senses, or learns, when to be sympathetic and when to be tough. And there's no set formula. It varies with each individual.

While individuality and the unusual would seemingly be the touchstones to managing the creative process, there are certain generalities, rules, principles, and techniques that seem to be applicable to all creative people and the products of their minds. I will discuss much of this in the ensuing chapters.

IN SUMMARY

1.   Myths concerning creative people abound. They contain a limited basis for truth. That's why they're called myths. The truths are:

   a.   Creative people are not all sophisticated and worldly. Nor are they all cultured, well-read, and snobbish.

   b.   Creative people are not necessarily more intelligent than others.

   c.   Creative people are not necessarily disorganized.

   d.   Nor are they all witty, seldom boring.

   e.   Creative people seem to be no more or less involved with liquor and/or drugs than others.

   f.   Creative thinking (contrary to the perceptions of some creative people) is not stimulated by drugs and alcohol, although false confidence may be.

2.   There are certain characteristics that successful creative people in the business world seem to possess.

a.   They are prone to idea development;

b.   They are able to accept criticism;

c.   They can work under pressure;

d.   They can produce under a variety of physical conditions and in a variety of different environments; and

e.   They can work on more than one project at a time.

3.   The subconscious is an important creative reservoir, but a good creative person knows that it must be fed and allowed to work on its own.

4.   One of the more popular ways to allow the subconscious to function is by consciously filling the mind with something far removed from the subject at hand.

5.   Another popular and natural source of creative ideas is the train of thought, which can be stimulated by the individual or with the aid of outside sources.

6.   These sources include such devices as the focused group interview, where a panel of noninvolved people are led in a discussion of a given problem or project.

7.   Most creative people need more than money to reward their endeavors. These can include titles, publicity, and perquisites not available to others—things that overtly separate the recipients from the crowd and give public recognition to their efforts.

8.   Advancement, however, can be the wrong reward if the new job responsibilities do not coincide with the creative person's talent.

9.   Good creative managers make it their business to know everything they possibly can about their creative cohorts because the creative process (and the creative product that they are ultimately responsible for) can be influenced by a wide variety of outside sources.

10.   Tact is perhaps one of the most important qualities for any creative manager. If it's not inherent, it must be developed.

This chapter is perhaps not as focused as those coming up. But that's because the workings and plottings of the creative mind and the creative person are far from focused. But now that we've done some surface and, I hope, practical exploring of why and how creative people act the way they do and what to do about it, we'll concentrate on more specific areas. Onward!

2

CHANNELING
THE CREATIVE
FLOW

Ever notice the ritual you go
through before attacking a
creative project? Any creative task, from writing a letter eliciting funds for the Little League, to a series of
employee evaluations, to a
detailed memo on the po-
tential of a new business
prospect, evokes the same
activities. You sharpen pen-
cils and arrange them
neatly beside a new yellow
legal pad. Or you clean

your desk or room or office ("can't create in a messy room"). You see how many birds you can identify out the window. You pay bills or fill out expense accounts. You stare at the ceiling. You do anything to keep from starting.

The way to overcome this foot-dragging, mind-deadening malaise is not to sit down and start writing. While this might get the creative juices flowing, it could get everything moving in the wrong direction. So, the first thing that must be done is to decide on the objectives. What do you really want to accomplish? And often what you want to accomplish is different from what you might think at first glance. In the following chart I've divided the examples above into two columns. The first column is what you might feel are the obvious objectives. The second is what the real objectives turn out to be.

Project	Obvious Objective	Real Objective
Letter to Little League parents and friends	Raise money	Increase the average gift by 20% from previous year
Employee evaluation	Delineate employee's strengths and weaknesses	Delineate employee's strengths and weaknesses in a manner that will be beneficial to the employee
New business prospect	Ascertain profitability	Ascertain growth potential

You'll notice that in general what has happened is that the objectives have been more sharply focused. And this focus often leads to creative executions (as they used to say on the way to the guillotine). For example, in the case of the Little League letter, the fact that you want to increase the yearly contribution might direct you to a creative approach that opens with a listing of the increase in the costs of bats and balls over last year (and thus the need for more money). With the employee evaluation, you will probably write it quite differently when you know the subject is going to read and discuss it and, you hope, benefit from it. And the new business prospect report takes on a completely different coloration when you're talking about growth prospects rather than what the bottom line will be in six months.

In the world of advertising and marketing this listing of the objective is known as "the creative strategy." And in the entire creative process there is probably nothing more helpful than developing the creative strategy. For without it we often don't know where to go. In a way, a strategy is like a road map. It points out our destination and suggests a variety of ways to get there. But it doesn't tell us how to make the trip. That's a part of the creative execution.

THE CREATIVE STRATEGY—AND WHAT IT ISN'T

COPYWRITER (in large advertising agency):   Hey Fred, I'm ready to go on the car commercial. Where's the strategy?

ACCOUNT EXECUTIVE: Got it right here, Kiddo. Listen to this: (reads) "The object of television advertising for the Pegasus 6 is to convince the consumer that it's the ultimate in styling, performance, and comfort."

COPYWRITER: Huh?

ACCOUNT EXECUTIVE: Take it away, Chollie. There it is—simple and direct.

COPYWRITER: What the hell, Fred. I mean, that's all over the place. That's the kind of thing that leads us to write pap like: "Introducing the new Pegasus 6 with contour styling reminiscent of the space age—and a powerful new twin-cam, fuel-injected, six-cylinder engine that comes on like thunder and lightning—and the kind of comfort that makes taking a long trip like riding in your living room. The new Pegasus 6. Try one and revel in the ultimate driving experience."

ACCOUNT EXECUTIVE: Ummm. See what you mean. Well, let's look at the strategy again and see what we can do.

And so the account team and the client and the creative people put their heads together and worked it out. They decided that the one thing the car had that put it wheel and hubcap above the competition was the new twin cam, fuel-injected, six-cylinder engine. And so the new strategy read: "The object of television advertising for the Pegasus 6 is to convince the consumer that it's capable of outstanding performance as a result of the new twin cam turbo-charged, six-cylinder engine." Although it's longer than the original strategy, it's simpler and single-minded, and therefore it should guide the creative people into concentrating on a number of different executions, all pointed in one direction—performance.

In this example, notice that we included creative people in the development of the strategy. This is most important. It seems to me that not doing this would be like a group of engineers designing a new process for making beer without involving the brewmaster. Yet it's surprising how many sophisticated managers forget to include the thinking of their creative people in strategy development. ("What the hell. They're a little flaky anyway. And strategy is a businessperson's responsibility. Let them worry about how we're going to do it. Not what we're gonna do.")

From this example we also see that a strategy can simply be defined as a simple statement showing the one thing we'd like our creative efforts to accomplish. Ah, but that phrase "one thing" is what's extremely bothersome to many people, because it calls for the process of elimination and selection. Ask someone what the one thing is that they like about spring and you'll get an answer like, "Oh . . . I like the spring smell in the air and the first yellow daffodils and the blue skies and white clouds of April and the peepers singing at twilight and. . . . " "One thing," you say. "Well," they say, "that's hard because there are lots of things I like. . . . " It's hard because they are being forced to make a choice. They must first think of all the things they like. Then they must weigh them against each other, narrow the list down, and once again go through the comparison process. And even then they may not be able to make a clear-cut choice. "I dunno," they say, "it's a tossup between apple blossoms and the smell of fresh-cut grass."

Every day, advertising and marketing people are faced with this selection process. And it's made all the tougher when the beckoning (and expensive) door of time stands wide open. ("Listen, we've got 30 seconds here. You mean to tell me that all you're going to do is talk about how powerful the Pegasus 6 is. Can't we spend just a little time romancing the styling. I mean, at these prices, we ought to be able to talk about more than one thing.") And there is the temptation and the problem.

And so the first thing a creative strategy is not is a compendium of everything you know about the subject at hand. Remember, it's a road map pointing the direction to your objectives. Now, if there are a number of different directions, then we should have a number of different strategies. For example, in the case of the Pegasus 6, the objective may be to get people to the showroom for a test drive. As we said earlier, one route or direction might be "performance." Another might be "styling." And another might be "comfort." To remain single-minded, each calls for a separate strategy so that the execution (the television commercial or print advertisement) will have a strong single-minded thrust. Of course, this results in three different approaches to the objective of getting people to the showroom—each one single-minded in its own way. But still, there are three different approaches, which tends to dilute the overall impact of the advertising and is more expensive than concentrating on one approach. The problem, therefore, is to make the decision as to which of the three routes is the most effective—an important part of managing the creative process that will be covered later.

WHAT ELSE SHOULD A STRATEGY DO?

Presenting, in a single-minded way, the direction to a stated objective may be the key role of a strategy, but there are other thoughts that will help us arrive at this direction and should be included in the strategy format.

1. Who is our audience? To whom are we talking? In the case of raising money for the Little League, we are probably talking to parents. But not necessarily exclusively. We might also be talking to local business people and retailers, friends and neighbors who could build goodwill supporting the team. These specific prospects could affect the tonality and structure of the letters. As mentioned before, the audience for the employee evaluation would be the employee himself as well as management. The new business analysis would be written exclusively for management.

In the last two examples, you can see how the specific audience can influence the attitude of the message. If the subject of the employee evaluation is introverted and insecure, the criticism, perhaps, should be tactfully sugarcoated. If the subject is a no-nonsense professional, then a more direct evaluation might be considered. Similarly, how you prepare the new business analysis depends on whether or not your management is conservative or adventurous and how they view your role. If they tend toward conservatism, they might want you to give an opposite point of view. In general, good managers do not hire good people just to agree with them. The audience we're trying to reach, therefore, can play a most important part in our strategic thinking. And, as you can see, the more specific we are in describing the audience, the better direction we give to the creative people executing the strategy.

2.   What reaction do we want from our message? What do we want our audience to do? Again, in the case of the Pegasus 6, we know that we can't ask the consumer to make a buying decision through a magazine advertisement or a 30-second television commercial.

The action we want them to take is to come to the showroom and see for themselves. An impulse purchase item such as chewing gum or a popular magazine might ask for an immediate purchase—but not just "buy my product," instead "buy my product rather than a competitive product because I taste better, or last longer, or am better for you, or contain more 'how to' features," or whatever the real or perceived product advantages may be.

This section becomes the "objective" section of a strategy. It's where we want to be after we've taken the specific route the strategy recommends. Refer to the previous chart and you'll see how the "objective" in the case of the Little League letter, the employee evaluation, and the new business analysis is what we want our audience to do or think.

3.   What is the principal thought we wish our audience to be left with? This is the "core" of the strategy—whether it's for a report, a TV commercial, a letter, a newspaper advertisement or lyrics to a song. We covered this earlier, but we mention it here because of its importance. Again, the single-minded aspect is the key to the success of the strategy and, ultimately, the creative execution. One final example of what I'm talking about. Recently a group of us completed a one-week trip to Japan to learn everything we could about Toyota's then new larger-sized car, the Camry. The examination and indoctrination were to be instru-

mental in formulating the positioning and strategy for introducing the car to an American audience. In their impeccable and thorough way, the Toyota people took us through everything from the original design concepts, to the engineering features, to a number of innovative developments. We were impressed. The final night in Toyota City, just outside Nagoya, we were guests at a "sayonara" cocktail party given by our hosts. I found myself talking pleasantly to the chief engineer of the project. Suddenly he asked me what I felt was the single most important feature of the car. I thought of the week we'd gone through and everything that I'd tried to learn. I thought of the electronically controlled automatic gear shift, the twin glove compartments, the squared-off steering wheel, the no-lip tail gate entry—all new, all innovative.

"It's innovative," I said.

"What?"

"It's a car full of innovative ideas."

He looked at me and grinned. "Every Toyota has innovative ideas. Why did we make this one? Think again."

"Room?"

"Room! We made this car because we feel the public wants the choice of a family sized Toyota. Room is the reason for the Camry's existence. And 'roominess' should be what you emphasize in your advertising."

"Hai," I said.

"Hai," he replied, "you understand?"

The student understood and we introduced the car as "The Family Camry from Toyota." Our hosts had pointed out the single-minded thrust of the strategy.

Because the core idea is the guiding light of the strategy, I often write it across the top of my rough copypaper so that I can always be reminded of what we're trying to do.

4. What is there about the product or service or message that will help the audience believe the principal thought? This is the "because" statement. The proof:

"The Little League would like you to increase your contribution this year *because* the price of bats, balls, and Band-Aids has increased 20 percent since last year."

"I am writing this evaluation for you to read, as well as management, *because* I want you to know exactly how I feel about the progress you've made since our last evaluation."

"This analysis of a new business prospect will be concerned with the long range growth potential *because* to be successful, our company must look to the future rather than a quick six months profit."

"The Toyota Camry is for the family *because* it has as much or more head room, leg room, hip room, shoulder room than any other compact car sold in America."

Of course, the problem comes when there is no "because," when you're involved with a parity product or situation. In some cases, the "because" section can be eliminated. But the lack of "reason why" does not mean we don't have a strategy. If this were so, a good number of very good products would not be marketed. In some cases the "because" section can be based on emotion or on impression rather than facts. In advertising, this establishment of an emotional "because" section is most important for products with no discernible (or at least believable) points of difference because it obviously creates, within the mind of the selected audience, a reason to buy the product. This becomes all the more important for products that tend to have an image transfer to their users. Cigarettes, beer, perfumes, and high fashion accessories are sometimes purchased not for what they offer but rather for the image they project. A Marlboro smoker envisions himself as a man with the spirit of the cowboy. A Camel's smoker is a macho individualist. A Barclay smoker, a smooth man of the world. A True smoker, a sophisticated intellectual.

Hamm's beer is pure and refreshing because it was born in the "land of sky blue waters." The "land of sky blue waters" has been a part of this beer's advertising for the past 30 or 40 years. It connotes the good things people want in a beer. It relates the beer to the kind of atmosphere beer drinkers would like to be a part of—no matter where they are. Blue lakes, lofty pines, the smell of camp fires, the rugged outdoorsman. It creates a positive image and makes the beer a part of that image. It's an established emotion that's been a part of Hamm's heritage, and, as such, it has earned its right to be the "because" section of Hamm's strategy.

Miller beer has been the beer for the working man because it's the beer that has welcomed you as a reward after a hard day's work. Lots of beers position themselves as a reward. Busch has taken the Marlboro approach and has offered itself as a reward after a hard day on the range or in the corral. Budweiser has saluted a wide variety of professions with the implications of reward for jobs well done ("This Bud's for you"). But it has been Miller that preempted this "reward" area by establishing the end of the day as "Miller time." A "welcome to Miller time" version continued this thrust originally established in the early seventies. These emotional "reasons why" are interesting proof that when developing a strategy, we should be very careful before deciding that a "because" section is not needed.

5.   What's happening in the marketplace, or what perceptions do people have that might influence the creative execution of the strategy? This is a completely separate area that has nothing to do with the first four sections of the strategy format. It could, however, be most important in giving executional direction or setting the tone of the creative approach. Again, some examples.

For years, Burger King, the fast food giant, emphasized individual choice ("Have it your way") as their single-minded core idea. Now, if we were to have a sudden gas crisis, obviously eating out would suffer, as it did in the mid-1970s. Burger King would not want to change its basic strategy, but somewhere as one of the guidelines, they should make note of what's going on in the marketplace that could influence their key objective—to get people to come to Burger King rather than to McDonald's. And so the gas crisis and its resultant decrease in pleasure driving would be recorded in this section of the strategy format. This could, for example, lead to a TV commercial that would set aside different days for different neighborhoods to car pool to Burger King, thus saving gas. "Monday night is the night for the Bronson Avenue Bash at Burger King. So grab the kids and neighbors, squeeze into the station wagon, and car pool to Burger King where you can still 'Have it your way.' "

This section would also include perceptions that people might have about a product or category of products that could influence the attitude, but not necessarily the core idea, of the advertising. If, for example, in the case of the Little League fund raising project there had been some bad publicity concerning parent interference with the coaches or parent over-exuberance at the games, this should be taken into consideration. It might be decided that this would have no bearing on your fund raising letter, but, on the other hand, you probably would not include in your presentation lauditory compliments concerning the great cooperation and spirit of togetherness between parents and coaches. These perceptions or statements are facts of life that should be noted—perhaps acted on—but never ignored.

THE CREATIVE STRATEGY—A SUMMARY

If I seem exuberant about this matter of a creative strategy, it's because I mean to be. In my experience it is perhaps the most important step in channeling creative thoughts. It not only gives direction but organizes the mind. In review, then, here are the five steps that can help in developing a strategy:

1. Figure out to whom you're talking—and be as specific as possible (the audience);
2. Figure out what actions you'd like them to take (the objective);
3. Figure out the principal thought you'd like to leave them with (the core idea);
4. Figure out why the principal thought is valid (the "because" section); and
5. Be aware of any influences or perceptions that might affect the creative message.

BACK UP THE TRUCK

I've talked about what a creative strategy should and should not be, but now I want to go back a step and discuss what should be done before any strategy development begins. I have purposely inserted this section after the strategy discussion so that you will see how this first step can apply to the different sections of the strategy format.

First, before tackling any creative subject, you must gather information. Seems obvious, but it's amazing the number of people who start writing or drawing or composing or even developing a strategy without complete information on the project or problem. In fact, some people are afraid that information might bog them down. ("Don't confuse me with the facts. Just let me get on with it.") They somehow feel that they can work it out as they go along. The fact is that there *is* such a thing as too much information, and some creative people use this information gathering process as an excuse to keep from starting to produce. But that's where managing the creative process comes in. Knowing when it's time to stop gathering and start producing.

How much information is needed? This varies according to the project or problem. Obviously, one would need more for the introduction of the new Pegasus 6 than the composing of the Little League fund raising letter. But that doesn't mean that the Little League project is not without its needed facts.

How many people contributed last year?

What was the average contribution?

What percentages were parents, friends, relatives, businesspeople in the community?

How many parents continue to contribute after their children leave the program?

And so forth. . . .

In the advertising business many people develop a series of general questions that can help the fact-finding process. A sample:

The Background

What is the history of the product category?

What competitive products are available?

Who is the leader in the category?

Why are they the leader? (Superior product? Better distribution? Larger advertising budget? Consistent advertising over a period of years? Better public image? High brand awareness?)

What is the history of the public's perception of the product category?

The Product

Why did it come into being?

How is it manufactured?

How would you define/describe it?

How is it priced?

Is it competitive?

What are its key advantages?

What are its disadvantages?

Why should anyone buy it?

Current Climate

What is the market for the product?

What is the current perception of the product category?

What is the current perception of the company? (As we know, these perceptions can change almost overnight. The tragic Tylenol case in 1982, while costing the parent company, Johnson & Johnson, millions of dollars, made a positive impression on the public for the way that Johnson & Johnson handled the problem. Ford, on the other hand, suffered from the adverse publicity it received on the Pinto gas tank rear-end collision incidents. In fact, this series of unfortunate accidents and resultant lawsuits were, I believe, one of the reasons for the company's eventual phasing out of the Pinto and the subsequent development of a corporate "quality" advertising campaign.)

What is the current demand or need for the product? Are there legal ramifications that we must be aware of? If the product is new, what product testing has been undertaken?

Has there been any testing for consumer perception of the product?

How are the competitors advertising their products? (Media used, budget breakdowns, complete samples of their advertising.) For the creative people, this item is most important. We must know how our competitors are advertising, where they're advertising, and what all of their advertising consists of. And we say "all," so that, in developing new campaigns, we don't innocently adopt a theme or approach already in use. This could not only be embarrassing from a professional standpoint but from a legal one as well. And, if they have an approach that seems to be working, we'd like to know what it is and why it's good.

As you see, the answers to such a checklist can often be used to fill in the key strategy questions. If you know that the first question in your strategy format concerns your potential audience, you're certainly going to spend some time in the information-gathering process finding out everything you can about that audience. And if one strong product advantage keeps surfacing in these question and answer sessions, you know that it will be a candidate for the core idea of the strategy.

Finally, a tip on what to do while you're gathering this information. *Take notes.* I was once in a briefing with two other agencies in competition for an account. We were being given the background for a creative assignment. The potential client representative said, "Everything we're going to tell you is included in these books we'll hand out later." Mary Wells, the successful founder and leader of the Wells Rich Greene advertising agency, said, "Do you mind if I take notes? I don't feel comfortable without scribbling something. I figure that if I don't, I'll miss something that's sure to be on the exam." I agree. But Ms. Wells was doing more than taking notes. By writing things down, she was helping to burn them into her mind—both the conscious and subconscious. And, like most creative people I know, she was using this technique to stimulate ideas even as she learned.

In writing this book, I used a variety of methods—longhand on legal pads while on planes, word processor in my home/office. But wherever I was and however I did it, I blocked off part of the page for related or unrelated ideas that might or might not be used later. And some of these unrelated ideas were "back burner" thoughts that had been bubbling along and suddenly boiled over. They would quickly go into the special section on each page (actually, all I did was use only three quarters of the page for the actual manuscript, the other quarter was ruled off and saved for the extraneous thoughts). At the beginning of each writing session, I would glance through these thoughts to see where, if, and when I should use them. It let the left side of the brain give a helping hand to the right side, or perhaps vice versa.

THE CASE OF THE RAT'S GUILLOTINE

Now, as a final exercise, let's see how we might develop a strategy for a specific product. Here's a brief digest of the salient facts:

> The product is a new high quality spring-type rat trap. It has a long-lasting oak base, a strong steel spring and "wicket," and an exclusive release mechanism that can be put on "safety" until the trap is baited and then put in cock or ready position with the tip of a pencil. Its advantages are that it will last longer than the average rat trap because of its quality materials, it is extremely efficient and thus humanitarian because of the strong spring, and it is less accident prone because of the safety feature. Disadvantage: It costs more than other rat traps. We also know that rats congregate in urban areas and along waterfronts, are not partial to cold weather, and have insatiable appetites.

Going through the strategy format point by point yields the following:

1. *The Audience.* Obviously, this includes apartment house owners and managers, food store owners, restaurant owners and managers, and people who live near or on waterfronts. And so our "audience" statement might be: "The advertising is directed to all people who are particularly susceptible to rodent problems."

2. *The Objective.* Here we could hope that our audience would buy our rat trap rather than using poison. Or we would hope that they would pay more money for ours because it's more efficient and lasts longer than other spring-type traps, or that they would buy ours because of the safety features. Now, these are all laudable objectives. But if we use all of them, they will begin to force us into three-headed advertising. So, let's try and narrow our choices.

People who use poison often use exterminators, and these are people who want nothing to do with the baiting and setting of traps. They are not our market. By saying, "use our trap rather than poison," therefore, we would be heading in the wrong direction. (If, however, there were a "Spring-type Rat Trap Association," we might consider a general association campaign against poison, based on the potential danger to other pets, or the chance of having an unlucky rodent scarf up the poison and then retire to sleep it off and expire—in one of the walls.)

As far as efficiency, research tells us that most people believe there's very little difference in the efficiency of rat traps, and the one or two seconds gained by our product is not important to them. As for long lasting, no one likes to think of rat traps lasting a lifetime. ("One or two years with old Rat-O-Rama here and we'll have them all cleaned out," they say.)

So that leaves us the safety features. Talk to people about rat traps. Ask them what they don't like about them. I'll bet 9 out of 10 will say: "I hate to set them. I'm scared stiff one is going to go off and de-finger me." And so our objective statement might read: "We want our audience to buy our rat trap rather than competition because of the safety feature."

3.   *The Core Idea.*   This becomes easy now because we've set up or arrived at it through the above deduction. The safety feature becomes the one outstanding difference between our product and competition. And we know that it's a meaningful advantage, while efficiency and long-lasting are not. And so: "The principal thought that we'd like to leave with our audience is that our rat trap is safer to use than any other."

4.   *The "Because" Section.*   Here we explain or prove our point. "It's safer to use than any other because it has an exclusive release mechanism that can be put on 'safety' while you set and bait it."

5.   *Influences and Perceptions.*   What influence in the marketplace might affect the creative message? Well, we know that rats don't like cold weather, so that means that their presence in houses, stores, and so on, will be increased in the north, as cold weather arrives. This might influence the creative direction, but it would probably be more applicable to media decisions. Concentrate the advertising in the fall rather than year round. If there's a health scare caused by something like a garbage strike, as New York City experiences from time to time, a special creative approach might be called for. But it should never overshadow the core idea. For example, the increased rat menace due to excess garbage could be alluded to in an illustration of rats feasting on broken garbage bags (how did we ever get on this subject?) with the headline saying something like: "NOW, A SAFE RAT TRAP THAT CAN'T HURT YOU. BUT IT SURE HURTS RATS." This, of course, is a simplified example based on logic, deduction, process of elimination—and no research. Obviously, research into the audience likes, dislikes, wants, needs, and attitudes is most important as a background for developing any strategy.

But so are your experiences and instincts and the creative use of the research.

As you can see, the strategy for the rat trap does act as a road map guiding the direction the advertising should follow. But don't mistake the strategy for advertising. Unfortunately, some people do. If the core idea is "This rat trap is safer than others," the headline should not be "Introducing a rat trap that's safer than others." How about: "The trap that snaps at rats, not at your fingers." Again, the strategy is a guide. The advertising must dramatize the strategy in a way that gets attention, holds attention, and puts across the core idea in a way that the audience will remember.

WHO CREATES?

You're an architect. You enter a competition with two other prestigious firms to design a new college library. You take two of your brightest young stars with you to the briefing and early fact-gathering meetings. Briefly adapting the strategy format, you might say that your audience is the university's special library committee and the board of trustees. The objective is to have them accept your concept and help "sell" it to the university family and the public. The core idea is to create a design that's exciting, yet will blend with the rest of the campus. You believe this will be possible because you're going to include a number of new advanced features inside.

Outside you will create a most contemporary structure that makes a dramatic statement while harmonizing with the other structures through the use of the same facade building materials. You set your people free, letting them think and experiment with different approaches. Meanwhile, you have a concept working on the back burner. You'd like an atrium to be the focal point containing the central desk, a reading-lounge area, and an open exhibition gallery. The stacks, computer room, and various reading rooms all open on the atrium at different levels. It's an inward designed building, leaving the facade free for a design in keeping with the overall look. After a few weeks your "stars" come up with their plan. It's different from yours but equally as intriguing. They're experimenting with glass walls that face away from the campus, looking out over the surrounding countryside. Again, the frontal facade is free to blend with the other buildings. The projected cost is about the same. The advantages for each balance out. You decide to present both to the client. But you know that eventually you'll have to recommend one. Which one?

You recommend theirs.

You have to. Because that's an important part of managing the creative process. If the creative contest is between you and your minions and everything comes out equal, they must win. That's what you hired them for. If, on the other hand, your idea is superior for whatever reason, select it and explain the reason to them. They'll understand. They may not be happy, but they'll understand.

But if you're the kind of person—even genius—who comes up with the big idea or concept every time, then managing the creative process should be within yourself, not among others. You should probably surround yourself with assistants who will do exactly as you tell them: people who want to learn by watching, not by doing. The problem here, of course, is that these assistants, if they're any good at all, will eventually develop their own talents. Now, if you are in a situation where an independent thinker is working for you and she's very good, give her all the help you can. Give her mechanical assistants if that's what she needs. Back her in her efforts. But don't put her in charge of other people who might compete with her. She won't let them.

I once knew a very creative copywriter in an advertising agency who exemplified this problem. He was a star. He'd turned out campaigns and ideas that had won national acclaim. But he wanted to be a creative director. And he was very convincing in his arguments to this end. He got along well with clients. He was a good salesman. He knew how to position and present his ideas. People liked him. And he'd earned the right to advance up the corporate ladder. Unfortunately, there was one big problem. He was unbelievably competitive. But he was given the chance. Within two weeks none of the people working under him would speak to him. Here's how it happened.

He and his team were assigned a project. They talked over various approaches. He suggested and assigned ways of proceeding to each of them. In a few days they returned with their ideas. He listened, commented, gave constructive criticism. Their work was presented on a Friday to the account group. They had some thoughts which were to be incorporated over the weekend and reviewed again on Monday. Came the meeting and the creative director arrived with his team. He smiled as his people presented the revised campaigns. The account team agreed with the revisions. They gave their recommendations as to which one should be presented as the lead campaign to the client. The creative director watched and said nothing. Then, as the meeting drew to a close, he held up his hand and said "Uh . . . hold on a minute. I really wasn't too happy with the work we showed you on Friday—or this morning—and so over the weekend I worked up a campaign that I think answers some of our problems." He then proceeded to present a brilliant idea that, in fact, did answer the problems. The effect was electric. His people, who had worked, following his guidance, all weekend were aghast. The account team that looked to the creative director for leadership was embarrassed and confused. The result was that the creative team stalked furiously out of the office. The creative director's advertising was presented to the client and eventually appeared before the public. And the creative director eventually lost his responsibility and had his duties changed back to what he really was—an individualist who was brilliant while working alone.

TIME AND DEADLINES

You're the sales manager of a medium/small manufacturing company. You sell mainly through a group of one hundred independent distributors. Your job is to see that these distributors are motivated to sell your product rather than others that they carry in the same field. To do this you decide that you need to stimulate them with some kind of a sales contest. You call in your sales promotion expert and give him the assignment. You'd like to have his suggestions as soon as possible. Problem: How much time is as soon as possible?

YOU: . . . and so that's the assignment, Bert.

HE: Ummmm.

YOU: Ah . . . and as you might suspect, I need it as soon as possible.

HE: How about two weeks?

YOU: Two weeks! I was thinking of two days.

HE: C'mon, Jack. It's a lot of work. I've got to see what's available. I've got to research what other manufacturers have done for our distributors so that we don't give them the same thing. I've got to come up with something novel, and ideas aren't sitting around waiting to be discovered.

YOU: But two weeks!

And so it goes back and forth with the final compromise being five days. But is that right? Have you really allowed your sales promotion manager enough time? Or has he wheedled an extra few days out of you to ease the strain? How much of the time is padded time? How much has each of you added to the schedule just to be safe?

The secret here, I think, is to know your creative cohort and his working habits. Does he work best under pressure? If given adequate time, will he procrastinate until the last minute?

Some people must constantly build challenges for themselves, and often the challenge is the minimum amount of time possible. Others look as though they're doing nothing—but remember the back burner. Be careful, it may be working. They've put raw material into the pot, and it's simmering while they read the paper or handle the expense account or check proofs for the annual Christmas card, while you simmer and wonder whether you'll ever have an idea given to you for the sales contest. Only by knowing your cohorts' psyches and working habits can you match your demands with their productivity. Oh, if they're professional the job will get done. But how much better would it be without the browbeating, heartburning bickering that often goes hand in hand with discussions of time and deadlines between two who don't understand or haven't bothered to understand each other's proclivities? This kind of understanding, I might add, is also very good for the digestion and blood pressure.

WHEN AND WHEN NOT TO BE PATIENT

Time and patience seem to be companions and adversaries in all our lives: companions when we have enough time for a given project and therefore can afford to be patient, adversaries when time is short and the creative people on whom we depend seemingly are involved in a discussion of the coming football season or Wertmuller film. It's easy to be patient when everything is going right. And often that's at the very beginning of an assignment. It's not easy when the pressure begins to build. Obviously, the shorter the time, the shorter the patience. And of course, that's when calm and cool are most desired and needed.

In dealing with anyone, we must always be aware of the transfer of emotions. We've all seen it happen with temper tantrums. Someone comes in the room in a state of high decibel with arms waving and fists shaking. The smart recipient, after offering the obligatory surprised look, sits back and listens. The ranter rants, but the crescendo begins to work in reverse and descends to mutters and mumbles and an embarrassed apologetic grin. If, however, the recipient matches the mood of the shouter we have a scenario that can lead to loss of control (saying things we didn't mean to say), ill feelings, strained relationships, and loss of productivity. And, unfortunately, the creative psyche is often so delicate that this kind of confrontation can obfuscate the thought process for longer periods of time than you'd think. So a general rule is to control the situation by controlling your feelings and temper. This doesn't mean that the temperamental cohort should, after the periodic explosion, always be agreed with. Sympathy, yes. Agreement, possibly. Because if the low threshold-of-patience people always get their way by shouting and stamping, the temper tantrum will obviously become a steady ritual.

On the other hand, patience can sometimes work against creativity. Because of the very nature of the creative process, most people look for any excuse to keep from getting started. And if, like most creative people, they are normally involved in a number of challenges, the project of the patient person can get pushed so far behind the back burner that it falls off the stove. Squeaky wheel and all that. So if you calmly give an assignment with plenty of time and then, in checking as time goes by, find that nothing is really being done, get tough. But lose your temper only as a last resort (known as the controlled or planned tantrum, or, as they used to say in the field artillery, "Fire a couple of rounds for effect"). The occasional display of emotion by anyone in a supervisory position can have an amazing effect on the supervisees. But use it discreetly. No one really likes to work for a screamer. And good creative people are hard to find.

WHEN HONESTY MAY NOT BE THE BEST POLICY

It seems to me that the only time to lie is when honesty will hurt the end result of the project on which you're working. Example: You're a textbook publisher and you have a particular artist in mind who specializes in anthropomorphic animals for the jacket of a new book on evolution. Unfortunately, the artist is unavailable, so you call in two or three others and look at their work. You select the alternate and then proceed to tell the truth. He's been selected because the person you wanted is unavailable and you certainly hope that the end result will have the quality of the original artist. Tactless? Of course. But worse, this kind of honesty can so inhibit the artist that the result will be less than satisfactory.

When you choose or hire people to perform a creative task (or any task, for that matter) you should give them all of the help and encouragement that you can. But beware of going too far. The "we're expecting-great-things-from-you" approach (with its implication of "so you'd better be good") can freeze the creative mind just as quickly. When working with creative people I think that the "it's-good-to-let-them-know-exactly-what-the-score-is" approach should be used more judiciously, perhaps, than with any other group of people. But don't confuse honesty with objectivity. Here, in managing the creative process, is where you can be most helpful and perform an invaluable function.

THE BACKBOARD

Usually the creative process is a lonely one. If it's not one person at the piano or word processor or drawing board, it's a team of two or three who isolate themselves and become mutually enmeshed in the challenge. At some point halfway or so through the project they decide it's time for someone else to look at the approach they're taking "just to see if we're on the right track." Sometimes the someone is a creative cohort. But that can be sticky because creative people don't like to hurt other creative people. They even build in excuses: "Ahh. I think that's nice, Gordo. It seems a little usual, but then I don't know the strategy or circumstances surrounding the problem." And Gordo says: "That's right. It may seem a little square, but you have to know the circumstances, and I don't have time to go into it now, but thanks anyway for your reaction."

What has happened is that in being nice you've given him the excuse (there are "circumstances" surrounding the problem) that allows him to slide by with something that isn't as good as it should be. The result is that some time somewhere in the middle of the night Gordo will stare at the ceiling and finally say, "Nuts, it isn't right" (or words to that effect) and get up and start over, having wasted time and effort because he didn't or couldn't face the moment of truth and did not receive the kind of advice that would help him make the decision. And that's, again, where you as a good manager can help. You know the background and those elusive "circumstances" that are a part of every project. You are involved—but not so deeply involved (at this point) that objectivity is lost. So you become the sounding board. The listener. The appraiser. The advisor. And if you're good, the creative people will take heed.

But now another problem surfaces. Once the uninvolved manager becomes involved in the creative solution, objectivity begins to slip. And this is why a number of organizations have so-called review boards to screen and comment on ideas. In the advertising agency business, these boards are sometimes looked upon as unnecessary evils by those that must parade their wares before it. "They inhibit" is the cry. "They're jealous" is the mutter. "They don't understand" is the wail. And unless the review board is carefully structured with very precise guidelines as to what they should and shouldn't do, the cries and mutters and wails could be right.

THE REVIEW BOARD

Some organizations have a standing review board, usually made up of senior executives who can utilize their years of knowledge and experience. Unfortunately, many of them utilize years of built-in prejudices, as well. And the constant working together and applying their own principles against a variety of different problems destroys objectivity and begins to build a rigidity of judgment. It has the inherent problems of a jury system with a permanent jury.

In the advertising agency business, some use a changing review made up of peers of the creative people drawn from both the business side and the creative side of the agency. The various teams that present the ideas to the board are also composed of both business or marketing and creative people. And the board is not permanent. The members rotate from a pool of senior marketing and creative executives. One day a creative director might be sitting on the board commenting on some advertising, and the next day the role might be reversed as the same creative director presents new campaign ideas to a different set of people on the board. From a morale point of view, being judged by one's peers seems to be better than by a permanent group of elder statesmen. Obviously, the composition of these boards in different fields of endeavor would be dictated by the expertise required. But the principle of a rotating board of working specialists is, I think, a good one.

What they say and what powers they have is also a matter of need and policy. Back to the advertising agency example. In some agencies the board acts in an advisory capacity only. In others its word is binding. My experience has been that unless the board has some power, the presenters have a tendency to say thank you very much and do what they originally intended anyway. If, however, the board is to have some discretionary power, the rules by which it judges the work should be simple, direct, and understood by all. And they should be broad enough not to inhibit ideas.

THE GREAT WALL OR MENTAL BLOCK

We hear about it all of the time. We've all probably experienced it, in one way or another, in our own lives. Creative people know that it's always there, ready to crawl out of their typewriter or keyboard or felt-tipped pen. They fear it and hate it but, if they're successful, have learned how to surmount it. It's the dreaded mental block. The moment when nothing happens. When the next idea does not appear on the screen in the back of your head. When you don't know which way to go or how to get there. And it comes in a variety of sizes and goes under a number of different names . . .writer's block, musical black-out, painter's block, the great wall of nothing, the dry well. But whatever we call it, the effect is the same. Panic (if you're new at the game), depression (if you're moderately experienced), resignation (if you're an old pro).

This block should not be confused, however, with lack of confidence or fear. I think that all creative people who tackle a specific project or assignment wonder, at one time or another, if they can really do it well. ("Do I have another book in me or is it all over?" "Can I come up with another great campaign for the Pegasus 6?" "Are all of my melodies beginning to sound the same?") If, on the other hand, the mental block inserts itself at the beginning of every project—if the creative person does not know where to start or how to come up with an idea—perhaps what we have is not a mental block at all but rather a simple lack of creativity. Reappraisal time. Perhaps the business of being creative for a living is not the right business for this particular person. Note the phrase "being creative for a living." Lots of very creative people are good at it in their spare time as a hobby. But the stress and pressures of having to produce to make money sometimes seems to turn out the light and dim the ideas that spring eternal during the off hours.

What we're concerned with is the block that challenges the creative person in the middle of a particular project. Most people have their own way of handling the problem. They walk away for a while. They work on another project. They take a long weekend in the country. That's fine if time is on their side. Most of the time it isn't. The challenge then is how the manager of creative people can help.

1. Act as a sounding board. When your cohort comes in with shaking head and rolling eyes sighing, "I'm stuck. I've been at it for six hours and nothing's happening", ask him to outline the different approaches he's taken. Then listen carefully. If any of them sound logical to you, ask why he has discarded them. If he says, "It just doesn't sound right" but it seems plausible to you, urge him to proceed on that particular course. Much of the time all that creative people need is some confidence and encouragement. They've enmeshed themselves so thoroughly in the project that they've lost their sense of balance and reason. You, somewhat removed from the scene of creative combat, may be able to bring objectivity back to the problem.

2. Check the facts—and the strategy. If, on the other hand, your cohort is right and, after going over all of the approaches attempted, you agree that nothing seems to be happening, see if he's on the right track. Much of the time a creative block is really caused by the creative person trying to do something that's impossible to do. Example: You're given the assignment to write a 30-second television commercial for a dried soup based on the fact that it's convenient. You're in trouble. No matter how hard you try, you can't make the convenience seem interesting, plausible, or believable. That's because it's not believable. And it's not believable because it's not true. No matter what you say or how you say it, there's no way to make preparing dried soup more convenient than preparing canned soup. This is a case where you should look at your strategy. Change it from convenience to fresh tasting and watch the creative block crumble.

3. Go back to the beginning. If reviewing the facts and strategy doesn't work, start a free-thought conversation with your compatriot. Don't just sit and stare and say, "What can I do?" Give him your impressions of the problem or project, of the audience you're trying to reach. Talk about what you think motivates people to act in a particular way. If research has been done on the subject, review the highlights—even though you may have gone over it in the beginning. It might start the bulb flickering. And have your source material handy in case he wants to do his own probing. Remember, most creative people are curious. Give them a chance to use this curiosity in helping to break the block.

If you have time (and sometimes, in cases like this, it's wise to make time), arrange focused group interviews with typical members of the audience you're trying to reach. Have your research people (or research consultants) probe them for general attitudes concerning the project. Once, when I was frustrated on the approach to an advertising campaign for Life Savers candy, we arranged a series of sessions to see if the attitudes of people toward Life Savers would give us some direction. We asked a number of questions to stimulate some thoughts. One of them, very simply was, "Why do you like Life Savers?" A variety of answers ("They taste good." "I like the way they feel in my mouth." "They have lots of different flavors.") came back. But sprinkled among those answers were such things as "Why wouldn't I like them. I've been eating them all my life." and "I've liked them since I was a kid and my grandfather used to buy a roll of peppermint and give me one." And there was the clue. Life Savers have a tradition of flavor and taste that has been a part of our lives . . .a tradition that no other competitive product could claim. Out of this came the campaign "Life Savers . . .a part of livin'." It was advertising that ran for about seven years depicting timeless moments in our lives where Life Savers had played a part. It was a sales-building, award-winning campaign. And it was generated by the answers people gave us to some simple questions.

4. Hold back nothing. When you're involved in any kind of thought-stimulating discussions with creative people, don't censor yourself. Don't worry about looking foolish or incompetent. Your objective is to help them—any way that you can. And you never want to be in the position of seeing someone, especially a competitor, come out with an idea while you say, "Gee, I thought of that—but I didn't feel it was good enough, so I didn't mention it." Again, you're trying to help your creative worker open the suddenly locked idea door and you never know which key will fit. Try them all.

5. Be an observer of the passing scene. Look at what other people have done on similar projects. Share these approaches with the creative people. I know, reviewing competitive approaches is a part of the early process prior to setting up strategies. But, strangely enough, some creative people don't really familiarize themselves with what's going on around them. They feel that looking at other people's work may contaminate and confuse their thinking. Of course, competitive awareness may also help keep them from conscious plagiarism. But they're willing to take this risk. Their ego suggests that even though someone else has used a certain creative approach, they will do it differently—and better. However, when the creative wall casts its worrisome shadow over them, they become suddenly amenable to any course of action that might help. Even if they are aware of what others are doing, a review may trigger a thought process that will lead to a light at the end of the tunnel. Often doing something just for the sake of doing something helps.

6. Creative block—or creative boredom? Often the block is a result of repetition and boredom. If you assign the same task to the same person time after time, yet each time ask the person to do it differently ("Give it a fresh feel, Kiddo.") built-in lethargy becomes almost inevitable. How many different ways can you write the Annual Floor Care Maintenance Guide or design the U.S. Information Booklet on State Department Deportment in Greece or reorchestrate the United Airlines jingle? At that point, probably the best way for a breakthrough is to put someone new on the project. There's always a different way to approach a problem—but not always from the same source.

IN SUMMARY

1.   Before any creative project is undertaken, the objective or objectives should be put in writing. The more focused the objectives, the better chance you have to achieve them creatively.

2.   In advertising and marketing, creative objectives become a part of the creative strategy. The more single-minded the creative strategy, the more effective the advertising.

3.   Also included in the creative strategy is a definition of the audience to be reached, a description of what action you want the audience to take, the principal thought that the audience should be left with after seeing the advertising, the "because" statement that gives the audience a reason to believe the principal thought, and the pertinent consumer perceptions concerning the product or product category or the conditions in the market place that might influence the creative execution of the strategy.

4.   Fact gathering is a most important step in developing any creative strategy. A check list that includes three main sections (background, the product or subject itself, the current climate in which the product or subject will be presented to the audience) is a most useful tool.

5.   An important part of any creative person's arsenal should be a note pad and pencil. Taking notes not only helps in the organization of facts but also in the idea-generating process.

6.   Often creative leaders also participate in the creative process along with the creative people they manage. In these instances they are in competition with their own troops. They must, therefore, make it a firm policy to favor their people's work over their own in any close decisions. Not to do this destroys their effectiveness as leaders.

7.   Know the working habits and capacities of your people so that you can accurately judge the time needed for creative projects.

8.   Know when and when not to be patient with your cohorts. Short tempers have a habit of transferring a high decibel atmosphere to the people to whom you're talking. Patience, on the other hand, is sometimes an invitation to advantage taking by the people working for you. Choose your moods carefully.

9. The only time to be less than honest when managing the creative process is when honesty will hurt the end result of your project.

10. One of the most important functions of anyone in a managerial position is to act as a sounding board for the ideas of the creative people. Objectivity is a key to success in this role.

11. Because objectivity can sometimes be lost through continued involvement, many organizations use impartial review boards as a final check on creative projects. This board usually judges whether or not the creative project is attaining its objectives and whether or not the creative execution is creative enough to gain the audience's attention and nudge them into the required action.

12. The creative block is one of life's major creative problems. Successful creative people have their own individual ways of hurdling these blocks. The creative manager can help by acting as a sounding board, giving encouragement and confidence, reminding them of facts and strategies and reinterpreting them if necessary, stimulating new approaches with free-thought impressions that might give them a new and different creative direction. Hold back nothing. This is the time when the creative manager can be most valuable. Finally, if the creative block cannot be broken through, be prepared to put new forces on the project. Managing the creative process has as its final objective good creative work that solves the problem at hand. A good manager uses all legal means to attain this goal.

While I will soon cover many other aspects of handling the unusual, channeling the creative flow through the various means covered in this chapter, it seems to me, is a key to getting things (including relations with the creative people) started positively.

3

HOW TO HIRE AND EVALUATE CREATIVE TALENT—AND HOW TO SAY GOODBYE

Everyone in a managerial position has, or will have, the dubious pleasure of searching for, sifting through, and selecting someone to fill a particular job. Some are fortunate enough to have trained personnel people to help in varying degrees. Others must tackle the job alone. This chapter is for all nonprofessionals (as far as the personnel field is concerned) who face the task of hiring someone or administering the hiring of someone to fill a creative role.

Your library or the business books section of a book store can provide much insightful information on the general subject of hiring, but not specifically on dealing with creative talent. What follows is not really earth shattering. In fact, some of it is pretty basic. What it is is a compendium of what I've learned over the years that has helped me handle this sensitive and often complex problem.

AN OUTLINE FOR HIRING

You're the new sales manager for a large lingerie manufacturer. As part of your job you've inherited responsibility for your company's annual buyer's show where the new line is presented with dramatic showbusiness flair to the country's leading department store buyers. Your predecessor handled the organization of this yearly extravaganza himself because he was good at it and he liked to do it. You don't feel the same. You have too much responsibility in the sales area expanding distribution, seeing that quotas are met, and so forth. Besides, your talents and instincts point in other directions. You are not experienced or comfortable in this theatrical role. For these reasons, and because of the importance of the annual show, you convince your management that you should hire a specialist, reporting to you, to handle the complete job. But how do you do it? Where do you go to look for this special person? What qualities do you look for? When do you need the person and for how long? And so forth.

Hiring is just as creative a challenge as many of the other subjects we've talked about. As such, it demands a written strategy as the first step. Not a creative strategy, however, but a special hiring strategy. What it will do is organize your thoughts and, like all good strategies, give good direction. One way to set up a hiring strategy is to answer some pertinent (and somewhat obvious) questions. Here's how it might work in the case of the search for the producer of the buyer's show.

QUESTION: WHAT IS THE JOB DESCRIPTION?

ANSWER: Producer of the annual buyer's show with responsibility for strategy, script, casting, music, direction, staging, filming or recording (if necessary), costs and overall budget. This would obviously include all subcontracting.

QUESTION: TO WHOM WOULD THIS PRODUCER REPORT?

ANSWER: Directly to the sales manager (you) but indirectly to the chief executive officer (through you). It's important that the applicant knows that the job is highly visible and that his efforts will be noticed by top management.

QUESTION: WHEN WILL THE JOB COMMENCE AND HOW LONG WILL IT LAST?

ANSWER: Some jobs are short-term projects and can be filled with freelance specialists. This position, however, looks like a permanent one because the planning and producing of each show takes about a year. Thus, as soon as the final curtain falls on one show, the idea sessions start for the next one. Because of this schedule, the job will commence as soon as possible, which means you really don't have the luxury of time in making your selection.

QUESTION: WHERE WILL THIS TASK BE PERFORMED?

ANSWER: Most of the time near the home office but there may be a certain amount of travel back and forth to Hollywood. This means that while you will be available for major consultation and decisions, the producer will also be on his own some of the time.

QUESTION: WHAT CHARACTERISTICS SHOULD THE CANDIDATES HAVE?

ANSWER: This is the big question. But the answers to the other questions have given us some direction. First of all, the candidate should obviously have some kind of show-business background with all of the implications of being able to work under pressure, with temperamental talent, and so forth. Knowledge of the field is also important for contacts, knowing whom to go to and where to go to get things done quickly, efficiently. As part of this background the candidate should have a feeling for the practical: be able to know costs and how to work within a budget. If you hire a pure creative genius, then you may have to find a business manager as well. The winner of this sweepstakes should probably be flexible and able to change direction to accommodate circumstances and whims of businesspeople not used to working in this area. Patience also becomes a virtue in these cases.

With this show-business flair, our person should also be able to present and sell ideas to management. While leadership is important because, as we said before, the person will be in certain decision-making situations, he will not be alone most of the time and will have you and perhaps other to fall back on for overall direction and decisions.

The candidate should also have stamina for long hours and concentrated work that are a part of this type of job—especially in the later days of rehearsals, script changes, and so forth. Stamina, by the way, seems to me to be an important attribute for anyone who looks forward to becoming a leader in almost any field of endeavor. And the creative area is no exception. As people grow in this field, they are called upon more and more to produce under stress, to make overnight changes to travel across the country or ocean for presentations, or to revise scripts or specifications or drawings or musical arrangements. And always their endeavors are governed by the clicking clock or flipping calendar. Their success often depends not only on their talent but also on the degree of indefatigability that's a part of their physical makeup.

Obviously, once you've jotted down the requirements for the job based on the preceding questions, you'll decide that no one person can fill the role. So you should probably weigh the requirements as to their importance. In this case we would probably give more importance to the experience in the field, ability to work under pressure, and stamina. If needed, you can step in and help sell management, guide the direction, give leadership when necessary, even keep an eye on costs. In the latter area, specialists from your accounting or bookkeeping sections can help.

The point here is that by organizing and writing down what you're looking for, you've developed a strategy for hiring that will make your job if not simpler, easier to attack.

FINDING YOUR CANDIDATES

Once you've defined your needs, send them in writing to your personnel director. If you're operating a small business and you're the personnel person, write the requirements down anyway. You may even want to include a profile of the person you're looking for based on these requirements. Then consult friends and business associates for any suggested candidates. This should be the first area of search because it's the best source for valuable opinions and evaluations. And you may even have a candidate in your own organization lurking somewhere behind one of the computers or sales charts. Obviously, if you can fill the job from within the company you've accomplished three important things: (1) you've saved yourself and your company quite a bit of "search" time, (2) you've also saved the time needed for the person to become familiar with and acclimated to the organization, and (3) you will boost the morale of your employees because you've demonstrated a willingness to promote from within. But be careful that in your awareness of these advantages you don't allow yourself to lean toward the candidate from inside and perhaps compromise some of the more pertinent requirements.

Talk to personnel agencies (there are a number of specialized agencies for almost any field in which you're interested) and/or run an advertisement in local newspapers or trade magazines in the particular field. Make the advertisement the kind of advertisement you'd like to answer. Be specific, but at the same time general enough so that you leave room for the applicant's imagination and ambitions to wander. And remember, the demands of your requirements can be in direct proportion to the salary you're paying.

In the case of the producer for the lingerie company's trade show, you probably would want someone with fairly extensive experience in the actual running of trade shows. You might start by talking to people who run the trade show divisions of other companies. And you don't have to know these people personally. Most everyone is flattered when asked for this kind of advice. We like to do favors for and establish contacts with people who some day may be in a position to help us. Of course, every now and again, the person to whom you've addressed your inquiry is interested in the opportunity personally, and voila—you have a good candidate. You might also talk to people in the theater. Stage managers and producers are often naturals for this kind of assignment. If you advertise, you would consider some of the convention and trade show business publications and perhaps local newspapers if you're located in a large metropolitan area. (The chance of finding someone with this kind of specialized know-how through a newspaper ad in a small town or city is probably quite remote.)

One of the best ways to find out what candidates have to offer is to ask for a letter explaining why they think they're the right person for the job. This gives them not only the opportunity to show off their wares and background, but also their ability to communicate and sell. If the letter is disorganized and sloppy, then the writer is liable to be the same. If the letter is precise and businesslike but unimaginative, that's probably what you're getting.

I once hired a copywriter because he answered my rather detailed ad with a letter that simply said, "I would like to work for you because I believe that every advertising agency should have a fly fisherman on its staff." Now this came in the midst of about 200 answers to the advertisement. It was startling. No résumé. No samples of his work. Just this simple one-sentence letter. It jumped out at me. And it worked. Oh, I didn't pick up the phone and hire him. But I did have him come in for an interview (and that, after all, should be the primary objective of the applicant) because I was intrigued and curious—and also because I wanted to see his face when I told him that I agreed with him and that I was the fly fisherman in the agency. The interview was marvelous. He wrote the letter because he didn't have the experience needed for the job but felt he could handle it, and he knew he had to attract my attention. He obviously did. His next move was to say: "It's Friday. Let me show you what I can do and how I think. Give me an assignment. I'll have an answer in the form of a campaign on your desk Monday morning." I did, and he did, and it was great, and he was hired.

HOW CAN YOU TELL IF THEY'RE ANY GOOD?

You've received a number of answers to your quest for excellence. You've narrowed them to a short list of five or six. This culling process itself has taken time and thought. You've done it from a review of their qualifications: the obvious nonqualifiers going into a reject pile, the possibles into another pile. And at this stage, if there's any question as to whether applicants have what you're looking for, give them the benefit of the doubt. It's easier to eliminate later if someone else is better; but in the beginning, you don't want to overlook any possibilities.

Now, before inviting the finalists in for an interview, take an important intermediate step: a sample of the candidate's work. One of the advantages of hiring someone for a specific creative task is that, unlike many other occupations, creative people usually are engaged in an activity that allows them to display the results of their endeavors. Musicians can submit sample tapes or records, composers their compositions, woodworkers photographs of their furniture, writers their accomplishments, and so forth. Most people like to accompany their samples to explain why and how and what. And it's true. Sometimes these explanations do help. But often you can tell much of what you want to know from the work without the explanations. It's a great time-saver. You don't have to nod and make positive or noncommital mutterings to the nervous candidate. You don't have to be polite.

If, at first glance, you can see that the work is not what you're looking for, you don't have to spend a lot of time going through it or explaining to the applicant, as tactfully as possible, why it's not right for your particular needs, which usually results in a desperate counterargument. ("Perhaps, sir, you don't understand the underlying philosophy of my efforts. Let me explain it to you.") Again, you can often tell quite a bit about the person in the way the sample work is presented. If it's true that a certain amount of explanation is needed, then the candidates who clearly and concisely explain this in writing, all things being equal, should be looked upon with interest. They are not only creative but have a good grasp of how to sell.

In the advertising field, putting a sample book together is an art in itself, which we don't get into here because it's really not a key part of managing the creative process. However, for those who may be interested in some tips on this subject, I can think of no better guide than my friend Maxine Paetro's book *How to Put Your Book Together and Get a Job in Advertising* (Hawthorne Books, New York, 1979). Having washed my hands of this type of project, I will offer one valuable format tip—at least it impresses and helps me when I'm screening creative applicants.

Include with each sample of your work a general outline of the problem your advertising was designed to solve and a critique of how well you feel it accomplished its task. Include in this any negatives that you discovered, with a suggestion as to how you might improve or eliminate them. This kind of thinking not only shows off a person's creativity but also gives the interviewer some insights into the workings of the applicant's mind relating to logic, objectivity, and organization.

THE INTERVIEW AND HOW TO CONTROL IT

Much has been said, taught, and written about the art of the interview. I think that all of us have been in the role of both interviewer and interviewee at one time or another. And we've all thought of all the wonderful things we should have said and didn't. There's no secret method or formula. But it is good to have some kind of plan before the quaking candidate gives you the sweaty handshake. Jot down on a pad exactly what you want to find out from the applicant. Here are some guidelines that I use when interviewing people for a creative position.

1.   Put the candidate at ease. I really don't adhere to the theory of applying pressure to see the effect of stress on the candidate. The reason is that when dealing with creative people, we are often in touch with a lot of emotion, which can be triggered the wrong way in the stressful interview. This obviously can give the wrong impression of the candidate and the wrong impression of you. Remember, you are also being judged in this interview. She's forming impressions, and she knows that the best work is the result of the right chemistry. And if she's good, you may be competing for her talents with others. Starting out with any kind of confrontation could jeopardize a potentially good future with the applicant. When interviewing creative people, I first familiarize myself with their résumé, looking for some trivia that will help break the ice, such as a mutual home town or college or acquaintances at former places or employment.

But be careful about the latter. It can boomerang. If the objective is to put the interviewee at ease, reference to a former cohort with whom he might have had some differences could lower a cloud of wary tenseness over the interview. His thought process could go something like: "Oh oh. He's just mentioned old Iron Pants. Is he a friend of old Iron Pants? Does he admire him? If so, I don't know if I want to work here. On the other hand, this might be a test. Maybe he knows old Iron Pants is a sonofabitch to work for and is fishing for my opinions. Whatever, I'd better be very, very careful of what I say."

As you can see, this is hardly the way to relax your candidate. On the other hand, later on in the interview after a certain rapport has been established, you might want to use this approach to get some attitudinal feelings from your candidate. This, of course, assumes you know a bit about the track record and reputation of the mutual acquaintance. If the candidate is cautious and tactful about old Iron Pants, then you've gained an insight into her approach. If she's blunt in her assessment, you might conclude that she's honest and perceptive but short on tact. If she's laudatory of Iron Pants, you might think that she's either a poor judge of character or she's lying, hoping to play it safe with you—or she might honestly like Iron Pants and agree with his controversial approach. Any of the latter answers could be warning signals in your possible future working relationship.

2.   One of the clues to the creative drive people might have is what they do with their free time. I've found very simply that good creative people can't help being creative: the writer who paints when not writing, the lawyer who writes poetry, the art director who builds boats, the film maker who raises orchids. If you're interviewing someone who, when asked what he does when he's not working, replies: "Sit and look at TV. When I'm through at the end of the day, I'm burned out. I don't want to do anything"—be cautious. Such people might be good managers or businesspeople or even competent creative people, but I'll bet they don't have an overabundance of creativity bubbling and bursting to get out.

3.   This creative restlessness and striving for excellence often are seen in the applicants' opinions of their own work. After looking at candidates' samples, ask which are their favorites. If the answer is: "I like this one and this one. I think they're both 90 percent of what I wanted, but I'd like to have had a little more time to make them perfect," you have indications of someone who's always reaching for the stars, never quite satisfied. You may also be talking to someone with a certain amount of

objectivity—a welcome commodity in this world of hard sell and opinionated intensity. In addition, you'll get some idea of your candidates' ability to present and sell, of their articulateness and deftness in making a presentation or explaining a position—if good, it can be a happy talent.

4.   Spend as much time as is needed in the interview—and allow for this time in your busy schedule. Don't give it short shrift. The position is too important, and the interview is probably the key step in filling the position. If you're interviewing a number of applicants, I think it's wise to arrange the sessions so that there's time in between—if possible, as much as a day. Back-to-back interviews tend to become a blur and can cause confusion.

5.   What about luncheon interviews? Sometimes, when dealing with a high-level position, the luncheon or cocktail meeting is a polite and accepted way for the principals involved to get to know each other and their respective philosophies. I personally think that the first meeting should be in the office. It provides privacy with fewer distractions. And one doesn't have to strain to hear over the babble of voices and clatter of dishes. In addition, if some sample work is to be reviewed, it's almost impossible to do it in the London Chop House or The Oak Room. If you do have a meal meeting, again make sure you know what you wish to accomplish. A premeeting outline will help, even if the encounter is to be informal.

6.   After the interview, spend a few minutes making notes on your impressions. Go over the checklist of what you wanted to accomplish to see how your candidate fared. Many companies have interview forms that can be used. Whatever you do, make sure that your notes are not so cryptic that they'll be a mystery at later meetings. They can be most valuable in eventually comparing candidates, refreshing your memory.

7.   When you've narrowed the qualified candidates to a short list of the final two or three, you might want to arrange to have a second opinion from one of your cohorts. But don't give him any of your impressions beforehand unless there's something specific you wish to have him look for or find out. Most of the time, however, you want an objective second opinion. Make sure that it is objective. After your compatriot has given you his thoughts, discuss the candidate; discuss concerns if you have them; ask for impressions you may have missed. Then add these thoughts to your notes on the candidate.

SOME TIPS ON REFERENCES

One of the problems with references, of course, is that the candidate does not knowingly list a reference who's going to give a negative or even slightly tainted report. A phone call to the reference can usually elicit more of what you want to know than a letter because a letter demands an answer and gives respondees a chance to compose exactly what they want to say. The phone call can often catch the person unaware and thus get closer to the unvarnished truth. Remember, what you're looking for from the reference are possible problems. It's really a disaster check. It's assumed that by the time you get to the checking of references you've pretty well decided that the person is right for the job. And don't let the references' enthusiasm, or lack thereof, sway you unless you know them personally. A bubbling endorsement or a lethargic response may be the natural everyday attitude of the person. Ask direct questions, particularly if you have cause to believe that there may be some problem areas. Then, if the reference seems to hesitate a bit, probe some more. This is often an indication of nervousness about an answer because the reference knows there's a problem but doesn't quite know what to say, or is hedging for legal reasons.

I think that one of the most important pieces of information to try and get from the reference is whether or not the applicant, in fact, has done or has handled the duties claimed. I recently heard of a case where a creative person, working on one part of a very important advertising account, was unintentionally given credit for work on the entire account by a prospective employer. While the candidate did not further this impression, he naturally did not deny it either. Unfortunately, the hirer did not check with anyone, or rather did not ask the important questions, "Hey, did this guy really run the entire such and such account?" The result is that it was not until after he was hired that the truth surfaced. Very awkward. The new employer could not let the person go saying that the man had misrepresented himself, because he hadn't. He personally had never been asked the direct question. His résumé didn't reveal it. But nevertheless, by not checking, the new company had not gotten what it thought it was getting. This is where the personal contact can play a most important part, much more important than the reference. Obviously, it's often most difficult to call a contact at the candidate's present place of employ without risking trouble for the candidate. Be careful. Never do this unless you know you can trust your contact implicitly. A better way is to ask a third party if they know of anyone who works with or is familiar with your applicant. In almost all creative areas, people in the business know who does what and how well.

Finally, I've found that one of the most productive questions to ask a contact is whether or not they would hire the person if they felt the person fulfilled the requirements for the job. This is where you get such answers as: "Yes. She's very good, even with her quick temper." (Aha. You didn't know about the temper. But Fred says she's good, and I believe Fred, so I'll be prepared for the temper.) Or: "I think she's terrific, but watch the stress. She works very well at one thing at a time. But when she gets multiple assignments, she tends to pull her hair and throw things." (Good to know. I'll hire her and keep her on one project at a time.) Again, what you're trying to discover is whether there are any hidden mine fields that may affect performance.

By following these steps in the suggested interview process, you, in your search for a producer for the annual buyer's show, have put your candidate at ease by reminiscing about great moments in the theater, discovered that in his free time he likes to experiment with baking bread (a most creative undertaking), have looked at videotapes of and listened to his intelligent critique of the last two industrial shows he's worked on, called your secretary and canceled a 2:30 meeting so that you can hear more about his ideas, said goodbye—and been impressed. After the interview, you quickly made notes on your impressions for future reference and comparison, arranged for the candidate's interview with two other members of your organization who would be working with him, and, on checking, found that his references were most laudatory. With that, your methodical and patient search reached its climax. You hired the candidate and were freed from the responsibilities of even thinking about him and his challenges—at least until your company reminded you of its employee evaluation system.

EVALUATIONS AND HOW THEY DIFFER

All of us are familiar with the periodic evaluations used in most businesses to chart an employee's progress, or lack thereof. They come in many forms, but most of them are based on the "goals" or "objectives" theory. Usually, certain annual goals or objectives for the employee are agreed upon between the employee and employer. These are normally based on the employee's position, responsibilities, and experience. The evaluations simply chart the individual's progress toward these goals. Obviously, the more specific the objectives, the easier it is to measure progress. And this is the basic catch in evaluating creative people. It's extremely hard to set up specific objectives. For a salesperson we can say: "Sales goal for the year: Increase sales of product by 20 percent." Very specific.

But what do you say to a copywriter? "One of your goals for this year is to come up with a new campaign for Superskin Pantyhose," you might say to one of your creative stars. And, after reviewing all of the facts, strategies, and so forth, she might come up with an excellent approach—only to discover at the last minute that a competitive manuever has forced the client to completely change the strategy nullifying the work of the copywriter. So she starts again. But now time is working against her. The original assignment allowed two months for the creative work. Six weeks of the two-month time period allocated has been used in the original and now defunct approach. Just two weeks left. Oh, she gets it done all right. But it's not as good as it should be. Everything has been rushed. The idea has not been polished and honed. The client knows it. Her management knows it. Unfortunately, everyone forgets the conditions under which she has had to produce her somewhat wayward epic. They see only what is in front of them in print or on the air. "Hmmm. OK . . . but not really our best effort. Who did it? Gloria? Gee, she can do better than that. Hope she's not slipping."

And we'd better hope that this individual is not responsible for Gloria's evaluation. Because, according to the goal (come up with a good new campaign for Superskin Pantyhose), she has succeeded. She came up with a good new campaign. But, through no fault of hers, it was not used. And so she came up with another campaign for Superskin, in one-quarter of the time. Therefore, actually, she exceeded the goal by 50 percent. (She had done two campaigns in the allotted time, but because the last one did not completely satisfy the "good" criteria, we've deducted 50 percent.) She should be rewarded and congratulated. Instead, she was probably mildly chastised.

The point is that it's extremely hard to establish specific creative performance goals for creative people because there are really no finite ways to judge this kind of performance. Is it public acclaim? Or research results? Or sales performance? Or innovation, no matter how impractical? Or management satisfaction? (Of course, if the goal is as simple as composing a company song that the president will like, and you happen to know that the company president is partial to college marching songs, your job—and the resulting evaluation—may be simple. But, as we said, most creative goals are not as definite.)

For these reasons, a number of different approaches have been devised for creative evaluations. One of the more popular is the listing of criteria relating quite specifically to general performance. In the case of advertising copywriters, for example, this might be broken into four different sections:

1. Conceptual talents (ability to come up with ideas),
2. Performance talents (ability to do what has been assigned),
3. Salesmanship (ability to present work),
4. Compatibility (ability to work with others).

The importance given to each of these sections depends on the nature of the job requirements. If the copywriter has been hired basically as a rewrite mechanic to work principally in the back room, then the second section should carry the most weight. If the person has expectations for advancement to a creative leadership position, then all of the sections should be given equal weight. While these sections are designed as suggested criteria for evaluating copywriters, the same general principles can be applied to evaluations in other creative fields.

For example, back to your new producer of the annual lingerie buyer's show. Although you hired him essentially as a person to pull together and manage the actual production of the show, he has surprised you by going much farther. He created and developed the actual theme and then wrote a good portion of the script himself, thus saving the cost of a free-lance writer. And so you are delighted to rate him higher than you thought you would in the "conceptual talents" section.

Because the show got produced on time, within budget, and was well received, you also gave him high marks in the "performance" section.

He exhibited the flair to be able to present his ideas with a certain amount of showmanship, although he sometimes belabored this process. You gave him OK grades in the "salesmanship" section, noting the long-winded characteristic. You made a note to discuss this with him.

As you get to the evaluation's "compatibility" section, you are about to rank him high. He's always been easy to work with, takes suggestions and directions well, and does not seem moody. Then you vaguely remember hearing something about a temper tantrum during one of the rehearsals. So you check with people who were more involved and find that not only does he have a temper, but he tends to be fairly autocratic. More inquiries and people admit that to get the job done he had to run the project with a firm and often tough hand. But everyone could do without the ranting and hair tearing. You note this in the "compatibility" section. When you've finished, you weight the different sections. To you, the most important section is "performance," so you weight that by four. "Salesmanship" is next and gets a three. "Conceptual talents," in the context of this job, is not as important, so it gets weighted by two. "Compatibility" is weighted one. Now, if in each of these sections you've ranked your director from 1 to 10 (with 10 high), you would then multiply the rank by the weight score of each section. For comparison, you can see that under this system, a perfect score would be 100 (10×4, 10×3, etc.). This gives you some basis for comparison while keeping a somewhat realistic perspective on the individual's overall performance.

In the archaic past, many employers kept these evaluations secreted behind lock and key, to be used only when needed. Today, happily, most of us are more enlightened. Evaluations are and should be shared with the evaluee. Some people ask the employees to fill out their own evaluation, and then the two evaluations are compared and discussed. In the case of the creative person, we have another particular quirk that is not common when evaluating noncreative workers: the creative ego. What you say and how you say it in a written review takes on new dimensions when that review is shared with the person. You must be truthful and honest. But here tact is most important because a blunt evaluation could create mental blocks, turn off the creative psyche, and create more harm than good. An understanding of the employees and what makes them work best is most important because the evaluation, besides being the guide to progress, can also be a stimulator for improvement.

HOW TO SAY GOODBYE

There comes a time in every manager's life when, for one reason or another, you have to dismiss one of your people. When dealing with those in the creative field, this is most difficult because the majority of the time these terminations are for nonperformance. And nonperformance by a creative person may be uncorrectable. It may be that the creative person is just not creative.

But, you say, presuming they're not beginners, how did they get there in the first place? Or how did they get as far as they did without being discovered? The answer is that there are different levels of creativity. And, unfortunately, one level is called competence. It consists of the mechanics who know enough to perform the function but never seem to grow. The bassoon player who plays competently but never puts any fire or feeling into it. The artist whose design concepts smack, too often, of what's been done. The architect who imitates, never innovates. The author who wrote an interesting novel in 1954—and has written it over and over in five succeeding books since then. The copywriter who started writing package backs for children's cereals and can't seem to get around to the front.

In business we often say "Someone's got to do this work." Yes. But the problem is that if that person performs the same role year after year without developing, he outprices himself. He keeps getting cost-of-living raises and minor "sympathy" increases. Suddenly, someone less experienced, and thousands of dollars less expensive, appears on the scene. She's full of excitement and determination and will "gladly tackle any job, sir, just for a chance to show you what I can do." And now you're in a box: old faithful, who has been outstanding and is now costing money, versus inexpensive newcomer enthusiasm and great potential.

The first solution is to try not to get into this situation. Try and evaluate the talent working for you as you go along. If, after a few months, you suspect what you've been afraid of, call for a conference. Go through the evaluation procedure. Be direct. Explain what you want and why you feel you're not getting it. Be specific. Thus, if the problem is correctable, the subject knows what the problem is and can take steps to correct it. But if it's not—if, in your opinion, it's a matter of lack of talent—at least the person knows your feelings. Then, after a reasonable period of time, if the work doesn't improve, you can take whatever steps are necessary in good conscience. You've not only warned your employee, you've tried to help by outlining the problem. You've probably done all you can.

Now, if you reach this conclusion early enough in a person's career, you may be performing a major service. Unfortunately, in many fields the "mechanics" can hide behind the usual for some time, often moving from one job to another while so doing. But eventually the moment of truth arrives. The problem is that they have entered the "old retainer" stage, or at least are approaching mid-life with the responsibilities of family, debts, and the like. They've been hiding in a creative career they never should have entered in the first place. So if you can help these people get out of the business they're not suited for at an early age, you'll be hated at first—and toasted after.

However old or experienced or set-in-his ways the nonperformer is, the personnel evaluation and review are a must. If done correctly, they let people know where they stand, what they're up against, and possible courses of action. However, I've noticed that often people handle these kinds of discussions brilliantly—right up until the "possible course of action" section. Then they mumble and wander and become outstanding examples of vagueness. Instead of saying, "But if the situation doesn't improve, we can't go on. You'll have to find another job," they come out with things like: "We'll have to reevaluate the situation," or "seek another solution," or "work out something else."

The recipients of this information, as we know, hear what they want to hear. While the manager may think that being vague is being kind and that the employee really "knows what I'm saying," the employee will be quite shocked when the warning period is up and the day of termination arrives. The manager will then hear such things as "but I had no warning," or "I thought 'work out something else' meant you'd give me another assignment," or "To me 'reevaluate' means we'll discuss it some more." Here's an actual scenario of what happened in a major advertising agency.

The scene: a copywriter's office. Bent over the typewriter is a writer of long standing and limited talent working on a tediously dull brochure for a client. Enter a very warm and human and embarrassed vice president. He hates the job he has to do.

VICE PRESIDENT: Hi, Claude. How's it going?

CLAUDE: Oh, hi, Fred. Working my tail off.

VICE PRESIDENT: Something I'd like to talk about.

CLAUDE: Yeah? Wassat?

VICE PRESIDENT: Ahh, we're contemplating a little reorganization in your area, Claude, and I thought I'd come down here and tell you about it.

CLAUDE: Oh, OK, Fred. Thanks. Appreciate it (turns back to typewriter).

VICE PRESIDENT: No . . . I mean this . . . ahh . . . reorganization may affect you, Claude. So I'd suggest that in the next six months, you . . . ah . . . keep your options open. If something comes along that looks good, you might want to consider it.

CLAUDE: Oh?

VICE PRESIDENT: Nothing immediate. I just wanted to let you know so . . . ah . . . you know (mumble, mumble).

CLAUDE: Yeah. Well, thanks, Fred. I really appreciate your talking to me.

The scene is now six months later. Claude is still bent over typewriter.

VICE PRESIDENT: Hi, Claude. How's it going?

CLAUDE: Oh, hi, Fred. Working my tail off.

VICE PRESIDENT: Say, remember that little talk we had six months ago.

CLAUDE: Yeah.

VICE PRESIDENT: I . . . ah . . . wondered what progress you'd made looking around.

CLAUDE: Fred, I haven't had a chance. I mean, do you know what the workload has been here? I've had to turn out three maintenance booklets, do a sales training brochure, and change the entire mat service guide from present to past tense.

VICE PRESIDENT: Oh.

Now, this may have been the greatest ploy of all time by the copywriter, the most creative achievement of his life—buying six months more time before being fired—but I don't think so. I think it was the gentle, kindly verbal bumbling of the vice president that caused the problem.

And so we return to the importance of the written evaluation. Tell your people how you feel, then show it to them in writing. Discuss problems and then have them sign the evaluation. Make sure that in the evaluation you clearly state the terms of your discussion. If you are providing a warning period, spell it out. Then when the time period is up, there should be no misunderstanding. Even if they haven't listened carefully to what you've said, even if you've been embarrassed and, therefore, less articulate than usual, the employees have signed and thus tacitly understood the evaluation and the terms of the warning.

HOW NOT TO SAY GOODBYE

Another scenario. It's the office of the vice president for business affairs of a medium sized midwestern university. He is about to face the termination interview with the head of the public affairs staff. While he doesn't relish the task at hand, he's prepared. He's had earlier talks with her, given her—and had her sign—a written evaluation stating that she would be dismissed after a given period of time if her performance didn't change. Making the task more difficult is the fact that he likes the person and enjoys working with her. Enter the public affairs lady.

VICE PRESIDENT: Sit down, Claudia. (At this point one approach would be to ask her how she thinks she's doing. Not recommended. The odds are that she'll say she thinks she's improved, or she'll give reasons for not having improved, putting you in a defensive position where you'll have to disagree. The one thing she won't say is that she hasn't improved and, therefore, she'd better leave.)

CLAUDIA: Is this it, Fred?

VICE PRESIDENT: Ah, I'm afraid so, kiddo.

CLAUDIA: Oh . . . and I thought things had improved.

VICE PRESIDENT: It's not all your fault, Claudia. Circumstances. As you know, we're expanding the job so that it's no longer what you were hired for. And since they are going to add the athletic public relations duties to the job, they really want someone with more experience in this field—you know, a guy who was a jock at one time or another, or at least who has an affinity to varsity athletics.

CLAUDIA: I see. And I guess it's understandable. Obviously, I'm disappointed. But I've enjoyed working with you, Fred.

VICE PRESIDENT: Me too, Claudia. But, as I said, you're very good as a writer. It's just that this has grown into more of a managerial and contact position. And then there's that athletic thing.

CLAUDIA: Yeah . . . well, I guess I saw it coming. You gave me a good warning. Thanks anyway, Fred.

She leaves, and Fred, though sympathetic, breathes a sigh of relief. The uncomfortable situation has not been as bad as he anticipated. Wrong. The next morning Claudia's lawyer institutes a suit against the university. Can you guess the grounds? Read the dialogue again. One innocent word cost the university a few thousand dollars. The word "guy." (" . . . you know, a guy who was a jock at one time or another"). The charge: sex discrimination.

Oh, it never went to court. The vice president told the university lawyers that he'd only casually mentioned "guy." And besides it was true. They did want a man—not a woman—who was qualified. They wanted the insights of someone who had participated in men's varsity sports. From a public relations standpoint, they wanted the ruboff of an ex-star, a man whose name might still open doors. And there was nothing in writing. He hadn't included any of this in the evaluation. The lawyers just shook their heads and sighed. To whom will the jury listen? The big, nicely endowed university with athletic ambitions or the hard working, loyal employee. In cases like this, jurors' sympathies usually skew to the individual. And so it was settled out of court, and the former employee took a nice, long, relaxing vacation in the Bahamas courtesy of the university. All because of one word.

Of course, all of this could have been avoided if the university had had a more open mind regarding qualified applicants for the position in the first place. The sooner the less enlightened become more enlightened, the easier it will be on everyone, except, of course, the legal profession. Unfortunately, litigation in these types of cases is becoming more and more popular, a warning to all of us concerning our attitudes and what we say, write, or promise when discussing an employee's future.

The four categories that should instantly wave red flags to everyone are sex, age, race, and religion. The ones that seem to be most precarious are sex—as illustrated above—and age. Happily, changing attitudes and times have practically eliminated race and religion as causes célèbres. As touched on earlier, one of the best reasons for evaluation and termination of a less than satisfactory employee while comparatively young is so that the ogre of age doesn't have to enter the picture at a later date. If you find yourself in this spot, if a person has been a loyal—albeit short-talented—employee who has outpriced himself because of longevity, find a way to transfer him to another area of responsibility. You will be doing him—and your organization—a service while avoiding the wide-eyed question: "After all these years, how can you do this to me?" It's a question that's often a prelude to another session with the lawyers. And it's always a prelude to soul searching on your part. How can you do this, indeed?

The Bad Guys—And the Good Guys

I remember that just before starting my freshman year in college I was invited to the dean's office for a brief discussion of study habits. He was a blunt man (later to become respected friend), who opened the conversation by asking me if I enjoyed going to football games. I said yes. He said: "Then you should enjoy about 70 percent of the season because that's about as long as you'll last here based on your high school record and what I perceive to be poor study habits." I was stunned. He went on to impress me with the seriousness of the matter by wondering how I'd been accepted. He ushered me out of the office by telling me unless I changed my ways, he really didn't think I could hack it.

I left his office numb with apprehension and fear, when a voice called to me from another office and asked me to step in a minute. The voice belonged to a kindly, rumpled man, smoking a meerschaum pipe. He introduced himself as the freshman advisor. "Pinky tell you you were going to bust out?" I nodded. "That's the tough guy treatment. He may be right—but I've been looking at your record and I don't think so, because you're smart enough to realize how important college is. Want me to give you some tips that might help?" Anything. Anything at all, kind sir. I don't want to be a failure.

We spent the next hour or so together, as he gave me suggestions for study schedules, how not to get bogged down in details, outlining, skimming. I left with hope and determination replacing trepidation. But "Pinky" had laid the groundwork, gotten me in a frame of mind (stark fear) to listen to and accept help. He was the bad guy. The advisor was the good guy.

IN SUMMARY

    1.   Before setting out on the hiring trail, organize your selection process:

        What is the job description?

        To whom will the candidate report?

        When do I need this person, and for how long?

        Where will the creative work be performed?

        What characteristics should the candidate have?

    2.   Carefully delineate the needs of the job and relate them to characteristics, attitudes, attributes, and weaknesses in your applicants.

    3.   In the search, use associates, personnel agencies, friends, competitors, and advertising as sources.

    4.   Ask for something in writing from the candidates giving reasons why they feel they are right for the job.

    5.   Ask for samples of the candidates' work.

    6.   Use certain guidelines in the interview:

        Put the candidates at ease

        Look for outside creative activities as an indicator of creative drive

        Ask the candidates to judge/criticize their own work

        Allow ample time for the interview

        Beware of luncheon or cocktail interviews

        Debrief yourself, and make notes, immediately after the interview

Get a second opinion of the finalists

Check references carefully

7. Concerning evaluations:

Be as specific as possible

Beware of unrealistic goals for creative people as a basis for evaluations

Use conceptual thinking, performance, salesmanship, and compatibility as guides to the evaluation

Share the evaluation with the employee

Be careful that the evaluation doesn't turn off the creative faucet

8. When termination becomes a necessary evil:

Give ample warning

Give it in writing

Review the evaluation with the employee

Have the employee sign the evaluation

Be careful what you say, promise, or how you say it

Eliminate race, religion, sex, and age from any thinking concerning hiring, performance, or firing

There is much written about the general subject of personnel management. I'm assuming that many of you are familiar with the field. In this chapter, I've tried to alert you to some of the differences that occur when dealing with creative people. I think it's a key part of managing the creative process, because if you don't know how to go about hiring the right people in the first place, your creative efforts may end up in last place. And if you have problems evaluating them as you go along, working relationships will suffer. And finally, although there is no right way to say goodbye, making it as fair and businesslike as possible may be making it as easy as possible.

HOW TO BE A CREATIVE JUDGE

In most people's business lives moments of truth abound, moments when decisions have to be made that can influence the future directions of many lives. And what we, as decision makers, all hope for at these crucial times is to have the pros and cons of the various options placed neatly before us in order of importance. Choice making, while not always easy, can thus become a bit more logical. Even though one still has to bite the bullet, the chance of dentures hitting primer is somewhat less.

Ah, but what about making a decision on a creative project? Approving the initial draft and layout of the annual report before it's shown to the chairman. Giving the go-ahead to the annual dealer's show. Saying yes to a film treatment, or to the lyrics of a song, or the recommended graphics for a hospital reception area, or for a new creative approach for an advertising campaign for a fast-food chain. How do you make these decisions? How do you know what's right and not quite right, what's going to work and what won't, what will make heros and money—or duds and losses?

Obviously, if I had the answers I wouldn't be writing this book. I'd be lolling on the foredeck of my 105 foot yacht in Mediterranean splendor. But there are some rules or guidelines that can make creative decision making somewhat easier. These guidelines are designed to help people who give the following answers when asked how they make these decisions:

"When it's right, I can feel it in my gut." (Fine, if indigestion isn't lurking in that decision-making organ.)

"I don't make the decision. I let the people who are doing the work sell me." (This makes for creative work that's only as good as the personalities and presentation skills of its creators.)

"If my wife understands it, then I know the general public will, too." (No comment.)

And too often, when shown the work, the key decision maker will respond something like this:

"Very interesting. If you don't mind I'd like to think about it overnight." (Translation: Help. I don't know whether it's good or bad, so I'll play it safe and say nothing and maybe someone else will give me an idea of what to think.)

"It's . . . ah . . . certainly different. But for some reason I don't feel comfortable with it." (Translation: I've never seen anything like this before, and therefore I don't know how to judge it.)

"Fascinating. Tell me, is this really what you want to do?" (Translation: Sell me. Give my brain some ideas and opinions. Tell me why I should like it.)

"I think we should test this idea against two others and let the public tell us which one is right." (Translation: You think I'm going to make a creative decision? Not on your life. This is the safe way. If it doesn't work, we can blame the research.)

With the exception of the person who made the last statement, all of these so-called creative decision makers could be very astute administrators. They've just never been exposed to what goes into making these particular all-important decisions. Some of them will learn from experience. Some will be lucky enough to learn through the guidance of good creative people. Some will never learn. (The last quotee—the one who wants to play it safe through research—will have a tough time. He'd probably do better in warehouse inventory control or the shipping department.) For all of these people, this chapter will attempt to give some specific help in the way of practical (and often obvious) guidelines that will, I hope, clarify what you should look for and be aware of before making any decision.

Rule 1: *Make sure the creative effort is pointed in the right direction.*

Strategy again. Notice that throughout this book we keep referring to the directional plan that a good strategy can provide. I think that it is perhaps the single most important tool to sound creative effort. Let's say that you're the chairman of the board of a drug company and it's time for the planning of your annual report. Now you, as an astute leader, know that the annual report can be used for much more than delineating the financial status of your company. It's a chance to project an image or attitude to your stockholders and the financial community. In your case there are two points that you'd like to consider focusing on. The first is to show the development and expansion of your new research center with its implications for the constant search for new drugs in the continuing battle against disease—a point that could favorably influence the financial public's feeling toward your company. The second is to put forward a new attitude toward Third World countries to help counteract the growing opinion that your company is taking advantage of underdeveloped nations for profit.

You decide that the latter is the more important task and write a strategy statement showing the positive side of your concern with and help to the peoples of these areas. A month later you're presented an interesting creative approach. Graphically the format centers on a test tube. The cover uses the stylized test tube pouring a liquid. The liquid forms a map featuring the names of the various branch offices, research centers, and manufacturing locations around the world. The main text describes the facilities and what they produce. It's striking, well-written, and certainly shows the scope of your company's worldwide activities.

But is it right? Is it what you intended? Does it fulfill your strategy? Your treasurer thinks so. He says it talks about Third World countries and, in addition, it shows the financial community the breadth of your worldwide activities. You agree. But you point out that international expansion is not a part of what you want to talk about. It's not a part of the strategy. And by including this thrust in the annual report the feeling of helping people has been minimized.

And so you ask for another approach: an approach that stays true to the strategy, an approach that focuses more on what you are, can, and want to do for the underdeveloped countries rather than how big and all-encompassing your company is.

You've just made a creative decision. You've just said the creative approach is not right because it's not on strategy. Thus, again, the importance of the strategy. If there had been no written strategy, if you and your board had said, "Time for the annual report, let's see what kind of a different look our creative people can come up with this year," you might have accepted the test tube approach—or any other that was graphically intriguing. But you would have been missing an opportunity that thinking through and writing a strategy helped you arrive at.

On the other hand, every now and then a creative execution will be developed that isn't on strategy but is so intriguing it can't be denied. Then is the time to reconsider the strategy. An example: The campaign for Life Savers candy discussed earlier.

The core idea of the strategy was to promote the wide variety of Life Savers' great flavors. We came up with a number of approaches: "What flavor would your mouth like to be?", "One of life's hardest decisions—choosing a Life Saver flavor," and so forth. Then we came up with "Life Savers—a part of livin'." As I said, it had to do with those moments when the candy with the hole in it played a small role in our lives: moments that are universal, moments that are nostalgic because they remind us of our past. But they are also moments that could happen today, or tomorrow: a mother giving her six-year-old son a Life Saver to keep him from squirming in church, a father giving his son a Life Saver to help ease the disappointment of losing a hockey game, a teenage boy wondering how he can surreptitiously get a Life Saver in his mouth before his first good night kiss on the front porch. It was a great campaign idea because it touched people's emotions, it related to Life Savers' ubiquity and to the heritage of the product.

But it did not center on the variety of great tasting flavors. It was off strategy and therefore should have been rejected. Everyone who had anything to do with it, however, was convinced that it was right for Life Savers because it grew out of a provable, believable product advantage that no other hard candy had: Life Savers have been popular since the early part of this century and therefore must be a superior product. So rather than try to force the variety of flavors into the creative execution, the leaders of the Life Savers Company agreed to change the strategy and run the new idea in selected markets. But first they ran a quantitative test to see how many people remembered the advertising and what they got out of it. The results were that the "part of livin' " campaign idea beat six "taste strategy" approaches. As a result of this and the intuitive feeling that everyone had for the campaign, "Life Savers—a part of livin' " became the national advertising campaign that helped build product awareness and sales.

So the first rule is to make sure that your creative efforts are going toward the objectives that you've set. If they aren't, you have two choices: You can easily make a creative judgment and reject the creative approach; or you can change the strategic direction. It has been my experience that if the strategy is well thought out and planned, it's usually wiser to work out a new creative execution. But not always.

Rule 2: *Make sure that the creative effort will appeal to the people you want it to appeal to.*

Another part of the strategy? Perhaps. Particularly if, in the strategy, we carefully define the market we wish to talk to. But it does deserve special consideration because often we'll have creative effort that seems to

be attaining the right objectives but may be appealing to the wrong audience. One of the dangers of advertising for low calorie soft drinks, for
example, is that while it's usually directed to young female adults, it's
often replete with catchy music and curvacious ladies in revealing bath-
ing suits. Attention getting. And appealing. But to whom? Possibly, if
not done carefully, more to men than women. In fact, the more provocative it gets, the more danger there may be of turning the primary market, young women, off. Mumbles of "sexist" might well be heard rum-
bling in the background. Perhaps it would be wise to include equally
intriguing shots of young men in this advertising.

In the aforementioned example of the drug company annual report,
the market to be reached was the stockholders, particularly those who
felt that the company was taking advantage of rather than helping Third
World nations. By asking yourself, "Will the approach showing the pro-
liferation of our worldwide offices appeal to the people who are ques-
tioning our attitudes toward underdeveloped countries?," you would
have to say "no" and again reject the test tube graphic approach.

If you're writing the Little League fund raising letter to the business
community in the neighborhood and it comes out with a father-son-
family-togetherness emotion, you might consider it wrong because no
matter how well it's written, the businessman would probably be more
responsive to a what's-in-it-for-me slant. So if you decide that the creative efforts for any project are not directed to the correct audience, you
can make another creative judgment.

Rule 3: *If the time or space in which the creative message is to be presented is limited, make sure the message is single-minded.*

We've talked about single-mindedness in the section concerning strategies. We stressed its importance to getting the core idea of a message
across, in particular in the world of advertising. But it's applicable in
most other fields as well, wherever you have limited time or space to
make your point. Another example. You have a friend who's a psychiat-
ric social worker who has been told that she has five minutes in a town
meeting to convince the neighborhood of the need for a community day
care center. Previous meetings have shown that a good number of people are opposed to the idea, not because of the cost (a government grant
will help) or the location (an old house with a big yard is available), but

rather because they're conservative and believe that day care centers cannot replace a mother's love. They feel that a mother's place is in the home, especially during the child's early years. Your friend has prepared her argument to fit the five-minute time requirement and asks you to critique it. The strategy of the persuasive proposal is built around a number of key points.

1. Children need socialization before entering the school system. It helps prepare them for the educational process and helps make them more receptive to learning.

2. Children get additional stimulation from trained teachers and from more sophisticated teaching aids and equipment than are available at home.

3. Children will learn to relate to adults other than their parents and begin to learn some of the realities of life.

4. Because of the constantly increasing number of working mothers, there is an urgent need for the services day care centers can provide. The alternative is to park the children with relatives, friends, or informal baby-sitting centers that too often provide the stimulation of warm milk, soggy crackers, and six hours before the TV set.

5. Recent studies have shown that the fastest rate of learning occurs in a child's first five years. Therefore, the professional help provided by day care centers can be extremely valuable.

6. In day care centers children receive a constancy of discipline often lacking at home due to the stresses and emotional moods of the parents.

She rehearses the speech, and you are impressed. She is a well organized, convincing speaker. When she's through, and you've murmured "very good," she asks what you've taken away from the presentation. You say there's a definite need for a day care center because . . . ah . . . children need it because . . . ah . . . they develop faster when they're young and they can have the advantage of special equipment and teachers and . . . ah . . . wait a minute . . . oh yes, it's good to have them learn something about people and the world before they go to kindergarten—and outside discipline. She looks troubled.

SHE: It's not going to convince them.

YOU: Ummmm . . . think you're right.

SHE: Why isn't it working?

YOU: It's all over the place, Betsy. Too many points. I couldn't remember a lot of them, as you saw.

SHE: What'll I do?

YOU: Why not pick the one point that'll convince them and then drive it home? Expand on it. Dramatize it. Make that one point so convincing that they can't forget it.

SHE: You're right. But what's the one point? I think all of them are important.

YOU: Think about your audience. They're conservative. They probably are not in love with the more advanced techniques of child rearing. But there is one fact that they can't deny.

SHE: What's that?

YOU: More mothers are working than ever before and therefore the need for some caretakers for their children is greater than ever before. The day care concept fills that growing need. Day care centers are not only a good solution, they're a most practical solution. You might also touch on the fact that children without any supervision or teaching in the early years may be the ones most liable to bring trouble to their community as they grow older. It's probably an unproven but logical conclusion. And it could clinch the argument with your conservatives.

SHE: Wow.

And you've just made a creative judgment: a seemingly impressive proposal was found wanting because it wasn't focused, it wasn't single-minded, it didn't leave the audience with one compelling reason why they should vote in favor of the day care center.

In the example, notice how by concentrating on the audience we were led to the core idea that would be most effective. It was this strategic analysis that gave the direction that was needed. In writing this book I've become more convinced than ever that if every challenge was given a strategy outlining whom we want to reach, what we want them to do, what we want them to remember from our message, and why they should believe what we're saying, managing the creative process and making creative judgments would be somewhat simpler.

Rule 4: *Make sure that you know what the creative people have in mind.*

One of the largest problems in trying to decide whether or not someone's creative effort is going to be effective is understanding exactly what's being proposed and how it will appear to the public. There's seldom a problem if it's a speech or simple letter or mailing piece. You can read it or look at the rough layout or art work and pretty well figure out what it's going to be. It's right there in front of you, and therefore you can concentrate on the appearance and content before making a judgment.

But what about those creative proposals that include something more? Something that involves music or special audiovisual effects or even personalities? Then it's most important that you know exactly how those other elements are to be used, how they will add to the ambience or creative impact. Without this complete understanding, you may be making judgments based on misconceptions. And if, as the case may be, you turn down something because you thought a flutter cut meant a butterfly darting across the screen, you may be losing an important creative concept. Here are some suggestions that could help avoid some of these problems.

1.   If the creative approach that you're critiquing involves music, the terminology can sometimes be baffling—unless, of course, you have some musical background. Ask to have it explained in simple ordinary language ("brisk" rather than "allegro"). Don't feel inferior. And don't try to impress your colleagues with your knowledge of their craft unless you know what you're talking about. Pride can be disastrous if it gets in the way of good creative judgment. If you're responsible for the special music to be composed for your community's bicentennial and you're thinking John Philip Sousa and it ends up with strings carrying the melody against a Latin beat, you may feel that you haven't gotten what you

wanted. In a way you could be right—and wrong. Perhaps, you haven't gotten what you expected because you haven't understood what the composer/arranger meant when he said: "I'm thinking of a contemporary march theme, with a kind of reggae beat, and a very rich, full liquid melody carried under and highlighted by staccato accents of trombone, trumpet, and Fender bass guitar." You heard the words "march theme" and "trombone" and figured all was, well, exactly what you wanted. Oh woe.

In cases like this, ask for an example of what they're proposing. It doesn't have to be an expensive demonstration tape. A record or something similar will help. If they're proposing a swinging big band sound similar to Jimmy Lunceford in the 1930s, ask them to play a little Lunceford. There were a lot of big bands in at that time—and there was a big difference in the swing of Jimmy Lunceford, Glenn Miller, and Kay Kyser.

Obviously, in the world of advertising, if music is being used in a commercial, it's even more important that you know exactly what the creative people have in mind. If you're not as conversant with music as you'd like to be, have someone else help interpret for you. Again, ask for an example. In many cases, a simple demonstration—particularly if there are lyrics involved—is desirable. A creative tragedy is seeing a good concept aborted because the music hurts rather than helps the idea.

The time, by the way, for a clear-cut understanding of exactly what the creative people have in mind is when they are presenting the concept for the first time. Don't wait until everyone is in the studio to give your advice and suggestions. Chaos will result. And chaos costs money. A popular misconception is that musicians are free-flowing spirits who can work up "head" arrangements or improvisations on the spot. They can, but it will probably have little to do with the original creative idea—not to mention the strategy.

2. If visual devices are proposed, again ask for a demonstration of what they're talking about. Sometimes a simple storyboard or schematic diagram will suffice. In other instances, "scrap" from magazines can create the mood. If, for example, your creative presenters are advocating a sales film illustrating the type of woman they picture as the user of a new

perfume, they might want to illustrate the idea with a number of photographs clipped from various magazines setting the scene and illustrating the life style of their model woman. Anything that helps explain and illustrate the basic idea should be asked for.

A few years ago, we faced the challenge of introducing a new model Toyota Celica. It was, for the time, a dramatic new styling concept, and in our television commercials we planned on using an outer space concept as our creative attention getter. (This was about the time that *Star Wars* had burst upon the scene with all of its exciting visual effects.) The storyboard called for the commercial to open looking toward the dark infinity of outer space. Suddenly, an object would loom overhead and roar away from the camera. It would be the new Celica, and the camera would follow it as it performed a ballet in space with stars and planets twinkling in the background.

The client was enthralled with the idea but was dubious that it could be produced as we envisioned. We assured them that it could. They wanted to know how (and, incidentally, "how much"). We retreated to our offices with a promise that we would be back with a complete explanation of how it would look and work. They were determined (and we agreed) that if the outer space idea was to be used, it had to look real—no shooting of the car and then superimposing it against a still photograph of the heavens. No models. The presentation had to be as authentically exciting as the new styling of the car.

We contacted one of Hollywood's most amazing special effects people. (He offered to levitate me when we first met. "Perfectly safe. A light charge on each leg which explodes downward. Lift you two feet in the air. Lots of smoke. Spectacular. Won't hurt you a bit." It was an offer I could refuse. And did.) He devised a special derricklike arm that, when anchored to the base of a flatbed truck, could extend out and suspend the car 20 feet off the ground. Through special gears inside the car and radio-controlled signals sent from the ground, the car could be made to rotate from side to side, and, in fact, flip completely upside down. Coupled with the movement of the camera and shot against a velvet backdrop with Christmas tree lights for stars, this would (and did) give the startling effect of a car zooming through outer space.

But first we had to sell the client. And he wanted more than words and assurances. We did a schematic drawing explaining the derrick device. But we knew that it wouldn't be enough. The final effect had to somehow be brought to life. And so we built an ingenious little model.

It was nothing more than a one foot square piece of wood with a hole in it. Attached to it was a curved section of cardboard forming a kind of open-ended box, with the curve being the side opposite the board with the hole. This represented outer space. We draped the curved cardboard with black velvet and poked pinholes in it. A flashlight behind was the light source. Star-spangled outer space.

Then in front of this backdrop we mounted a toy car with a crank that went through the backdrop. By turning the crank the car moved in a series of nonconcentric circles. Touching the front of the car would cause it to flip while turning. By looking through the hole, you could easily imagine you were looking at the scene in the dark heavens. And the "hole view" obscured the wire arm and the crank. The client looked through the hole and applauded. It took some thinking and some doing. But it was worth doing. It demonstrated how we intended to handle the problem and what the result would be. The model cost us about $4.50 in materials. The actual commercial was a bit more.

Rule 5: *If the project calls for a number of creative pieces, make sure that they work together.*

A seemingly simplistic piece of advice. If you're running a sales contest for your company, you don't want the first week's graph showing results to be a red thermometer on a gold blackground and the second week's a brown football advancing toward the goal on a green gridiron. The various pieces should have a graphic continuity that works synergistically to build an impression. If the thermometer is the theme, make sure that it's used in all of the material involved: announcement, instructional folders, posters, flyers, leaflets, everything. Obvious.

But not quite as obvious for the advertising field. All of us, at one time or another, have come up with a simply smashing idea for a commercial, usually at a cocktail party.

HE: Hey Stan, you're in advertising, aren't you?

YOU: Uh . . . yeah.

HE: Got a great idea for a product name and a commercial. Listen and tell me if you think there's anything in this.

YOU: (politely) Um.

HE: It's for a hard-working deodorant. The scene is at the Indianapolis 500, got it?

YOU: Um.

HE: Lots of quick cuts of the pit crews rushing around, changing tires and all that. Sweating. And lots of flashing armpits in coveralls, know what I mean?

YOU: Yeah.

HE: And the announcer says something like, "If you have a deodorant that'll handle this kind of action, you know it'll handle whatever you can dish out in everyday life." Got it?

YOU: All the way.

HE: And the name of this product . . .

YOU: . . . is?

HE: Pit Stop! Get it? "Stops perspiration in your . . ."

YOU: Got it.

Pit stop. Interesting. In dubious taste, but interesting—particularly if you're aiming at the youth market. But where do you go from there? The name almost forces you to use the auto racing motif. And how many times can you shoot arm pits at a race track? One of the big problems is that often in the advertising business we come up with one good idea for an advertisement. But that's all. So, for the next advertisement in the campaign, we come up with another good idea. But it has nothing to do with the first one. And if we allow these disparate ideas to appear before the public, we will be diluting our efforts. Imagine the waste if Marlboro cigarettes were to run an advertisement featuring the famous cowboy and then follow it up with another one starring a man in a tuxedo. The impact of ideas is directly proportional to the number of times the public is exposed to them.

So, when you're judging creative efforts—if you're in advertising—make sure that the individual pieces can work together to build and reinforce an idea or impression. The principle, I think, is a good one in other fields as well. A good interior decorator always keeps the sum of all the parts in mind as well as the effect of the individual rooms. She's aware of the impressions of her efforts from a variety of points of view:

from the center of the room itself, looking at it from another room, looking at it through a picture window, from the hall, from the stairs. And she designs with all of this a part of her scheme of things. If one room uses a soft pink print wallpaper she might think twice before recommending an orange print for the next one.

Similarly, a casting director is always aware of how the individual actors come together as a whole. Again, she makes sure the various creative pieces (the actors) can work together to build to the desired impression or effect.

A conductor or arranger may not select a brilliant musician for his orchestra if the musician's tone or ability works against those of the rest of the orchestra. There are many who believe, for example, that the two great jazz musicians Sidney Bechet on soprano sax and William "Wild Bill" Davison on trumpet did not make astonishing music together because each played in a hard-driving, soaring, tumbling style hitting every beat and allowing no holes for the other to sneak in and do his stuff.

Again, if you're judging a creative project, make sure that the various parts work together—no matter how good they are individually.

Rule 6: *Make sure that the technique doesn't overpower the message.*

We once created a delightful commercial for Skippy peanut butter in which the entire action focused on a four-year-old boy seated at the kitchen table awkwardly but carefully spreading the product on a slice of bread. Throughout, the voice of the boy's sister could be heard off camera urging him to tell the audience why he likes Skippy. "Go ahead, Timmy, tell them about the taste . . . ," and so forth. She pleads with him to say something good about Skippy, but he's too busy spreading and eating. Finally, he acquiesces, looks at the camera, and says, "Skippy . . . ." Off camera voice interrupts: "Mommy! Gerald's talking with his mouth full again." End of commercial. As I said, delightful. Full of human interest. A little piece of drama with a surprise ending that, throughout, makes the product the focal point of the commercial.

Ah, but does it? To our amazement, research showed that few people even remembered the product name, let alone why they should buy it. When asked what commercials they remembered having seen in a given time period, viewers referred to this one as, "That wonderful commercial where the sister says, 'Mommy, Gerald's talking with his mouth full again.' " They even remembered the kid's name—but not the product. They said the commercial was for jam or crackers or honey or something—and this with the Skippy jar staring at them throughout. A classic case of vampire video where the technique sucked the lifeblood from the sales message.

This rule, it seems to me, is valid in a good number of fields of creativity. We've all heard musical arrangements where the arrangement overpowers the basic melody, and I'm not talking about improvisation after a theme has been established. I mean an arrangement that obscures the composer's intentions from the beginning so that the melody is a mystery. Sometimes it takes a sharp ear and mind to catch this. Once I had the privilege of sitting in on a recording session with the magnificent jazz pianist Earl "Fatha" Hines. I believe he was in the middle of doing something with the great standard "Rosalie." Suddenly, the writer, critic, and jazz authority Stanley Dance, sitting in the control booth, turned to the engineer and said "He's lost it." Earl, in about his third improvisational chorus, had wandered away from the theme and chord structure. He was striding away in another imaginative direction. Stanley said that he often did this. It was part of his creativity as he built his marvelous improvisations. "He'll come back," Stanley said, and he did, somehow cleverly slipping back into the familiar "Rosalie" theme. The critic explained that sometimes they left these wanderings in the final recording—but most of the time they mentioned it to the grinning performer, and he rerecorded.

We've all seen movies where the editing overpowers or distorts the simplicity of the storyline, or annual reports where the complicated graphics cloud the message (come to think of it, this may well be planned in many cases), or novels where the author's need to impress forces the reader to spend as much time with the dictionary as with the novel itself. Therefore, in judging any creative effort, make sure that the creative people don't get so involved with form or technique that it obscures function.

Rule 7:   *Make sure that the creative efforts can get and hold the audience's attention.*

Having made this point, I'll now make life even more confusing by contradicting myself. For those involved in wooing the public through advertising on television, the challenge is growing more intense and more complicated because the public is becoming more jaded, less interested. There was a time when we thought that by making commercials relevant, newsy, informative, entertaining, impressive, or whatever, we stood a chance of gaining and holding the viewer's attention. And we were often successful, not because the vast audience was breathlessly awaiting our message, but rather because they knew that they had minimal choices. If they switched channels, they usually were deep in the heart of another commercial because the networks utilized the same time periods for commercial breaks. But with the growth of cable, all this is changing.

Choice had made switching an adventure. Where, at one time, there were three networks, one or two independent stations, and a public service channel to choose from in most areas, now there are those plus 15 or more cable stations to woo the viewer's attention. The problem is that even the hint of a commercial, no matter how entertaining or newsworthy, stands a chance of being turned off, unless:

1. The program that surrounds the commercial can rivet the viewers to the screen so completely that they won't want to leave for even a two-minute "swing around" for fear they'll miss some of the action. Unfortunately, commercial programming, in general, has not responded to this challenge.

2. The commercial has established a format that is so entertaining that people wish to watch it, even though they've seen it before, and even though they know it's a commercial. Recent examples of this are Mariette Hartley and James Garner and their work for Polaroid, the fast-talking Federal Express commercial, and some of the Toyota "Oh what a feeling" commercials. And so, while we don't want the technique to overpower the message, we also must be aware of the fact that the audience isn't really interested in our commercials. We must find ways to capture and hold their attention without detracting from what we're trying to say—a difficult and delicate challenge to all those whose job is to create advertising, and all those who must prejudge its effectiveness.

3. The commercial does not look like a commercial. And usually this means not mentioning or showing the product being advertised

in the first part of the commercial. This technique has been used in Europe for some time, particularly in cinema advertising where the rules require entertainment rather than hard sell. A classic example: the scene is the railroad station in a small Italian village. A family of four is saying good-bye to grandma as they put her on the train. Kisses and waving of handkerchiefs as the train pulls away. Suddenly the little boy discovers grandma's suitcase still sitting on the platform. Pandemonium. Wringing of hands and waving at train to come back. Father gestures to the family, and they scoop up the suitcase and race to the car—a new Fiat sedan. With a string quartet playing softly in the background (a nice touch, I thought), they race to the next station over back country roads. Car slides around corner and accelerates uphill. Kids in backseat giggle and watch the olive groves flash by. Mother points hysterically to sheep blocking the road. Good braking action. Finally, they swing around a turn to the next station just as the train comes down the track. Kisses and shaking of hands as the train pulls in—and roars right on by. Incredulous looks and then back into the Fiat and off to the next station. As they speed away into the sunset, the Fiat logo appears on the screen. There has been no announcer telling us what's happening, and the logo at the end is the first and only mention of the product. A beautiful bit of entertainment that I defy anyone not to watch. And an interesting demonstration of the Fiat in action.

While certainly important, television commercials aren't the only places where gaining your audience's immediate attention is of primary importance to a creative effort. Think about the mail that arrives at your home every day. In one recent week, we received 48 pieces of first class mail. Only 6 were personal, 10 were bills, 32 were solicitations or junk mail. It's become so overwhelming that I don't even bother to open the "resident" or "occupant" envelopes. Or the "you-may-already-have-won" invitations. And I'm very selective about the rest. What a blow to those thousands of organizations and advertisers who aren't even getting the envelope slit. Because if I'm doing this, I'm sure that there are millions more doing the same. And more millions who are not getting beyond the first sentence. And the great majority who are reading everything—and doing nothing. How to break through this clutter has become a fascinating art. Thousands of specialists whose very existence depends on their ability to gain and hold the audience's attention are working to perfect this art.

In the theater it may be presumed that once people settle comfortably in their seats waiting for the lights to dim and the magic to begin, there is no reason to worry about capturing their attention. We are dealing with a captive audience. But producers, directors, and playwrights know differently. They realize that a good part of the success of their efforts depends on staging, lighting, and showmanship.

The people responsible for the famous Royal Shakespeare Company's production of *Nicholas Nickleby* wanted to get the audience immediately involved in the action. They felt that for the success of this marathon performance (somewhere in the neighborhood of eight hours) audience involvement was an absolute necessity. And so they open with actors sprinkled throughout the audience, standing in the back of the theater. The actors were merchants of the time and were responding to trade association officials running a meeting from the stage. The effect was electrifying. As the actors in Dickensian garb strode down the aisles shouting objections and comments ("What about crumpets?") and throwing crumpets at the stage, it was as though we were actually there. Immediate and instant involvement. Actually, it was so successful that many in the audience felt disappointed when the lights dimmed for the last time hours later. They'd become a part of the life of Nickleby and friends (and enemies).

The producers of television shows have more of a reason for gaining the audience's attention: competition for the casual viewer. These are the people who cruise through the channels, or do not change channels after watching one of their favorite programs. When the station break finishes there had better be something intriguing to keep them from switching. That's why many programs now open with a scene or a series of quick scenes—almost previews—of the upcoming shows instead of the title of the show. Even the popular program *M*A*S*H** used a series of scenes from life in a mobile army surgical hospital in the Korean war to gain attention: helicopters coming through a pass, nurses running, ambulances wheeling to the pad, and so forth. While this became a familiar program signature as the years went by, it was originally designed to gain viewer attention, to keep them from switching.

So whenever you're in a position to judge some creative work, ask yourself if it's truly creative. Put yourself in your audience's shoes (or seat) and see if you think the first few seconds or words would get your attention—and if the rest of the creative piece has enough news value, or information, or drama, or fun, or whatever to hold your attention. If not, you can make another creative judgment. Fix it!

Rule 8: *Keep personal prejudices away from the judgment process.*

This rule is difficult to follow because our personal likes and dislikes are almost always intertwined with judgment. We like an eclectic look. A decorator urges pure modern in our apartment. We will probably make a judgment against the decorator. We like the quiet beaches of Nevis in February. Our travel agent recommends the swinging scene on Martinique. We go to Nevis. We are partial to maroon in car colors. The dealer has a white one in the showroom. We wait for the maroon.

These judgments based on our likes, dislikes, and prejudices are fine because the decisions affect only ourselves. It's personal stuff. But it gets tricky when we get into the area of judgments of creative efforts that can influence a number of others. You live in a young community and are put in charge of the village dance. The committee wants nostalgia. You're personally partial to the glittering, vamping 1920s, and without consulting with the others, you line up a band that specializes in "The Varsity Drag," "I'll see you in C-U-B-A," "Black Bottom," and others of that ilk. However, to your youngish neighbors, nostalgia means the 1950s and bubble gum rock. The dance is a failure. And you are not a hero.

Now, correcting this mistake would have been easy if the only factor was your like for the music of the 1920s. You could have done what you should have done: consulted with your committee, discovered the desire for 1950s rock, and probably said fine, if that's what the community wants. No problem, unless you had a violent aversion to rock. That's the kind of problem prejudice we're talking about. You fight for the mood of the 1920s not just because that's what you like, but because you personally hate the alternative. But the majority of your friends and neighbors want rock. Whether you like it or not, it's what's most popular. This is the point where your personal prejudices should not color the decision. You should acquiesce.

As you can imagine, personal prejudices can have a devasting influence on creative judgments in advertising. Much of the time, but not always, these prejudices are a result of various generation gaps. For this reason, it's most important that we are absolutely sure of the target audience. If we are trying to reach young, contemporary adults, the creative approach should be skewed to appeal to them. A radio commercial with country swing or the new big band sound rather than your favorite middle-of-the-road Muzak is called for. You may admire the new miniskirt look and feel that it's attuned to your support-hose campaign, but the product target audience is older women who may not be as aware of the return of short skirts as their daughters are. It works both ways. The young copywriter is a great fan of *National Lampoon* humor and wants to use a spoof approach—a college dining hall "food war"—to demonstrate the cleansing ability of a new mop. Interesting. And attention getting. But probably wrong because the main mop audience is not the youthful college or early post-college crowd in this age of the advancing gray panther.

Personal prejudices may be the single most difficult roadblock to overcome on the path to imaginative creativity because these prejudices can become built-in rules that put the creative person in jail. It's called creative confinement.

ACCOUNT PERSON: . . . so that's it, guys. Use your imagination on this new campaign. No holds barred. Give it everything you've got. We need breakthrough advertising.

CREATIVE PERSON: Great. I want to talk to Arnold about music. Got an idea for a nice sound and . . .

ACCOUNT PERSON: Hold it . . . ah . . . no music or jingles. Client hates them. He had a bad experience with that tuba-harp duet couple of years ago, remember?

CREATIVE PERSON: Yeah, but I wasn't thinking of that. I had in mind . . .

ACCOUNT PERSON: Yeah, well stop thinking about any kind of music. Client gets apoplectic.

CREATIVE PERSON: (hesitantly) Anything else we can't do?

ACCOUNT PERSON: Nope. Sky's the limit . . . except for casting.

CREATIVE PERSON: Oh oh.

ACCOUNT PERSON: White bread. You know, freckle-faced red headed or blonde kids.

CREATIVE PERSON: One tooth missing and baseball cap on side of head.

ACCOUNT PERSON: You got it. Matter of fact, if you can give him a straight side-by-side demo he'll be happy as hell. No foolin' around with acting or humor. Just lay it out there. He's a meat and potatoes guy.

CREATIVE PERSON: But . . . but . . . I had a hell of an idea using cinema verité with a nice musical background of real people on a playground using the product. Candid and informal. Believable.

ACCOUNT PERSON: Listen. I'm not going to box you in. You're the creative genius. You can do what you think is right. But I'm just trying to help by telling you what I think he'll buy and what will turn him into a raging maniac.

The obvious prejudices in this example come from the client. But they seem to be compounded by the account person who, in his effort to be helpful, is trying to prejudge his client's reactions, a practice that certainly is inhibiting to creative efforts, no matter how practical it may be. These kinds of problems are indeed difficult to solve—but not impossible.

Rule 9: *Don't impose rules—and don't be afraid to break them.*

In the previous example, we saw some rules being formulated by the account person as a reaction to client prejudices. But prejudices aren't the only source of rules that may be inhibiting. In many areas, research innocently enough can be the villain.

As a result of research measuring the noticeability and memorability of television commercials, some people like to set up rules as creative guidelines. Like:

1. Always show the product in the first five seconds of the commercial. (One of the most popular and famous campaigns of the 1980s is for Federal Express. The client name is usually not mentioned until the last five seconds.)

2. Stay away from humor. It's tricky and often detracts from the message. (True, unless it's well done and relevant to the product. Again Federal Express is an example that comes to mind.)

3. Use people talking directly to the camera. They work better than an off-camera voice describing the action. (Sometimes, and sometimes not. It's according to how it's done. There are too many successful examples done both ways to make any definite assumptions, no matter what the research scores show.)

4. "Slices-of-life" (scenes with people discussing the merits of a product or service in a supposed lifelike situation) are most effective. Use this technique. (Again, "It ain't what you do—it's the way that you do it." Most slices-of-life are by nature unbelievable, and thus their advertising effectiveness must be somewhat suspect. It seems to me that this technique is most effective when there is something important to say about the product.)

5. Don't use low-key mood approaches. They are not as instantly memorable as a more strident creative effort. (According to research, this seems to be true. But, at the moment, there does not seem to be a measurement as to what disappears in the subconscious and may influence future buying decisions. The correlation of memorability and intent to buy is at best a fuzzy one. In addition, in this day of commercial clutter and strident lookalikes, the softer low-key approach may, just by being different, be becoming more memorable.)

6. And so forth.

I'm not saying that any of these points isn't worth serious consideration. They just shouldn't be made into rules. Or if they are, there should be a clear understanding that they can be broken. Of course, we're not referring to legal rules or rules of common sense. These must and should be adhered to. If you're an architect, and zoning says no building shall exceed four stories, you would be ill-advised to design a 16-story high-rise apartment rather than four 4-story structures.

Think of where we'd be if, down through history, everyone had adhered to the existing rules:

"C'mon, Orville, you and Wilbur are going against the law of gravity."

"A musical with a continuing story? That doesn't follow the rules. I don't care if you call it *Texas,* or *New York,* or *New Jersey* —*Oklahoma* just won't make it."

"Alright, Christopher, sail if you must. But don't come complaining to me when you drop off the edge."

Rule 10: *Beware of becoming a part of the creative process while attempting to judge it*

This is a particularly difficult rule to follow for those of you who have become creative leaders (and thus judges of a certain amount of creativity) after spending years as creative practitioners. The temptation to say "Here, let me show you how to do it" is strong, indeed. Particularly when deadlines loom. But the good creative leader resists. I once knew a marvelous copy chief (an archaic pretelevision title that seemed to always be held by wise, Mr. Chips types) who never, never put his pencil to anyone else's efforts. He would read the work over and then quietly suggest areas for improvement—if they were called for. He would never suggest how it should be done. That would be up to the writer. But, to make sure that he was right, he'd always tackle the assignment—and keep his work to himself. If the writer continued to have trouble, Mr. Copy Chief would make broad suggestions that could lead to the solution that was hidden in the bottom drawer. It was a failsafe device. And because he never put it into motion until trouble loomed, he avoided the problem of constantly imposing his ideas on his people. And even then, because the actual work was accomplished by the writer, the finished work could show the writer's originality—and the copy chief's direction.

Aside from denting the morale of the creative people working on the project, there are other reasons not to get involved in the actual creative process. You can easily lose your objectivity.

YOU: OK, what do we have for the costume for waitress in the second act?

DIRECTOR: Well, you know, a simple waitresses' dress. Semishort skirt. Not too sexy.

YOU: Listen, my wife has her old army nurses' uniform. Why don't we dress the waitress in that? And then we could design the restaurant set around a medical motif.

DIRECTOR: Huh?

YOU: I've been feeling for some time that the second act needs a little shot.

DIRECTOR: But don't you think that'll take us in a different direction? I mean this is supposed to take place in a small town in Ohio. Do they have restaurants like army medical units in Ohio? I mean shouldn't we talk this over with the author?

YOU: It's not changing anything. It's just adding an interesting touch, that's all.

DIRECTOR: Well . . . I really don't know . . . but you're the boss.

Your suggestion, enthusiasm, and ego have drawn a veil over your objectivity, promising trouble for the Annual First Baptist Church Little Theatre Group Benefit production.

As you can see, becoming a part of the creative process is not necessarily restricted to writing. Have you ever wondered why so many television commercials take place in San Francisco? Hills for dramatic street scenes? There are hills in Pittsburgh and even steeper ones in Ithaca, New York. Beautiful vistas? Yes, but vistas can be admired in Seattle or Palos Verdes or even the Hollywood Hills overlooking Los Angeles. Variety of architectural backgrounds? Any number of other locations can provide this. In addition, the weather in San Francisco is often abominable for film making. Fog rolls in when you least expect it. Rain can be a way of life. The vistas disappear and reappear at the whim of low-hanging clouds. The wind can do amazing things with dresses, hair, light reflectors, and other pieces of fragile camera equipment—not to mention the well being and comfort of the actors and crew.

Once while shooting a Toyota commercial on the Buena Vista hill in San Francisco's Haight-Ashbury district I ran into astonishing conditions. It was mid-August. Haight Street was a humid and uncomfortable 87 degrees, with practically no breeze. We were just four blocks away on a hill that couldn't have been more than 100 feet above the Haight Street level. But in that 100 feet the wind changed from a slight breeze to a steady 20 or 30 knots with gusts up to 40. And it was a wet wind off the Bay that kept pounding us all day. By late afternoon we had sent out for parkas, mittens, and hats. Eight hours of constant wind battering had turned us numb. And all the time we were shooting, people would wander by in tee shirts and shorts, happy for a few minutes' relief from the oppressive heat, and wonder what in the world had come over these mid-August refugees from igloos.

Ah, but I digress. There are many good reasons to choose locations like San Francisco. And one not so good one. San Francisco is often chosen because it's effervescent, stimulating, charming, entertaining San Francisco: the people making the commercials like to go there. Fine, if the location meets the creative requirements first. But don't let personal reasons get in the way of your creative judgment. Keep your objectivity.

Rule 11: *Do let money influence you.*

This doesn't mean to play it cheap. It does mean watch what you're getting for your money. Make sure that what you're getting is worth what you're spending. And equally important, make sure that you're not ruining or losing a good idea by keeping the budget too low. This is tough stuff because you are required to fill the creative judge-business person role, which often calls for Solomon-like decisions.

We make creative decisions daily in our personal lives. You're putting a new entryway in your vacation home in Vermont. What kind of floor? Wood, vinyl tile, or slate? Wood is the least expensive, vinyl tile is in the middle, and slate is quite costly, all calculated on a square foot basis. Wood may be impractical because of the "mud season" problem in Vermont. Vinyl tile fills the bill, as does slate. But slate looks splendid and adds an understated but opulent first-impression to the entryway. But the cost per square foot seems prohibitive, except that the entryway doesn't require a lot of square footage. The actual cost is only $60 more. Sold! You choose the slate and are so happy that you want to spend more time in the entryway than in the living room. You've logically weighed the pros and cons, including the elusive psychic effect, in making your decision.

Now in the creative world you should pursue, as much as possible, the same logical approach. Even after 38 years of working at it, I find it most helpful to use a checklist.

1. Is the cost completely unreasonable for the potential of the idea? And what is considered unreasonable? Is it 20, 30, or 50 percent over budget? (As a rule of thumb, I've found that up to 20 percent is usually modifiable. More than that takes some doing.)

2. If the idea is a good one, what can be done to pare the costs with-

out seriously affecting the concept? Would the judicious use of two colors, rather than four colors, attain your objectives in the new sales brochure? Could we do without the expensive helicopter shot in the opening of the frozen peas commercial? How about doing away with the spectacular but costly hanging of the refrigerators from the ceiling at the dealer meeting show?

3.   Even after cutting as much as possible, if it's still over budget, is there some other way to amortize the cost? We had planned six different single-page ads. Could you use the idea in one double-page spread and run it three times, thus saving the production and creative costs of four ads? (We once did this for Hanes pantyhose. We wanted to inform our audience of the variety of different pantyhose available. The original concept was to do a series of advertisements, each one showing a different pantyhose for a different situation in a woman's life. Instead, we designed a spread, entitled "Hanes Explains," where we used stop-action photography to show four different types of woman getting dressed—housewife, socialite, career woman, student—each using the particular style of pantyhose for her needs. We made over 200 separate sequential shots of these four women getting dressed. Sensational—and expensive. But, in the long run, it was less costly than if we'd done the series of individual ads. And the impact of this provocative double page was much much more than the individual ads would have been.)

4.   Is the idea so unusual, so great and full of so much potential reward that it must be pursued, no matter what? Great ideas are often the best investment a company can make. DIET COCA-COLA received instant recognition, awareness, sales, and market share after turning a celebrity sprinkled introductory extravaganza in New York's Radio City Music Hall into a monumental television commercial. The expense would give even the most liberal company treasurer the vapors. Was it worth it? The counter question is: Would the product have received the instant success it did without it? And so, if you are presented with a great idea whose only negative is the cost, go with it—because great ideas are too rare not to be given a chance. But it had better be great.

Rule 12: *Make sure the creative efforts are not offensive.*

This is another tough one because, as we know, what's perfectly accept-able in some circles may not be in others. Ethnic jokes, no matter who your audience is, are unsafe and, in my opinion, a tasteless way to gain attention. Sexual or scatological innuendos can be equally risky. Various forms of nudity may be applauded in some parts of the world—including this country—but be careful of your audience. And, lurking in the path to success, there are often hidden mine fields that we haven't even thought of. Most advertising must appeal to a wide audience with varied values and tastes. Once, some years ago, we had the challenge of creating a new television campaign for White Cloud toilet paper. At the time, it was available only in certain areas of the country. We invented a grandmother character who traveled to various relatives' homes. As she packs to leave, we see her slipping a roll of the family's toilet paper into her suitcase. Her family is astonished. "Grandma, why are you taking the White Cloud?" they ask. "Because we don't have anything this soft where I live. Why, White Cloud's so soft it . . . it . . . it doesn't feel like toilet paper." Big breakthrough! For the first time toilet paper was being called by its true name on television. The familiar descriptive phrase, "bathroom tis-you," was being relegated to the archives.

But then the networks' censors stepped in and decreed that the pub-lic wasn't ready for the truth. They refused to let us assault the millions of eager viewers with the naughty words. Toilet paper may really be toi-let paper, but not on the sanitized cathode ray tube.

Then genius. We didn't change the dialogue. Grandma read it the same way. But she didn't say the offensive words. She just looked di-rectly at the camera and silently mouthed them: "so soft it doesn't feel like (silently) toilet paper." Victory! Networks agreed that we weren't saying the words, and another milestone in television history was achieved.

And then the letters of complaint started. But they weren't objecting to our clever subterfuge. No one was bothered by the pioneering use of the words "toilet paper." But hundreds of people were accusing us of advocating stealing. Grandma was lifting the stuff as she packed and left the house. Never mind that she just wanted some of that wonderfully soft White Cloud for her tender skin. Never mind that a lifetime of harshness was about to end. She was snitching in front of impressionable

America. Toilet paper today and who knows what tomorrow. Well, we weren't dealing with network censors now. These were the people talking. And, as any advertiser knows, letters can be a few cranks, or they can be the indicator of some deep-seated feelings. We waited a bit. And the letters kept coming. And so we agreed that we had reached a raw nerve and quickly discontinued and remade the commercials. (We had Grandma arriving at the relatives and as she alighted from the train or plane or taxi or whatever, her suitcase would pop open and the telltale roll would unravel across the floor. Kids giggle and point. "But Grandma, we have some at home. You don't have to bring your own." Grandma: "You don't have anything as soft as White Cloud . . ." and so forth. No stealing.

Our error seems obvious. But none of us, including the networks, caught it. Therefore, if in the creative material that you're judging, there is anything that you consider in questionable taste, get some outside opinions. Read the creative piece to people not familiar with what you're trying to do. Ask them what they think of it. If they don't bring up a problem, probe a bit more—but don't say: "Are you bothered by the fact that Grandma is stealing?" Of course they will be. You've forced them to be bothered. Let them tell you on their own. After some discussion, if they haven't brought up the questionable point, you're probably safe.

This kind of safety check is one of the most important functions of focused group interviews. The trained moderators can find out pretty much if there are disaster areas in various forms of advertising. Today, most successful agencies and advertisers use focused groups routinely to make sure, among other things, that they are not offending someone. But be sure these research sessions include a diverse audience, because, as I said before, what's anathema to one demographic group may be applauded by another.

Rule 13: *Beware of image change.*

This rule is particularly important for those involved in advertising. Every product that has been in existence for a reasonable amount of time has created an aura or image in the public's mind. This image can result from a number of factors:

1. Price. The money a person pays for goods or services can be a key part of this image. Thus, a Pontiac or Jaguar has a different image

from a Chevrolet or Volkswagen. A Brooks Brothers suit is different from one purchased from the old plain pipe racks of a discount store.

2. Target audience. The people selected as likely prospects for a product can, in themselves, become a part of the product image. Obviously, price plays an important part in defining this audience/image relationship—the Cadillac owner projects a different life style from the VW fan. But target audience is not always involved with price. The Chevrolet Corvette has long appealed to young lovers of automotive appearance/performance. And many of them will go into indecent debt to be able to own one. On the other hand, the Volvo positions itself as the thinking man's car and appeals to practical-minded people, many of whom could easily afford more expensive machines.

3. Usage. A product's reason for being can help form an image. A diamond is forever (or so we are told), and so are some of the newer steel-belted tires ("lasts the life of your car"). Yet even though both products have long-lasting attributes the image of one is luxury, the other utilitarianism and practicality. L'eggs Sheer Energy Pantyhose is a product that provides a therapeutic feeling to legs because of its unique massaging action. L'eggs Sheer Elegance Pantyhose was created to rival silk in appearance and feel. Both are pantyhose, manufacturered by the same company. But their product qualities are different. And therefore their appeal and their images in the public mind are different.

4. Positioning. Among parity products in the same category, the strategic positioning against competition can help form the image. Once more Marlboro cigarettes have positioned themselves differently from Tareyton or Benson & Hedges. The images are thus diametrically opposite.

5. Advertising. Probably more images are created by advertising, which can be considered the implementation of strategic positioning, than any other single factor. This, of course, is particularly true of products with no discernible differences. In the highly competitive dry breakfast cereal field, Wheaties positioned itself in the 1920s as "The Breakfast of Champions" and has remained that through advertising starting with Hudson High's Jack Armstrong, All-American Boy. Oxydol reached out

for the true-blue, hard-core middle American housewife through the popular soap opera "Ma Perkins" and, through the years, continued to capitalize on this tough, no-nonsense heritage. But creating images through advertising need not be restricted to parity products. The Volkswagen of the 1950s certainly was different from any other car on the market. But, as an outgrowth of Hitler's prewar "people's car," it was not sweeping the country. Then Bill Bernbach built his startling advertising on the car's appearance. "Think Small" and "The Bug" became some of the most talked about advertising of the time, and a cult image came into being.

Thus, with these and hundreds of other successful case histories staring us in the face, an obvious maxim is to build your creative efforts on the perceived image of the product, because if you don't, if you insist on changing the image in the public's mind, you're courting confusion, a decline in brand awareness, a resultant decline in advertising effectiveness, and possible disaster. Very risky stuff. Referring again to our old friend Oxydol, some years ago Procter & Gamble added enzymes to the detergent with its green bleaching crystals and then restyled the familiar green box. Enzymes were then fashionable dirt-gobblers, and it was felt that, with their help, good old Oxydol could become the all-American detergent. The product's cleaning range was widened to include all kinds of dirt and soil—not just the kind that detergents and bleach handle. The advertising was skewed to a much broader audience than just plain folks.

And the public became confused. No longer was good old Oxydol good old Oxydol. It stood for something else. Just what was not clear. What was clear, however, was that Oxydol was not the same product that helped make Ma Perkins famous. Brand awareness studies showed this. Awareness plummeted. Faster than you can say, "cleans and whitens like no other popular detergent," P&G removed the enzymes and remodified the packaging to reflect its original heritage, and Oxydol regained its position as one of America's most familiar washday companions.

With all of this logic and evidence before us, why would anyone want to change a product's image? Well, I think the principal reason is ego. A

new creative team wants to show that they are capable of doing something different. An account person or brand manager wants to contribute new thinking. New top management wants to make a clean sweep of
all that has gone before. A new president imagines friends saying, "Hey,
saw your new commercial. Exciting. Different." Unfortunately, what
they'll probably say is, "What new commercial?" They probably won't
have noticed it, no matter how different, because there will be no link-
age between the new look and the perceived image. That old devil
brand awareness, again.

Ego, however, isn't the only reason for changing the image. Some executives honestly feel that new and different is better. The competition
has done something different, why don't we do what they're doing. (This
can be one of the cardinal advertising sins because not only are you
changing the product image, you may be reinforcing your competitor's.
I have a good friend who, in an award winning commercial, played the
part of a grandfather coming to America and being welcomed by his
Pepsi-Cola–drinking family as he stepped off the boat. Very warm and
moving. But my friend tells me that time after time people would stop
him on the street and say, "Harry, you were wonderful in that Coke
commercial." Pepsi-Cola had moved into the arena of Americana that
was owned by Coca-Cola. They not only had blurred their image, but
they had reinforced Coke's.)

Another example of product success, failure through image change,
and rebirth through image renewal is Hamm's beer, a favorite regional
brew of the midwest. As I said in Chapter 2, it had long been a ssociated
with "the land of sky blue waters," the pines, balsams, and great outdoors of the Minnesota lake country. In the 1950s the Campbell-Mithun
advertising agency of Minneapolis developed a bumbling cartoon bear
character who was always seen innocently getting in and out of trouble
with his woodland friends. There was no apparent connection with the
bear except for the bear on the Hamm's label. But it did create an image
of fun and communicate the virility and purity of the wide-open spaces.

Then there was a management change, and an unfortunate strike hurt
Hamm's sales. The new management felt that the "clean sweep" technique was needed. They changed advertising agencies. The new agency
tried a number of different campaigns, all quite good, but none related
either to a bear or "the land of sky blue waters." One had a number of
people sitting around a bar singing "a beer is a beer is a beer—until

you've had a Hamm's." Another urged the public to "join the big beer brotherhood of Hamm's."

Advertising awareness, brand awareness, and sales continued to slide. In the early 1970s Hueblein, which had recently bought the brewery, awarded Dancer Fitzgerald Sample the account. Mindful of the problems of image change, we used research to confirm our belief that the Hamm's image was what we thought it was. In addition, we discovered that the Hamm's customer considered himself (Hamm's customers were predominantly male) a part of the "great outdoors" image. Whether or not his outdoor experience consisted mainly of waddling to and from his home to his garage or sitting, swaddled in mittens and scarfs, in various pro football stadiums, he identified strongly with the "land of sky blue waters" and all that it stood for. And if, as many people believe, beer drinkers wear their brand proudly on their sleeves, it became even more important for us to somehow capitalize on this feeling by building on the perceived Hamm's image.

An obvious approach (and one that we considered) was to bring back the animated bear and his happy woodland friends. But, at that point, the cartoon bear was considered old fashioned, out-of-date, the same old thing—particularly by many of the distributors, who are key to the success of products like beer. In addition, we felt that we needed some kind of a jolt, something completely new and different to draw quick attention to the brand and help to reverse the trend in awareness and, of course, eventually sales.

We considered a campaign showing the real beer drinker talking about the product and somehow relating all of this to the great outdoors. Some call this a "mirror image" campaign where television shows people as they actually are. This approach is often quite effective, and always somewhat risky because in many cases people don't like to stare at themselves. One of the truisms of life is that beer tends to be fattening. How many fat people have you ever seen in a beer commercial? They may be drooping over the sides of their bar stools, but they don't want to see that. They are Steve McQueen, Charles Bronson and Dennis Weaver all rolled into one.

And so we developed our own hero figure. A tall, lean bearded man of the outdoors. A man always on the move, but not a mountain man in raggedy clothes. He would wear a smart leather coat, hiking boots, and a wool shirt and carry a distinctive over-the-shoulder musette bag. He would be seen moving through the great outdoors, stopping to enjoy a Hamm's—sometimes in a rustic bar, sometimes in a logging camp, sometimes with fishermen around a campfire at twilight. But then he would move on his way through the "land of sky blue waters." And his faithful companion on this trip through life would be a live 300 pound Kodiak bear.

And so man and bear became the new embodiment of the Hamm's image. They were seen walking through the woods, riding in a canoe (the secret was to keep the canoe moving fast with a small outboard motor—the bear loved it and the speed kept it from tipping), tooling along in a jeep (the bear looked like man in a fur coat in the front seat), even arriving in a mountain lake in a single-engine plane.

This duo became the symbol for Hamm's for a number of years and traveled with us to location shootings in the Trinity Alps of northern California, the end of the Gunflint Trail near the Canadian border in northern Minnesota, the wilderness country of north Georgia, and the wilds of Moosehead Lake in Maine.

As you might imagine, these situations were ripe for adventure and a certain amount of creative improvisation. We did not want a trained dancing bear for this series. We wanted as much authenticity as possible, so Earl Hammond, the animal trainer, convinced us that he could "condition" a bear to follow a person in about six weeks. We felt that was fine because we would use the time to search for locations and to cast the right actor for the Hamm's man. We were somewhat taken aback when the trainer informed us that to condition the bear to follow a person, he would also need the actor for six weeks. They had to be conditioned to each other. Our first bit of creative improvisation was to abandon the idea of casting an actor and use the trainer himself as our hero. He was, after all, an outdoorsman. He was tall, lean, with a twinkle in his eye, and a nice smile. And he didn't have to talk or act. Just be himself with his friend, the bear. Built-in authenticity.

The first group of commercials was to be shot in and around Hyampom, California along the south branch of the Trinity River. I arrived by charter plane from San Francisco three days after our producer and the film company had discovered the location. ("Why," you might ask "did you not choose a location in the 'land of sky blue waters?' " Weather. As often happens, we had to shoot a commercial in mid-winter to be ready to run March 1 and throughout the spring and summer. Northern California was the only area in the country without snow that could duplicate the flora and terrain of northern Minnesota.)

As I got off the plane and surveyed the town (a combination general store/restaurant/Mobil station and Bob and Gail's Housekeeping Cabins), the agency producer greeted me as follows:

ROD: Jack, wait'll you see the locations we've got.

ME: Great. Where's the bear?

ROD: We'll open on a backlit shot of the crest of a hill. Use a telephoto. Man's head appears as he walks up the other side of the hill. Music builds. More of the man comes into view. And suddenly the bear is revealed ambling over the crest of the hill with him.

ME: Sounds good. Where's the bear?

ROD: Then for the second shot we'll do a down shot through that large oak tree over there. . . .

ME: Rod, the bear! Where the hell is the bear?

ROD: Ahh, uh . . .we dunno.

ME: Dunno? Whadya mean ya don't know? Is he lost?

ROD: Well not exactly. We just don't know where he is.

ME: You mean we've got a complete film crew, 22 people, all this equipment, not to mention the client out here in the middle of nowhere at about $22,000 a day to shoot this epic with man and bear and you're tellin' me we don't know where the Gahdamned bear is?

ROD: Yeah . . .well I hope he's somewhere between here and New Jersey.

ME: Argh!

ROD: See, we can't get any airline to fly him out here from the farm where he trained in New Jersey, but the production company's workin' on it.

ME: Argh!

But before I could faint or rip the large oak out in a raging pique, word came that the bear had been allowed on board something and was winging his way to San Francisco, where he'd be transferred to a small van, and he and Earl and his assistant would drive north—about a four-hour trip. They were due at around 9 P.M. We were elated but still a bit concerned. Suppose they got lost on the back logging roads, or had a flat, or worse yet, were stopped by the police for some reason. ("In the back, officer? Oh, he's wearing that fur coat because he's cold, I guess. Heh Heh.")

By 9 o'clock we were nervously watching the road. By 11 we decided to try to get some sleep (Ha!). At 1 A.M. we heard the first grunt of the van huffing up the hill to our camp. I was dressed and outside in 30 seconds and was tied for last. The van stuttered into the parking area and stopped. We all rushed up to welcome bear and friends. The front door flew open and out stumbled Earl and his assistant. They were gasping and groaning. We rushed up to them and got within 15 feet of them and the van, and suddenly we were gasping and groaning. The bear had gotten carsick. For 120 miles he had vomited and defecated over the inside of the van and its occupants. And they couldn't stop. They had to keep going because no one was quite sure about the laws concerning licenses for transporting bears on freeways. It was appalling. The whole thing slowed down our production by two days because it took that long for the bear to recover. He just lay on his back, with his feet in the air, moaning.

Incidentally, the key to training the bear to follow the man was marshmallows. He loved them (bear not man). The man would surreptitiously drop marshmallows down his pants leg leaving a trail behind. The bear would shuffle along scarfing them up. In the camera it looked as though he was just sniffing around. Marshmallows were the reason for Earl's musette bag. That's where he kept them.

The campaign ran throughout the 1970s. Brand awareness, brand image, and advertising awareness, as you might imagine, rose dramatically. Sales responded also—but then, unfortunately, leveled off and started to slide. There had been another sale of the brewery, and the new owners had some hard luck with the quality of the beer. A bad batch can destroy a product image faster than almost anything, particularly with the serious beer drinker.

And so when Olympia beer bought Hamm's at the end of the 1970s, they spent millions of dollars modernizing the breweries to reestablish the fine Hamm's quality. And they felt, and we agreed, that as much as we loved the bear, it was time for a fresh campaign because, unhappily, man and bear had become too closely associated with inferior quality.

("Love the advertising, wouldn't touch the beer.") And so once more we were faced with the classic advertising challenge: How to do something fresh without changing the image.

We brought back the animated bear. Oh, we updated the plot lines in the animation, and we added live personalities to help add appetite appeal and conviction. But it was still the old familiar cartoon bear bumbling his way in and out of trouble to the delight of his fans. Why could we do this now when we felt it was not wise 10 years before? Because now 20 years had passed since the bear's real heyday. He was no longer old-fashioned. He was a piece of nostalgia. Men in their twenties remembered watching the bear while sitting on their father's knees when they were watching the White Sox baseball game. Men in their thirties and forties remembered growing up with the bear. And they associated the cartoon bear with the beer when it was at its best as a piece of the warm and wonderful past. (It's a part of the they-don't-make-'em-like-they-used-to syndrome.)

The new animated campaign has been on the air about three years now, and Hamm's has become the fastest growing beer in America, at this writing. In the past decade it's gone through a number of ownership and management changes. But the image has remained steady, revolving about the wide-open spaces, the land of sky blue waters, and a bear.

Recently, another brewing company bought Olympia's properties, including Hamm's. They decided to consolidate their different brands under their own advertising agencies, and thus the beer leaves our hallowed halls. The new advertising agency may propose a fresh campaign. It will be interesting to see if, in so doing, they maintain the Hamm's image.

Rule 14:   *Stick with a good idea.*

Unfortunately, when judging creativity, it's not enough to say, "That's it," because all too often that's not it. What you'd thought would happen didn't. "Gee," you say, "the idea seemed so good. I wonder what happened to it. I wonder why it isn't working. Well, that's the way it goes. I guess we'll just have to start all over."

Wrong. If the basic idea is good and you've examined it from top to bottom and turned it inside out before presenting it to your audience, don't give up. Perhaps there's something amiss in the way that it's being presented. The after-dinner presentation you'd planned to make at the faculty meeting dealing with suggested changes in the rules of tenure seems less than inspiring when you try it out before a few members of your department. Your hypothesis is excellent, but you're coming on too strong. So you lighten the approach, soften the belligerence. But you don't change the main thrust.

The idea of two melodies working together in counterpoint to open the special gala for the local United Way Drive is excellent. But when you work it out on the piano, it comes out confusing. The counterpoint idea is a good one because it allows you to blend the benefits of those who give and those who receive. So you don't discard it. You rescore the two melodies, realizing that one must be done to a fast beat and the counterpoint to a slower one to be able to mesh successfully.

In advertising, particularly, it's too easy to panic if something doesn't work immediately. Real professionals know that it takes time for advertising to sink in. But they also watch research and public reactions carefully to make sure that the ideas have a chance to sink in. We recently proposed a campaign for one of our clients based on a spoof of soap operas. It was full of all of the clichés that have made this form of entertainment so popular from the early days of radio right up to the present: romance, conflict, seemingly insoluble problems, wide cast of characters, glamor, and, of course, suspense that keeps the audience waiting for the next episode.

We opened in typical soap opera fashion. Woman enters restaurant. She's upset. She spots a man at a table, throws her hands in the air, and says, "Ashley's gone." "Gone?" he says incredulously. "I've got to find him. It's his child." Involving opening. The commercial continued in the same vein. We were delighted. And most of the reaction we got from the public supported our delight. But not all of it. There was a definite group that disliked the commercial. We couldn't understand why. It was a delectable spoof.

And so we did some more research, only this time instead of showing our customers just one commercial and asking some pertinent questions, we showed a group of these commercials. And we discovered the problem. Some people did not get the spoof idea after just one showing and, therefore, thought the commercial was crazy and didn't like it. Once they understood it was a spoof, however, they loved it.

And so we cleaned up our act a bit. We added a title at the opening to implant the spoof idea at the beginning. And we added some ridiculous announcer lines at the end that further added to the elbow-in-the-ribs feeling. And it worked. Our amount of "dislikes" decreased in direct proportion with the number of people who understood it was a spoof.

But we didn't throw the basic idea away. We stuck with it.

IN SUMMARY

When judging creative efforts, whether they're yours or someone else's, keep the following guidelines in mind.

1. Make sure the creative effort is pointed in the right direction. In other words, be convinced that you're on strategy.

2. Make sure that the creative effort will appeal to the people you want it to appeal to.

3. Make sure that the message is single-minded.

4. Make sure that you know what the creative people have in mind.

5. Make sure that all of the parts work together. That means that, in advertising, if you're looking for a complete campaign, make sure that's what you get.

6. Make sure that the technique doesn't overpower the message.

7. Make sure that you can get and hold your audience's attention.

8. Keep personal prejudices away from the judgment process.

9. Don't impose rules, and don't be afraid to break them.

10. Beware of becoming a part of the creative process while attempting to judge it.

11. Do let money influence it.

12. Make sure the creative efforts are not offensive.

13. Beware of image change.

14. Stick with a good idea.

This has been a long but, I trust, interesting chapter because I've covered what I consider the real essence of managing the creative process, whether you're judging someone else's work or your own. As a copywriter, I have often used this checklist before presenting any of my ideas. It amazes me how often one or another of the rules (and seldom the same one) has helped me not necessarily come up with good ideas, but rather, reject the less than good.

5

SELLING AND
BUYING OF
AN IDEA

No matter how brilliant, inspiring, potentially moneymaking, revolutionary, practical, or astute an idea may be, it's nothing if no one does anything about it. Over the years, we've all come upon the results of ideas that we've had in our own heads at one time or another.

"Why didn't I do something about that idea I had 20 years ago about hooking a fan up to the power lawn mower to blow snow?"

"Look at that. A new product where they squeeze peanut butter laced with honey from a tube. I thought of that when I bought my first tube of striped tooth paste. Damn."

"Ethel, c'mere and look. It's my commercial. The one I tried to sell with a man standing in a boat in the toilet bowl. Now someone else is doing it. Damn."

Sometimes the idea is just a fleeting thought that we probably would never do anything about anyway. But too often, in the creative area, the idea has possibilities but dies because we haven't been able to convince others of its merits. Or, if we're on the receiving end, we haven't been sold. This chapter is concerned with both sides of the issue because those in the positions of managing the creative process are often involved in both sides. They are the seller and the sellee.

One of the definitions of "to sell" in the *Random House Dictionary of the English Language* is: "to persuade or induce someone to buy." And that's what we're talking about. Persuasion. A not-so-gentle but often complex, complicated, intriguing, and thought-provoking art that deals with both logic and emotion—an art that demands the utmost in presentation skills. There are a good many books available on the art of persuasion. Most of them deal with one-on-one selling: the process that was the heart of Willy Loman's life. What we're more concerned with when we're trying to manage and guide the creative effort is less individual selling (although there's certainly a place for it here) and more the process of presentation. The difference is that a presentation usually is a more structured, formal affair and calls for the involvement of more than the seller and sellee. The psychology of the process operates on much the same level, however, in both instances.

We must first prepare ourselves for the sale: know what we're presenting and why. The next big step is to prepare the sellee for the sale. Do the groundwork. This may take a period of minutes, hours, or days and could encompass a number of meetings with the sellee. The actual presentation of the idea or goods is next, always followed by the aftermath or rebuttal when the sellee has the opportunity to ask questions, discuss the proposition, consult with others and, we would hope, say, "Sounds good to me. I'll buy it." The final, and often overlooked, step is the follow-up. And it's not always merely the delivering of whatever you've sold. It's the addressing of the various caveats that are a part of the sale because no one ever really means, "Sounds good. I'll buy it." They mean, "Sounds good. I'll buy it, but . . .," or "I'll buy it with the following conditions . . .," or "I'll buy it if you can. . . ." There always seem to be strings attached. The follow-up should take care of the strings, or maybe even resell the idea.

"Second thoughts," the anathema of the seller (I've never heard any-one say, "I've had second thoughts, and I'll buy the idea.") can take place anytime after the presentation. Be prepared for them. It's usually the result of the sellee discussing the presentation with cohorts, who may or may not have been present. If you have to set up another meeting to "resell," make sure you know why. And if the reason is something you thought you had covered quite thoroughly and competently in the presentation, realize that you probably didn't. Dissect it. Try to figure out the problem. Then redo it accordingly. But we're ahead of ourselves. Let's go back to the beginning. What follows is a series of sections that may act as a guideline to successful persuasion. I'll talk about letting yourself be persuaded later.

WHAT ARE YOU SELLING?

Whether it's a product, a piece of music, a political candidate, or an idea—know everything there is about it before you even attempt to sell it. Too many times something good fails because the person making the presentation either can't explain what he's trying to explain or gets caught by not knowing his subject well enough to answer questions. This problem is more common when the originator of the idea or product or whatever passes his thoughts on to a middleman (often the creative manager) who in turn must make a presentation to some one or more final decision makers. In the advertising agency business these "middlemen" are often the account team. The creative person who has come up with the original idea usually participates in the presentation to the client in partnership with the account team. If, in the presentation, anyone stumbles or has problems explaining or answering questions, not only will the jist of the idea be imperiled, but the client may lose confidence in the whole procedure. ("They really don't seem to know what they're talking about. Can't be a very well thought-out idea.") So make sure you know all of the possible advantages and pitfalls of your proposition before trying to induce someone to buy it. In a way, as you see, this goes back to some of our early discussions of strategy where I talked about imbuing yourself with everything there is to know about the product. The market, the competitive situation, the public's attitude, and so forth.

In presenting a basic idea, it's particularly important to know what else has been done in this general area. Perhaps your idea is enlarging on something that's already been created. Or perhaps, somewhere in the distant past, someone else has done something similar and has copyrighted the idea. You'd better know that before you present it. Incidentally, because an idea has been used before or is even copyrighted, does not mean that your use of it is not viable. Some years ago we came out with an initial campaign for Toyota, the war cry of which was "You asked for it—You got it!" Now, when we developed the concept, we knew that the slogan had been the title of an old television show. So we contacted the people who had the rights to the show (and the name) and found out what it would cost to buy those rights. Then we proceeded with our creative development. We decided that the idea was so ideal for Toyota at that time that we would include a fair price for the purchase of the rights as a part of the estimate for the production of the idea. Toyota agreed, and "You asked for it—You got it, Toyota" became a part of the patois of the times. How embarrassing this could have been if we had not researched the background and carelessly opened ourselves and our client to the loss of a good idea and a lawsuit as well.

TO WHOM ARE YOU SELLING?

Consider our example of the day care center presentation a few chapters back. Remember, we analyzed the audience to find out which of the many reasons would help sell the idea of a day care center in a rather conservative community. By knowing to whom we were presenting, we were able to be single-minded in our approach. The same kind of thinking and research should go into the manner of presentation. Here's a suggested checklist that you might want to think about before starting to plan your next presentation, no matter what it's for.

1.   How many people will you be talking to? Watch a good stand-up comic in a nightclub. When he's talking to a full house, his whole attitude, demeanor, and approach will be different from when he's working an early crowd or playing to a half-empty establishment. And it's not just the amount of adrenaline that gets pumped up with big audience response. He knows that he can't come on larger than life and use the whole stage with a small crowd. With 20 or 30 couples the reaction time for laughter and applause is different than with 300 so he changes his timing, even his whole approach. That's not to say that he can't be effective. He probably becomes more intimate, less grandiose. He knows that if he does an overblown joke and it doesn't make it he'll have an overblown letdown, and he'll be fighting from his heels to try and rewin the audience.

2.   How many times will you have to make the presentation? By this I mean, will you have to present to a series of different levels of the group or companies to whom you're talking? When we were developing the Crime Prevention Coalition public service campaign "Take a bite out of crime," featuring America's best known (and perhaps only) trench-coat dog, McGruff, we made the same presentation at least 15 different times to groups varying in size from five to three hundred. When it got really tough was when we had to make two or three different presentations one right after another, particularly when the last or final presentation was the big one and the earlier ones were to lower working levels in the pecking order. In these not too uncommon instances many things can happen. You can give short shrift to the lower levels, but that is obviously a wrong tactic. You want them to be just as enthusiastic about what you're selling as you are. You want them, in fact, to help you sell as you go up through the chain of command. And that won't happen if they get the idea that you're showing them the stuff just as a courtesy.

But then you have the aforementioned problem of possibly playing a big presentation to a small audience, as is often the case in these matters where you're building up to make a final presentation to a committee or commission or board of directors or faculty or sales force. Do you change the presentation like the stand-up comic? No. Because then you'll be making a different presentation at each level. And the odds are very good that the lower levels won't like this. But if you give them the Radio

City Music Hall treatment, it's liable to fall flat. And that is hardly the way to start a successful clamber up the selling ladder.

In these cases, what I try to do is plan everything and rehearse everything for the big presentation and then, at the first level, set the stage. Ask the audience to imagine that it's the final presentation and there are lots of people in the room. In certain instances it might even help to dim the lights a bit, if you can, to give them the feeling of a little theater—and to help you imagine a lot of people out there. As you make the presentation, however, don't be afraid to throw some asides to your first-level audience—even to the point of breaking the flow to ask their advice on an integral point or approach. This makes them feel involved, eliminates the possible thought that all you're doing is rehearsing in front of them prior to flaunting your stuff to the big boys, and could elicit constructive suggestions. Obviously, you must be careful where you decide to break the flow.

The largest problem with multiple presentations is fatigue. After three or four times of talking like McGruff, your voice begins to go. Your enthusiasm wanes. Your timing slips a bit. You might even begin to skip some seemingly unimportant points to get through it faster. (Usually not a good idea. If you've built a good presentation, every point is probably pretty important.) The solution is to try and pace yourself. Use controlled energy the first time through. Build slightly as you go along. One of the things I try and do is have a number of different asides or ad libs. Nothing important, just little things. And I change these with each presentation. They help relieve the monotony among your cohorts and the initial levels you've presented to as they hear it time after time. They'll even begin to listen closely to see what little changes you may make the next time. It also keeps you, the presenter, more on top of things. A little device. But it works.

I don't mean to say that you change the sense of the presentation one whit. Just the flavoring. Example: "If we don't follow through with this program, we run the risk of having fewer people buying our product than would appear at the old folks' home for a screening of *The Rocky Horror Picture Show*." Next time you might want to change it to: "If we don't follow through with this program, we run the risk of having fewer people buying our product than there is dandruff on Telly Savalas' collar." On second thought, you might want to forget the whole thing.

3. What is your audience like—both as individuals and in its entirety? Individually, it can be helpful to find out some key things about the important decision makers. Are they receptive to different approaches—or do they have a tendency to the absolute mind set? Are they conservative or liberal in their thinking? Do they have senses of humor? Do they like showmanship, drama? (Not everyone does. Some people think that this approach masks the lack of an idea or, at the least, rather than spotlighting an idea, tends to concentrate attention on the presentation rather than the thought. They could consider it a form of the vampirism that I discussed in the last chapter.) Are they nervous when being presented to? Are they quick decision makers—or do they like to talk and think things over for awhile? (At one of our client meetings when an advertising idea is being presented, the brand group involved will listen, ask searching questions, and then caucus—without the presenters present—to discuss and analyze the proposal. They then reconvene with a unified opinion.) Do they like the challenge and stimulation of creative ideas—or do they wish the whole thing was over with as soon as possible? Are they able to concentrate on the proposition, even though the air and their lives may be full of real or imagined distractions? (In one memorable moment early in my advertising life, I had the misfortune of participating in a presentation introducing a new luxury fleet of ocean liners to the president of the company as one of his vessels sank in New York harbor—visible just over his shoulder through a large window. To make it even more difficult, we were stressing the safety of these vessels. As we reached the climax of our presentation, the subject ship rammed—or was rammed by—a garbage scow and went down in about 15 feet of water. The passengers walked planks to the shore. The president's assistant interrupted our dramatics to hurriedly point out this misfortune to his boss. The president glanced casually over his shoulder, ascertained that there was no serious emergency, turned sedately back to us and suggested we continue. Now there was a man who did not let distraction distract. It was, however, somewhat inhibiting to go on with our presentation on "the safest ships afloat.")

To answer these questions—questions that could mean the difference between selling and unselling an idea—takes research experience, amateur psychology, and insightfulness. If you've never confronted your audience before, ask people who have. Find out how receptive they were to the last presentation—and if it didn't go well, find out why. But don't stop your research with the most recent presentation. Try to get a feeling for the nature of responses your people have gotten from the decision makers over a period of time. If it seems to have fluctuated, probe some more. Find out if there were external influences at work. Or if the people or persons being presented to have a reputation for shifting moods. Or if the entire cast was the same. Sometimes, shifting people can cause a personality conflict and change the mood or receptiveness of a meeting faster than the mercury in a thermometer going from a sauna to a snowbank.

In your research, don't just concentrate on the key decision makers. The underlings can be most important. Their role can be to ask questions or make comments that can help their leaders make the final decision. Usually, there are one or two people in a meeting known for this. Don't ignore them. Talk to them and through them to their bosses. But know who they are.

And that brings us to the dynamics of the meeting as influenced by the individuals. You are planning strategy to urge your local zoning board to uphold the existing law and not grant a variance. Before going into the merits of the case, the leader of your cause opens the discussion something like this:

> We should know the composition of the board and how they've reacted in the past. This could give us a clue as to what their action will be in granting or not granting the variance. First there's Lou S.—a well meaning, happy soul who really doesn't understand his functions on the zoning board. He can't stand to hurt anyone and has habitually voted for giving variances. We must find a way to convince him of his responsibilities, perhaps even go into the basics of why zoning exists. Jane M. is next. Tough, no-nonsense. Asks the right questions. Seems that she will give fair, unbiased, intelligent judgments, but she has already voted to grant variances, because she's conservative and believes that people should have a right to do what they want with their own property, no matter how it affects their neighbors, or what the law says. I think that the only thing that might convince her to uphold the zoning laws is the threat of a lawsuit. . . . And so forth.

By paying attention to the individual reactions and interactions from the past, you will now be able to plan a more effective strategic approach and presentation.

The problem with most of us is that we often don't consider these factors. Think about this the next time you're about to present a budget for this year's sales contest. (How have the participants reacted in the past? Who sets the tone of the meeting? Who has the final say? Does she listen to her subordinates? Does everyone believe in sales contests? Do they fight over every penny—or can you sell the ideas first and cost second? What about Fred, who seems to drift off every now and then?) Research should also try and provide you with answers as to the best time for the meeting. Some people are at their finest first thing in the morning. Others like early afternoon affairs. The only generalization I can make is fairly obvious: try to stay away from late afternoon meetings where you have the debilitating effect of the wear and tear of the day working on your audience, as well as their possible desire to get the hell out of the meeting and home to a warm fire and cool martini. These can be pressures you really don't need.

Again, pay close attention to the track record of your audience to determine the interrelations of the people attending. And here we're talking about presentations where there will be some audience involvement. Normally, if you're simply presenting an idea more or less for informational purposes and don't expect or have to listen to comments or questions, the larger the audience the better because the large audience begets a willingness to accept drama, theater, show-biz. If the presentation is to gain agreement or approval of an approach or idea, then a smaller audience with the key decision maker or makers is often best. Reason: ego. The large audience may cripple the give and take of comments and questions because another factor has entered the mix: "How do I look in front of my superiors—or my subordinates?" It leads to thinking like: "I'd like to ask this question, but it may sound foolish. How can I rephrase it so that if the answer is obvious I won't look like a boob? Maybe I should just forget it, or I can talk to someone quietly after the meeting." See what's happened. A possible opportunity for creative discussion within a group of intelligent people on a subject of some importance to all of them has been missed. And perhaps the undecided questioner will not even talk to someone after the meeting because he'll suddenly realize the answer may be, "My God, man, why didn't you bring that up in the meeting?," and he'll feel that he'll look even more foolish. So what's happened is nothing.

Now obviously, this kind of thinking does not go through the mind of the chief decision maker. But she may have an even more dangerous problem. With a room full of her subordinates, she may feel it necessary, subconsciously, to show her leadership abilities, her incisive thinking, her creative agility. She may feel, again deep within her psyche, that she has to top what has been suggested or presented. She just can't sit and agree, even though she does. Her people must remain in awe of her. And so she contributes. Sometimes getting herself in a hole that's difficult to get out of. And that jeopardizes the presentation. Ego wins again—but the idea is in peril.

So, for the best results from a meeting where you're seeking the approval of an idea or proposal, try to keep it small, limiting it as much as possible to the final decision makers, who you hope will say "yes."

CAN YOU SELL THEM BEFORE YOU SELL THEM?

Talk to some of the successful old-timers in your fields of endeavor. Ask them about their successes, how they presented and sold whatever they were trying to sell. I'll bet you'll hear things like:

> "So I got together with old Bart the night before and planted the seed. I think I got him thinking it was his idea."
>
> "J. B. and I were fishing together when I got him in the right mood to at least listen to why we should have a new facade on the building."
>
> "If I hadn't talked to her about it over dinner, she might not even have known she needed a new approach."

It's the presell, and it can be as important an ingredient in your selling attack as anything else you do. Of course, preselling presupposes that you have someone in your organization who has built up some kind of relationship with the potential sellee. Significant in this presell is how far you go. The big danger, of course, is in getting carried away and jeopardizing the idea. After all, you do have a well-thought-out, detailed presentation to be made in the near future. There's no sense in trying to force the idea through single-handedly under circumstances and time constraints that could be working against you.

The presell should be used to get the sellee in a receptive frame of mind. It can be as simple as:

The scene: A corner table at Christ Cella's. You and your client are having coffee and strawberries after a delightful dinner.

YOU: Well, C. J., tomorrow morning I think you'll really be interested in what you're going to see. It's completely different from anything we've ever done before. And because of this, I think it has a chance to be a real winner.

HE: That right? Well, I hope we're not being different just for the sake of being different.

YOU: Not at all. As you know, I'm the last person to go along with something we don't think has merit. But this one does, C. J. It will astonish you and perhaps even scare you a bit because it's so unusual. But once you get over the initial reaction, pick at it and see if you can find any flaws. We did. And we couldn't. That's why I think it's got a great chance.

HE: Well, Sam, if you say so there must be something to it. I must admit, you've got me intrigued.

Of course, his final retort could have been:

"I dunno, Sam, I've gone along too many times with some nutty approach or another that you people have come up with only to have it fizzle." Or

"Sam, if there's one thing we don't need now, it's a chance." Or

"Sam, I admire your enthusiasm—but sometimes I think it gets in the way of solid thinking."

Implicit in any kind of presell strategy must be a trusting or at least respectful relationship between the two parties. With this relationship, any kind of salesmanship becomes easier. But trust must be earned. Notice from the first negative response ("I've gone along too many time s with some nutty approach . . . only to have it fizzle") that this had not been done through past performance. If this is your problem, you should analyze your techniques of assessing the ideas before they're presented. Questionable proposals are obviously getting through your internal screening process. The sellee has bought a number of them through your salesmanship, but they've somehow not proved worthwhile. Thus you haven't earned the right to the implicit "Trust me." While one of the tenets of a reaching-for-something-different is the acceptability of a certain amount of failure, you've got to have some successes.

If you're confronted with the second response ("if there's one thing we don't need now, it's a change"), you should be prepared. This is the kind of response that probably can be predicted from past experience with the sellee. He sounds like a person who tends to be conservative, is extremely cautious about changing anything without absolute proof that it will be beneficial. The presell should concentrate on changing that attitude, on using past and present examples where change has proven to be the correct answer. The presell should thus concentrate on setting up an attitude or atmosphere for the impending presentation but should not touch on any of the details of the actual presentation. With this kind of person, more than one presell meeting may be necessary.

In the third response ("your enthusiasm . . . gets in the way of solid thinking"), be aware of what could be a serious problem. The way it usually works is that the seller becomes known for his dramatics and for his involving presentations. People look forward to listening to and watching him. It's not that the enthusiasm masks good thinking, but rather that the sellees are so mesmerized by the presentation techniques that they miss the message, and therefore the good thinking has been overlooked. I've been in meetings where a prized presenter has been asked not to present to eliminate this pseudo-hypnosis. Sad. We've been reduced to having the agency dullard (as far as presentations are concerned) drone through the executions of a new campaign so that the client would not be distracted from the basic message. Of course, the danger here is that the client then thinks the premise is correct, but the execution is less than earth shattering. One way around this is to again handle a logical buildup of the premise in the presell without ever resorting to dramatics. Then, in the actual presentation, the calm analysis of the premise should be briefly reviewed before you reveal the skyrockets and pinwheels.

But what if you don't have an opportunity for the presell get-together? There are two courses you can follow. You can enlarge the "setup" section of the actual presentation to include your presell thoughts. The danger here, of course, is that the sellee won't have enough time to digest the information and embrace your point of view. For presentations that are dependent on the presell, I favor a second course: If you can't do it in person, put it in writing—or, if the sellee has quick access to a videotape playback machine, put it on tape. This should be a well-thought-out piece, as concise as possible, with an accompanying personal note explaining why it's important for the sellee to read or view the piece before the meeting.

There is, however, a deadly presell temptation, which, if followed, is almost always fatal to the idea and even the entire seller-sellee relationship. It's going over the heads of those whose heads should not be gone over! I have personally seen two major advertising accounts change agencies because one of the principals of the agency insisted on stepping over the chain of command and going directly to the chairman of the board when his agency's idea was, for whatever reason, blocked. It's a way to make instant enemies. The unfortunate plot, of course, is that eventually the chairman is no longer a factor and the chain changes. The people once stepped over reach the top. And they remember. Oh, do they remember.

So, when preselling, your objective should be to get the sellee in a receptive frame of mind, not to seek approval of an idea before anyone else has seen it.

PLANNING THE PRESENTATION

The first step in any presentation, no matter to whom and for what, is to decide on what you want to accomplish.

Objectives

This may sound basic and simple, but often a team will go into a meeting with different ideas of what the outcome should be. You laugh. OK, next time you see one of those "Now-there's-a-big-sellathon-going-on-at-your-local-Ford-dealer" commercials on television, ask anyone in the room what the objective of the advertising is. "Sell Fords," someone will probably say. Wrong. The objective is to let people know that Ford dealers are having a sale, for a limited time. If the objective of the advertising were to sell Fords, the approach would be different. More time would be spent talking about the product's advantages. But when promoting a sales event, the product is not as important as building the excitement at the retail level. Think about it. In this case which would be important? (1)"Watch how the Ford Mustang outperforms any car in its class" or (2) "We've got to sell 30,000 Fords in just two weeks. And that means your Ford dealer is ready to deal."

In the case of the sellee who resists change, the objective, as we said, may be to set up the need for change, saving the actual new idea for a later presentation. If this is not understood by all concerned, if one of the team thinks that the objective is to immediately sell the new idea as hard as possible, you may lose because the sellee has not been properly prepared to accept the new thought.

Time Constraints

Many people may feel that the next step in the planning process is working out the flow of the presentation. Be careful. The next step may be much simpler and more basic. But it should be the next step. Find out how much time you have to make the presentation. Then you can proceed with the outline, tailoring it to the time constraints. If the time given seems unreasonable, and it can't be lengthened, see if you can change the time of the meeting so that you will be allowed what you need. But if none of this works, or if it seems inappropriate to ask for more time (and this is often the case), then work around it. And this means planning and rehearsing (more about rehearsing later) and not straying too far from the script or outline.

For some reason, even though we all know better, there seems to be some kind of sublime confidence that comes to many of the more experienced practitioners of the arts of presentation that, boiled down, translates to: "I don't worry about time. I can adjust on the spot and just wing it." One of the more embarrassing moments in life is to be told you have an hour and a half to make a presentation because the key people that you're talking to have to make a plane and then, because you've digressed from the script and even repeated yourself (horrors!), have the audience smile apologetically and leave when you're only three-quarters of the way through because time's up. I know. It happened to me in a new business presentation. We didn't get the business.

In calculating the time needed, be sure to allow some time at the end for questions and comments. Knowing to whom you're presenting can be a big help here. Some people like to comment at the end, some like to interrupt, and some really don't want to comment at the meeting but would rather talk it over with each other and give you their thoughts later. Now, if time is tight, try to hold the questions until the end. If your audience starts interrupting as you go along, your schedule will be sliced up and you may not make the finishing gong. If they insist, politely remind them of the time schedule, set by them, and that they will have plenty of time to tell you what they think when you're through—but if you take time to reply to their most provocative thoughts now, there may not be an end. ("That is a most interesting comment, sir, and I do want you to remind me of it when I'm through if we don't address it to your satisfaction in the next part of the presentation.")

The nightmare of everyone making a presentation that's been well-thought-out, rehearsed, and timed to the second is to have someone turn to you, as you're entering the conference room and say, "Oh, by the way, old boy, the chairman and president have an emergency meeting that was just called, and so they only have half the time we thought they would for your meeting." When dealing with top brass, this happens more often than not. Therefore, it's a good idea, at this level, to have a condensed version of the presentation.

Role Assignment

After you've worked out the structure of the meeting, decide who's to say what. Assign roles. This, as you can imagine, can be ticklish business. Egos again. And these egos often come from top management ranks. In large corporate presentations they, like all of us, enjoy being in at the climax. The problem is that often they've not participated in the development of the idea and, therefore, are not as familiar with it as they might be and thus may not be as effective as someone of lesser rank who's wallowed in the idea since the inception. In general, if top brass is to be included and if they've not been intimately associated with the particular project, they should be used for the introductory remarks and for a recap or summary at the end. No more than one member of top management, not directly involved with the subject, should be included in your planning. There's no sense in having the platform sagging under the corporate weight of chairman, vice chairman, president, chief financial officer, and so forth. The exception, of course, is if any or all of these people have played key roles (not just approval) in the development of the project being presented. Then you should wheel the big guns out and fire away.

In most presentations you should go with the best you've got. Consider, for example, the three architects working on the college library project that I discussed a few chapters back. One of them is an imaginative blender of the traditional and the modern but blushes when asked to give the time of day. The second is quick, facile, fast, and adds to every concept with intriguing unthought-of details—but also talks in details—and talks and talks and talks. The third is not as accomplished an architect but has a good overview of what's being done and is concise and articulate when making her points. All of them would like to participate in the presentation in one way or another. And in lower, non-decision-making meetings, perhaps they should. But when it's into the big time, presenting the plan to the architectural committee of the board of trustees, you'd better depend on Ms. Articulate. Even though she may be the least talented architect of the three, she's the most talented presenter. And that's what matters at this point.

When assigning roles, there are some who believe that no one should be in the presentation who doesn't have something to do. At the top level, I agree. Eliminate the elder statesmen who sit and smile and nod and blink like toads when appropriate.

Unless, of course, they're someone like Dave Bascomb.

Dave became famous as a successful, imaginative, and irreverent creative figure in the advertising world of the late 1950s and early 1960s. Once I had the pleasure of being in a pressure presentation with him in St. Louis. We were on the verge of losing the Falstaff beer account. The reasons had to do with management changes and disagreement over marketing direction, but, as is often the case, troubles were blamed on the creative effort. We played the game. Even though it seemed to be a hopeless cause, we put a number of creative teams on the project to try to save the account. (We'd been their agency for 15 years.) Cliff Fitzgerald, our then chairman, made a brilliant and warm introduction lightly tracing the history of our relationship. Stu Upson, then the management director, gave a concise overview of the situation and reviewed strategy. Then Dave quickly introduced his team's creative efforts. The work was good but received stony reactions from the assorted brewery representatives. Halfway though the second campaign there was still no response. Suddenly Dave's hoarse stage whisper echoed through the room: "For God's sake, Whorehouse (we had an account man, Morehouse, seated at the end of the table), start muttering 'Gahdamned good. I like that stuff' and maybe they'll think it's one of them and we can get a groundswell going." It didn't save the business, but it sure broke the tension. And a lot of us felt a lot better. Dave was welcome at any presentation we made. Unfortunately for us, he decided that fly fishing was more rewarding. He may be right.

I do think, however, that it's a good idea whenever possible to have junior people at presentations as observers. This is one way to start early exposure to tasks they someday will have to plan and handle themselves. But don't overload, because people's time can be expensive. Andrew S. Grove, in an article in *Fortune Magazine* (July 11, 1983) adapted from his book, *High Output Management*, puts some figures to the hidden costs of meetings and presentations. He estimates that the dollar cost of a manager's time is about $100 per hour. If you have a meeting or presentation that includes 10 people averaging out at this level (yours and the sellees) for two hours, you're spending $2,000. That's as good a reason as any to make sure that everyone is necessary and that the whole thing is as efficiently planned and run as possible. But don't get so efficient that you forget the purpose of the meeting. The idea is to attain your objectives, not to see how smart a meeting you can manage.

As a final thought on the attendees, make sure there's a note taker. Sometimes tape recorders are necessary, but I find them inhibiting and somehow demeaning. And they sometimes bring out the exhibitionist in some. (I have a friend who could never resist doing a tap dance audition in front of the hidden camera in the lobby of his Chase Manhattan Bank.) According to the meeting, the note taker can vary in stature. In preproduction meetings for TV commercials we use a specially trained production assistant. In large presentations we'll use an account executive and a creative person. We use both of them to compare notes after the meeting to make sure all are hearing the same things. These notes, obviously, are the basis for reports, future action, etc.

Deciding on who's to do and say what, in any kind of presentation or meeting, can help channel the flow toward the objectives you've set up. Think of the number of family conferences you've had. The successful ones, I'll bet, result from you and your partner working out your different roles beforehand. Most of the frustrating ones, I've found, happen when the meetings are impulsive, usually the result of ticklish tempers. ("Chauncey, get down here this instant! Your father and I want to talk with you—and let me tell you, THIS IS SERIOUS! Now answer just one question: Did you or did you not take the car last night when we expressly forbade you. . . ? " Blah, blah, blah.) This is not to say that the well-thought-out meetings are always successful, but at least you don't end up saying, "Why the hell did I lose my temper? How did I know that you told him it was OK?"

Audiovisual Aids

I'm continually surprised at the number of books and articles written on the managing of meetings that refer to "acetates" as the accepted and somehow only visual aids. The fact is that you should use anything practical to make your point. Slides, videotape, music, film, models, actors, anything—as long as it helps. I touched on some of this in the last chapter ("Rule 4: Make sure that you know what the creative people have in mind"). But be careful you don't overdo it or put something in just for the sake of showmanship. And if you're presenting something graphic, like a TV commercial concept, be careful that the trappings surrounding it don't overpower the actual commercial. Easy to do, because commercials are usually presented in rough storyboard form, and they may look pale, indeed, if the buildup includes finished film or color slides conveying the mood you wish to convey.

Two diverse examples of how aids can help presentations. The first was a presentation by a conference-planning group to explain the general approach to a Toyota dealer meeting for 3,000 people. It opened with a graphic display of the theme stretched across the conference room wall. The model was unveiled to show the rather intricate staging in a theater-in-the-round. Finally, the broad outline of the program was read. At appropriate points, suggested theme music was played on tape. Then, informally but effectively, one of the presenters would sing specially written lyrics against the background tape. Nothing overdone. Always preceded with "then the song would go something like this." Sure, it was a little bit of show business—but every bit of it was important because it established the mood, feeling, logistics, and actual theme of the presentation. And it showed that the people doing it had thought it through.

The second example was a presentation we gave some years ago to win an agency competition for the Florida Citrus account. Our objective was to convince the commission that they should select us because we were packaged goods specialists—what we referred to as the hardball of advertising. Our presentation used baseball graphics. (I think the presentation coincided with spring training in Florida.) We did something with "Take Me Out to the Ball Game" and we ended with "We're DFS, the hardball agency. And we're here to play hardball for you." (Circular DFS symbol appears on screen, dissolves to baseball, dissolves to Florida orange.) As the lights came up we threw orange colored hardballs with our logo on them to the audience. Show business. But it played to our perceived advantage and theme and, we hoped, convinced them that we offered experience, sound business thinking, and executional flair. It worked.

If you're going to use these aids, decide early enough in your planning so that you have time to prepare them. It's most frustrating to say: "Hey, great idea. We're talking about the gentle time of day, in this approach. Let's set it up with a lot of different slides of sunsets" and then realize that the meeting is at nine the next morning and you don't have time to get slides made. Or if you do, you'll pay extra for them in overtime. Speaking of overtime, what about the cost of all this? Well, like everything, the cost is relative. If you're presenting for a multimillion dollar account like Florida Citrus, it's well worth the few thousand for slides, music, orange paint, and baseballs. If you're making a smaller internal presentation, even the cost of special slides may be too much. Don't let that discourage you. Clip photographs from magazines to help explain a feeling or mood. Letter charts or acetates yourself. Get some cohorts to help you act out commercials. Tailor your presentation aids to your budget. But if the idea is big and there's somthing extra that will help sell it, don't skimp.

The last word on audiovisual aids is probably one of the first things you should do. As the barkers in front of the old burlesque theaters used to say, "Check 'em out." Check out the facilities. Make sure there's equipment available for what you want to do. No sense in saying we'll mount the display material and pin it on the cork walls, or bulletin boards, or ledge around the conference room only to find there are no cork walls, bulletin boards, or ledges. If the meeting is away from your home grounds, try to bring your own equipment—particularly videotape recorders and tape decks. Then you know what you're getting. You can control the quality. And be sure that you or one of your people know how to operate the stuff. What a marvelous climax to a presentation to say; "And now the dessert. The actual creative work we promised you. Ta da!"

Silence.

VOICE 1: (hoarse whisper) Did you rewind it?

VOICE 2: I think it's rewound. This is not like our machine.

YOU: Our apologies, folks. Hold on for a minute while we . . . ah . . . straighten out this little technical. . . .

(Image appears on screen).

VOICE 1: There it is. But there's no sound. Check the sou. . . .

VOICE 2: It's running backwards!

YOU: Ah . . . this might be a good time for a little break while we straighten things out here. . . .

It's not a good time at all. Because no one "checked it out," a creative presentation suffers. And don't depend on the audiovisual person in the sellee's organization, no matter how good he is, to be psychic and guess what your program is. Cover it with him beforehand. If you have time for a last-minute run-through, be sure he's in on it if he's going to assist in any way. If there's no rehearsal time, at least have a quick talk with the man, explaining the scope of the project and letting him in on his cues.

Rehearsal

No one in their right mind will deny that rehearsal of any kind of presentation can be some kind of step in the right direction. Or, to put it another way, no rehearsal can be a giant step toward disaster. Rehearsal lets you know how you're doing from a time standpoint. It gives you time to change and adjust the presentation. It impregnates the flow and key ideas in your mind. It helps make the familiar more familiar, dries sweaty palms, diminishes the proclivity to panic.

Unfortunately, organizing rehearsals is not easy. One of the biggest problems is getting all of the participants together at one time. Conflicts keep looming. "Everyone can make it Tuesday except the V.P. in charge of sales and the chairman. Oh well, we'll rehearse their parts separately." Now this may be the way it has to be done, but if so, have someone stand in for them and read the missing person's part so that everyone will understand what's going on and, more important, will not include in their section something that's been said by someone else. In addition, if you don't know what everyone is saying and how they're saying it, a time bomb may lurk in the presentation, just waiting. Once it went off right in my face.

It was a year or so after World War II, and I was working hard in my first real job in the advertising department of the Armstrong Cork Company (now Armstrong World Industries). The head of the department was Cameron Hawley, a brilliant creative presence who later left the world of advertising to become the author of such best sellers as *Executive Suite* and *Cash McCall*. He had decided that the best way to inspire Armstrong's various floor covering distributors was to invite them to the home office in Lancaster, Pennsylvania and put on a flamboyant musical extravaganza centered on their, and Armstrong's, important role in the world's scheme of things. and it was something. Dancing girls, a 60 person chorus, blackouts, big orchestra, everything. And I was the stage manager.

One of our major problems was that at that time there were no facilities for these kind of goings on. No matter. Hawley insisted that we build our own. We rented Lancaster's Moose Hall and ran power in from the plant. We expanded the stage, put in foots and three borders, a giant screen, a customized switchboard, sound system, even a disappearing podium. The maestro was a perfectionist. He did not want the executive vice president for sales to make the welcoming speech and then, before we segued into the first skit, have some yokel in overalls stump out on the stage, smile apologetically, and remove the podium. And so we built an extension on the stage apron with a trap door and put a two-cycle motor in the bottom to raise and lower the podium, untouched by human hands. And now, patient reader, comes the denouement, the long-awaited time bomb.

The V.P. in charge of sales was not available to rehearse. "Never mind," said Hawley. "All you need is his cue to change things for the next setup. The cue is: We take you now to a wholesale warehouse in St.

Louis. The year is 1939. Spot out. Start podium down. V.P. walks off stage. Foots up and curtain open. Got it?" And we rehearsed that way for weeks, never going through the V.P.'s complete talk.

The big evening arrived. There were 300 people in the audience plus the press (this was big stuff in those days). The show opened. Podium came up. Spot on and V.P. started his welcoming address. Suddenly a light on the switchboard blinked. The intercom from the balcony. Would I sneak back behind the curtain and shake out a big wrinkle where it had caught on the American flag. I told my noble but nervous assistant (We were all nervous. Hawley had threatened banishment from the cork company for anyone who made a mistake.) to just follow the script, that I'd be back before any stage change was necessary. I wasn't gone more than a minute or so, but when I returned the assistant was babbling, "I think we're near the end. I lost my place when the intercom blinked again. He's going very fast." Suddenly I heard the cue phrase, " . . . St. Louis in the year 1939." With eclat I flicked switches and heard the podium start down.

To my horror, just as I was about to dim the spot, I heard the V.P. continuing. Impossible. He's supposed to be walking off. But not only was he going on, he was reading like a machine gun because the podium and his speech were sinking slowly into the floor. He grabbed the podium and tried to hold it, which caused a high pitched whine from the two-cycle motor as wisps of smoke curled around his feet. Luckily, he decided against this approach and let go. He then tried to follow the script down by slinking into a crouch, all the more intriguing because he was a giant of a man who seemed to be shrinking in front of the audience's very eyes. I stopped the podium. He was caught in mid-crouch—but he continued, nervously wondering what would happen next. I made a quick decision not to raise the podium and compound the problem. And so he finished in a half crouch and decided that if he straightened up to leave the stage, the mistake would be more obvious (more obvious? There wasn't a person in the audience who wasn't bug-eyed at the unusual performance.), so he slunk across the stage in a good Groucho Marx bent-kneed glide. The only things missing were the wiggly eyebrows and the cigar. And this man was not a comic. At least not until then.

Did the wrath of our leader descend on me? Not at all. He knew about managing the creative process. He knew that he had to depend on me for the next two days of the show and it would be unwise to blow my head off at that point. Later, perhaps. But later never came because the rest of the extravaganza was, as they say, boffo.

The point is that I don't think any of this would have happened had we discovered the false "St. Louis" cue in the middle of the man's speech in rehearsal. But, remember, we never rehearsed that part. We just rehearsed the final cue change. Ah well, had we done that, we probably wouldn't have had this memorable moment in advertising history.

The Presentation Structure

As we all know, most presentations consist of three main sections: introduction, presentation of the subject, summary—including questions and answers. But that's about all the generalizing we can do. What each of these sections contains and how involved they are depends on the subject. In my world of advertising, where presentations are a part of the essence of the business, we become quite detailed.

Introduction

This usually includes a very short and succinct statement explaining the purpose of the presentation, perhaps giving some general background concerning the market place, business trends, and conditions affecting the product (most of our presentations have to do with client products), and a brief outline of what the presentation will entail and how much time it will take. This portion is usually handled by the top management person involved.

Also included in the introduction may be a section with more specific background materials. Here would be an evaluation of the current situation concerning the product, including a reprise of the agreed upon strategy, detailed competitive influences, research findings, and any agreements or directions touched upon leading up to the presentation. This portion is usually handled by the account team, calling on experts as needed.

The Presentation

This is what it's all about, what you've been leading up to, preparing for, what the presell has been preselling. It's the idea, the proposal, the raison d'être. It should naturally evolve as the climax of your efforts. It's usually handled by one or more people (according to the length and complexity) closely associated with the idea development. And, as I said before, these should be your best presenters. Notice I said best, not necessarily most experienced. Experience is often equated with age. And age can be tricky in presentations. If you're presenting to a panel of elder statesmen, you may want to have a sprinkling of grey hair on your team. Not a must if your youth brigade is good, but something to think about. More important, however, could be the other end of the axis. Be careful of having the experienced old-timer as your key speaker—no matter how good he is—if your audience tops out at 39. The image you may project could pose an imagined threat to the energetic, enthusiastic, action-oriented audience. If you do use the weight of age, be careful how you position it. The danger is presenting a 55-year-old creative director as the day-to-day contact with a 39-year-old client. Most people do not want to deal with generation gaps regularly. They're bound to feel uncomfortable. And there are enough challenges in this business without starting off with an uncomfortable client.

Back to the presentation itself. In this creative section, you may want to give an introduction to the creative process involved—different from the business or marketing background in that it traces earlier creative thinking and probing. The objective here is to help the audience arrive at the same conclusions that you've arrived at by taking them through your thinking step-by-step. You may also want to do some mood setting. One of the big problems with presenting anything in rough form— which is usually the form that's taken in early presentation—is that whatever you present is just that—rough. For instance, if you want to show a chorus line tap dancing its heart away as an idea to sell the durability of pantyhose, a simple storyboard with rough drawings of the action might not do it justice. A film clip from *42nd Street* or *Chorus Line* could be used to illustrate the look you're striving for. This mood setting also becomes a part of the philosophy I talked about in the section in the previous chapter on making sure that you know what the creative people have in mind.

Other devices that we've used to help set the stage for the idea to be presented have included the following.

1.   *Demonstration tracks or live performances of music.* (I realize that we've discussed this before in general, however, we'll be a bit more specific here.) The live performance is usually the composer on piano or

guitar with a singer or singers. Because of the lack of visual rapport with the audience, the sound tracks may offer a bit more: rhythm section, piano, and singers. Of course, this can vary with the importance of the presentation. I've heard demonstrations for presentations used to help gain new business or new accounts that consist of a full symphonic orchestra or the entire USC marching band. To set a mood the tracks need not be original. Stock background music with flutes, oboes, and cellos might be used to evoke a pastoral scene. When you do this—and if you eventually wish to have original music—be sure that the sellee understands your thinking. When you play "I Want to Hold Your Hand" to project an aura of the 1960s and say, "Our music will be something like this," be sure that the client takes note of the "something like this" clause so that when he sees the finished version he doesn't ask where The Beatles are.

2. *The showing of film clips to illustrate particular techniques.* There's a new process called Intravision where certain action can be frozen while other action continues at the same time. In the past, to accomplish this effect everyone in a particular scene would be told to freeze in one position while other actors might move through the scene. Obviously people could only hold the freeze for a certain amount of time and then only in certain positions. The whole thing would fall apart with the slight movement of a leg or twitch of any eyebrow. In Intravision, actors can actually move among the frozen people. And they can be frozen in any attitude that's desired: jumping, standing on one foot, sliding. As you can see, it's difficult to describe, let alone visualize. An actual example would help immensely.

3. *Still photographs to illustrate a setting, atmosphere, or character.* If you're presenting something reminiscent of *Casablanca*, how about a series of stills of the Casbah and the wonderfully decadent, mysterious, romantic Hollywood-Moorish interior of Rick's? If you'd like to open your commercial with a low shot skimming over icebergs in Alaska's Glacier Bay and suddenly reveal a car on one of them (as we once did for Toyota), start your presentation with a photograph of a panoramic view of the whole scene to establish the majestic, dramatic effect. But be careful of overpromise. Before you get involved, be sure that what you're recommending is practical and can be done. Don't show them the scene in all its natural magnificence and then have to end up with a Styrofoam replica in Marina del Rey. And if you want an

Orson Wells-like character, get one and show his picture. Don't show a picture of the corpulent master himself. Overpromise.

4.   *Competitive advertising to point up the environment you'll be entering.*   This could be particularly useful as a reason for taking a different creative approach. Ed McCabe, the president of Scali, McCabe, Sloves, put it nicely in an article in *Pencil Points*, the monthly newsletter of The One Club for Art and Copy. He complained of the faddishness of certain humorous commercials. He even mentioned a specific sound—"the flat, gravelly, understated yet full-of-feeling voice" that seems to appear in a good number of these similarly constructed approaches. Show these commercials together to illustrate the sameness of what's being done today. The faddishness of advertising. It can be a nice jumping off place for breaking away from the usual.

5.   *Videotapes to get reactions to casting.*   For normal nonstar casting it's always wise to show videotapes of your choices taken from the casting sessions. But beyond that, if needed, you can get audience reaction to help make your selection. A few years ago during the oil crisis, we wished to present a campain for British Petroleum built around a character known as the BP Miser. A most important part of the advertising was the character himself. We cast three different types, videotaped them giving rough readings of the commercial, and then showed the tapes to test audiences. Their reactions helped us. All of this was done prior to the client meeting. When we made the presentation and described the BP Miser, we had visual proof and reactions to our recommendation.

After the creative introduction, we have the presentation of the idea. This should be done as clearly and dramatically as possible, again using anything that's needed to help sell it. I'll talk about some of these techniques later in this chapter.

Summary and Rebuttal

Now you've finished presenting the big idea. You've given it your all. You've reached the climax with upraised arms. It's done. You look at your audience. Some look interested, some perplexed, some noncommittal, some nervous. Silence. At this point several things can happen.

1. *The leader of the sellees speaks:* "Well, that certainly is interesting and dramatic. I can see you've given it a lot of thought. And we all appreciate your efforts. Now, I'm sure many of us have some questions and comments we'd like to make. So let's start with. . . ." Very good. They've acknowledged the effort, the important discussion period is about to get underway. But, most important, they've given you some breathing time.

2. *No one speaks.* To fill the void, you start to talk—only you don't know what to say because you've just said it all. So you find yourself repeating your presentation in a different style. Very bad. You're unselling. No matter what happens at the end of the specific presentation of the goods, the presenter should not have to ad-lib through a silence.

3. *The leader of your team speaks:* "Well, ladies and gentlemen, that's it. We invite your thoughts. But before doing that, I'd like to summarize the strategic objectives of this advertising and ask you to weigh those objectives against the points we made in this commercial to see how they match." This does several things. It breaks the silence. It relieves the actual presenter, gives him time to think. It focuses the sellees' attention on what the advertising is supposed to do. It obviously reviews the key objectives. And it sets up what we refer to as the "selling ballet."

Very simply, this ballet is a verbal dance between at least three people. In this case, they might be two members of your team and, at the beginning, one from the sellee's side. After the leader of your team reviews the strategic objectives against the points in the commercial, the key sellee spokesperson comments and asks a question about some action in the commercial. Now, having relaxed for a few minutes during all of this, you are ready for a calm, thoughtful reply. You give it, and perhaps there are a few more thoughtful exchanges between you and the sellee. Then a curve ball comes at you: "Why did you decide against a demonstration in this approach?" You pause. And your leader slides in with: "Because we feel the demonstration is not dramatic enough to warrant the time that it takes in the commercial. And our competition is already using a more compelling demo that we can't match." Sellee: "Is there a different kind of demo that we could develop?" You: "We've looked at a number of them and would be glad to show them to you, but we honestly don't think they're competitive." And so it goes. From your leader to sellee to you to sellee to leader to sellee to you. While one is in conversation, the other has time to think, to regroup, to anticipate, to give ammunition to the explanation and eventual sale. As you can see, this can work with any number of people beyond three. But it must be handled carefully.

The leader must be sure that the team does not make extraneous comments that may lead away from the main objective of selling the idea.

But what if you find yourself in the unenviable spot of being the only one available to make the presentation? The first suggestion is don't let yourself or any of your team get in that spot unless it's a one-on-one situation. Here the ballet is a simple back and forth. Every now and then, however, it happens. Dates are changed suddenly. Your people are out of town. The sellee's team is arriving in three hours. You're it. One against three.

You must control the meeting. You do it by planning not only your presentation but the beginning of the rebuttal as well. You pause when you're finished—and if no one says anything, you make the overall "strategic objectives" statement or some such that summarizes your case and asks for their comments. Then, as the ballet starts (from sellee one to you to sellee two to you to sellee one to you to sellee three to you . .), slow down. Don't get excited and oversell or overtalk. Try and keep answers concise. And listen. They may have good, logical things to say. But you can't respond to them if you're too busy trying to think of the next thing you'll say. And be fair. If a point is well taken, acknowledge it. As a selling tool, I once knew an art director who always made a mistake, a tiny something wrong in his layout, so that a client would have something to correct—and feel good about—and thus know that she had contributed to the success of the ad. ("Helluva good idea the agency presented. But it's lucky I saw the dark milk coming out of the cow or somebody'd think we made chocolate milk."

Anticipation—the Mother of Success

One of the keys to success is figuring action and reaction: anticipating what the sellee will think, do, question, and say to your presentation. Obviously, this takes a good sense of the opinions and attitudes of the sellee team based on the experience you or others in your organization have had with them. To prepare for this, some organizations use a role-playing session. In the advertising agency business, members of the account team or senior creative people become members of the sellee team. They try and think like the sellee. And the game of "what-if" proceeds. "What if old Brad says, 'I'm not sure this is on strategy'? What if the treasurer won't buy the cost? What if the ad manager remembers the speech he made a year ago against the use of children in soft drink commercials—and we're building the whole thing around an eight year old's birthday party? What if . . . ?" The anticipation should not just cover the content of what you're presenting but any procedural steps you're taking as well. ("What if she decides that we ought to test both these approaches, but we don't have time if we're going to make the air date? What if he stalls and wants to hold off making a change? What if she's scared? What if he likes it so much he wants to go ahead with no testing? What if she doesn't think the product's up to the advertising?") When the role playing is over, when all the possible questions and answers have been given—the actions and reactions described—then you should sit back and do some deep thinking.

Analyze What You've Done—and What You're Going to Do

Now's the time to reassess your entire presentation with an eye to the most important of the possible questions and answers that have come out of the role-playing session. Because this role playing has been a part of an extemporaneous exercise, some of the remarks may not be as pertinent as others. Sort them out. Zero in on the ones that could be threatening to your idea. Then provide answers. The answers may be in developing more persuasive selling arguments, or better ways of demonstrating what you need, or even the modification of the basic idea. Obviously, it's to be hoped that any basic problem with the idea is discovered before this phase of the presentation preparation. As I mentioned earlier in the "Creative Review Board" section, in Chapter 2, having noninvolved personnel participate in this role playing and analysis can sometimes give more objective points of view and uncover weaknesses that may not be as apparent to those deeply involved.

When you've worked all of this out and decided on how you'll react to any possible comments from the sellee, you should end the presentation with a review or summary of what you've done and a firm recommendation of the next steps. And these should be as specific as possible. Not just, "And we recommend that you endorse this idea," but "And we recommend we proceed with the idea by authorizing the making of a test commercial, cost not to exceed $20,000, put it in three markets for recall, and then test it for comprehension and reaction. If it passes, we recommend going into full production with the objective of getting on the air 10 weeks from today." Specific. Actionable. A recommendation that demands an answer.

THE TECHNIQUES OF PRESENTATION

How you do it can be as varied as the presenters, the sellees, the situation, the idea. Obviously, every presentation should take these factors into account and be slanted accordingly, but there are certain technique guidelines that I think can help.

Presenting Words and Pictures

In the advertising business today a large part of what we do is concerned with television and, therefore, the presentation of television commercial ideas. Up until the early fifties, no one had even thought about this. Presentation consisted of holding up magazine or newspaper layouts and letting the client read the copy, or listening to demonstration radio commercials. But television brought a whole new challenge to the world of presentation, to say the least. And people somehow started their presentation of these big television ideas by describing the pictures first. They would usually do this from a storyboard or, if in a large presentation, by flashing the pictures sequentially on a screen. Then they would go over the whole thing again, this time reading the words. Bad news. Big bore. Think about it. You're presenting an idea for a TV commercial that's supposed to have elements of humor and surprise—except if there's any visual surprise in the thing, it will be given away or at the least confused by doing the visual without the words. Most television commercials are designed so that words and pictures go together. Why then separate them? Imagine this kind of presentation for one of our more infamous (and certainly popular) commercials.

YOU: First I'll describe the pictures, then I'll read you the copy. We open on a down shot of these three little old ladies looking at a hamburger bun. Then one of them notices that the beef looks small in the bun. She looks at the others and says something. Then she looks off screen and yells something. Then we cut to product shot and then we go back to the three ladies and the one that's been hollering yells something else. OK? Now. . . .

CLIENT: Wait a minute. What's she looking at off stage?

YOU: Oh . . . well, she's asking a question of people in the back of the store.

CLIENT: What kind of a question?

YOU: Ah . . . let me read it to you and I think it'll be explained a little better.

See what's happened? The client has gotten confused about the flow of action. The pictures, without the words, are a letdown. He's got to be momentarily disappointed. Now, the words may put it all together for him. But why build up to the climax of your presentation, the idea itself, and then do something that even momentarily bogs down your sale? Wouldn't it be better to do it this way?

YOU: We open on three ladies looking at a big hamburger bun. On it, as you can see, is a comparatively small hamburger. One lady says, "It certainly is a big bun." Second lady says, "It's a very big bun." First lady: "Big fluffy bun." Second lady: "It's a very big fluffy bun." Third lady—the little one—says, in a deep voice while staring at the bun, "Where's the beef?" And the line is again repeated: "Where's the beef?" as she looks toward the back of the restaurant. And so on.

The client does not interrupt because he's involved in the flow and development of the commercial, as he should be. Every commercial should be presented so that it reflects, as closely as possible, the mood and effect that the public will see on television. And just because it's a 30-second commercial doesn't mean that it has to be presented in 30 seconds. Take all the time you need. If you have to interrupt the flow of words to describe some more complicated visual effect, do it. And then

once you've gone through words and explanations of action, do it over—
this time just reading the words and pointing to (or flashing on the
screen) the pictures. The only time that I vary from this is when there is
a rather difficult visual effect to explain, an effect that may be important
to the whole concept. Then I'll briefly allude to the effect and the pictures first. ("This entire commercial will be a visual extravaganza of the
Rockettes dancing on the rooftops of the city. As you can see, there'll be
a number of exciting shots from a variety of angles. OK, it goes like
this. . . . ") But if there's a visual punch line at the end that depends on
words and pictures going together, I'll stop before I get there and do the
words-picture approach.

As final proof of the validity of the words-pictures together approach,
think of reading "Dick Tracy" aloud to a child. Would you say: "OK, kid,
your father and I are going to read you the funnies. First, I'll take you
through the pictures and then Dad will read the words. In the opening
panel we see Dick talking to Tess and through the door we see a man
with a flat head. He says something. In the second scene the man with
the flat head pulls a gun and says something else, and Dick says something, and Tess says something. In the third scene we see that Dick
shoots his gun, and the bullet goes through the man with the flat head's
head. In the last scene the man with the flat head is lying on the floor,
and he says something, and Dick is kissing Tess, and Tess says something as her eyes are rolling." Think about it.

Presenting to the Large Audience

If you're talking to more than, say, 15 people, there are a number of
techniques that I've found quite helpful. Good books on public speaking
and related subjects can give you a lot more—but these have given me
comfort and confidence. I like to stand and use a podium, if at all possible. Standing gives assurance. Unless, of course, everyone else is standing. Then you have two choices: Tell them to sit down or climb on a
chair or something. The podium also takes care of the what-to-do-with-
the-hands problem (if it is a problem). You can grip the edge of the podium or hide them behind the front lip. If it's not a problem, use them.
And I don't mean wave them around like a symphony conductor. Try a
simple flick of the wrist here, a backhand gesture there, a fist for emphasis. Jack Benny was the master of this. He often used his hands (and

eyebrows) to replace words. If you have access to a videotape camera, have someone record you during rehearsal and see if you can improve your hand and arm technique.

Usually microphones are used when speaking to large audiences. Don't worry about them. They're engineered to pick up your voice and amplify it. You don't have to speak louder to make them work. My grandfather subscribed to this theory with the early telephone. When he was talking long distance his voice rose in direct proportion to the distance between his phone and the other party. (Gramp, top decibel: "Hello Chauncey, how's the weather in San Francisco?" Chauncey, aside: "Migawd, it's John B. from New York. Get my ear plugs, Bess.") And you don't have to lean into the mike. It'll work just fine when you stand erect behind the podium. If you like to wander while you talk, use a lavalier mike. Just remember that you'll have a cord trailing behind you. When you drift from the lectern and your prepared material, make a check mark in the speech at the point where you've departed so that you can find your place quickly when you come back.

If a sound system is not available, talk to people in the back row. Project. Don't shout. Speak from your stomach, not your throat. And if you have questionable speaking habits—the words come out like a 33 record played at 78, or you slur them, or drop your voice at the end of each sentence—rehearse, rehearse, rehearse. Again, videotape can be a tremendous help. There's nothing like seeing yourself bumble along to give an impetus for improvement. Most of us, even professional actors and announcers, tend to slip into a speech pattern or rhythm. And this can be like waves slapping gently against the side of a ship. Predictable. A great doze inducer for the audience.

In any situation, no matter how large or small, use eye contact. Talk directly to a person in the third row. Then shift to another pair of eyes at the other side of the room. It has an amazing effect on the impact of what you're saying. And it helps establish a rapport with the audience. If you have a tendency to stage fright (and who doesn't), eye contact somehow makes the whole thing easier, more personal. By looking directly at someone rather than at a bland sea of faces, you can see and feel their reactions.

If you have visual materials, make sure you can see them. Every now and then you may run into a situation where the speaker's station is parallel to or slightly behind the screen. Inch forward a bit so that when something appears that you're referring to, you know that it's there. I once suffered through an entire presentation with the speaker one slide out of sync because he couldn't see the screen. And when you're cuing slides from a script and controlling the slides yourself, circle a word in the script about four words ahead of when you want the slide to appear to allow for the time lag in the projector. (Obviously, the actual timing can be worked out in rehearsal.) It can make for a sharp presentation because the slide will be hitting on the exact word you want. If you're referring to a number of points with slides, refer to them, paraphrase them, but don't read them. The audience, presumably, is not idiotic. And besides, reading aloud what they're already reading slows things down and can move you into a boring mode.

Presenting to the Small Audience

Of course, much of this is applicable to any sized audience. But there are certain variations in technique that should be considered when talking to a smaller group. Strangely enough, I find this often more difficult because you're exposed. No lectern to hide behind. No distance buffer between you and the first row. You're right there. Face to face. They can see the sweat beginning to form on your upper lip, the shaking of your notes as you pick them up. The answer: be more prepared than ever, particularly as it's tough to read from a script around a conference table. The intimacy of the situation demands a more personal approach. This is one reason to try to involve the people who participated in developing the idea. They should know what they're talking about. And thus they should be more at ease in presenting their thoughts. The basic philosophy of talking to a small audience is more conversation than presentation.

Be Prepared To Be Flexible

You may have interruptions that can eat into both your thought process and time constraints. You must be able to handle them and at the same time be ready to adjust your presentation if necessary. Prepare for this by marking the parts of your presentation that can be cut if needed: an example here, a summary there. Underline the key thoughts so that if time is running short you can get them in, even if you have to sacrifice the elaboration. If the questions keep coming and become more and more interruptive and the "hold them until later, please" request fails, use the "selling ballet" approach described earlier. It can give you time to think. While someone else on your team steps in, you can check the script and adjust accordingly.

Improvisation Can Save the Day

If things aren't working, do something that can bring them together. If the room is too hot and people are beginning to drift into nodville, stop the show. Ask everyone to stand up and stretch, take their coats off, loosen ties, open windows, open doors, take a five-minute break— anything to get the blood moving again. Be prepared to describe your ideas without the aid of audiovisual equipment in case the power goes out. I once had this happen at the Amos Tuck School of Business Administration at Dartmouth. We continued the lecture on the lawn beside Tuck Drive. Because we knew the subject quite well, we were able to describe and act out some commercials we'd intended to show to illustrate our key points. One of the ancillary benefits of this was to immediately gain the attention and sympathy of the listeners because they knew we were battling tough odds. They were with us. And so were some passersby, including a golden retriever and fat beagle who showed interest in a dog food commercial I was acting out.

If a point can't be made because of logistics, again do something about it. There's no sense in going on with a presentation and discovering that you can't dramatize the key issue because the room is arranged so that only three people can see what you're displaying. A classic example of the kind of quick thinking that can save the day happened some years ago in a marketing conference room at General Mills. We were presenting a promotional concept for one of the children's cereals, Cocoa Puffs. The idea was to get children more involved with the product by introducing them to the Cocoa Puffs quick step: a nifty little piece of soft shoe that we hoped would titillate and entertain the kids of America. We planned to describe it on the back of every package of the product. (Lift left foot off ground and slide forward twice on right foot. Then, take three little steps quickly—left, right, left. Then with both feet together, take three little jumps. While you're doing this chant: "Huff Huff Cocoa Puffs, yum, yum, yum, yum! Slide-slide, step-step-step, jump-jump-jump.") We would have actors demonstrating this on Saturday morning television. (I spent one memorable Friday trying to teach it to the ring master on the clown show "Sealtest Circus with Bozo, the clown—live, from She-Caw-Go!") But first, we had to sell it to the client. And to do that somehow we had to demonstrate it. Now, this was before the days of the popularity of videotape. So we figured we'd have one of our people demonstrate it in the General Mills conference room in Minneapolis. Except that there was not enough space. And the sellees were all seated around a conference table where they couldn't see the presenter's feet. Then, in a masterful stroke that has lived in the minds of those who saw it forever, the chap making the presentation said "and it goes like this," removed his shoes, hopped up on the conference table and did the Cocoa Puffs Quick Step, the entire length of the table hitting the last "yum" perfectly—inches from the lap of the vice president in charge of cereal marketing. Unfortunately, the presentation was more successful than the winning of the children of the country to our cause.

Knowing Your Audience, as I Said Before, Can also Help in Your Presentation Techniques

Tune your delivery to their wave length. If you're experienced, you may be able to pick up something that has been said before and use it as a part of your opening. This can not only help you ease into your part but will also establish you, subtly, as pretty quick—a person with a fast mind that picks up nicely on something that's just been said or done. Of course, we don't always have that opportunity. But if you approach your presentation with the idea of doing this, you'll find that more opportunities exist than you'd thought, because you're looking for them. I once saw one of our people pull off a brilliant coup when suddenly faced with an unexpectedly diverse audience of a contingent from New York, Atlanta, and London (he'd thought he was selling only the New Yorkers, with whom he was familiar. He knew nothing about the others). He opened with something like "I'm delighted to see all of you here and to make things as simple and clear as possible I shall speak to each of you in your own native tongue." As he got to the end of that sentence he broke it into three different accents, turning first to the New Yorkers (side-of-mouth "inyerown"), then the Atlantans (syrupy and slow "nay-iv"), and the British (clipped "ectsually, tongue. Quite cleah, what?"). It was a piece of inspired improvisation that won the group over and set the stage for a warm and interesting presentation.

A FEW PRESENTATION DOs AND DON'Ts

Do be bright. Which means don't stay up so late the night before rehearsing that you can't remember the name of the people you're presenting to the next day. And this also means beware of having a rousing evening the night before. This is particularly tempting when the presentation is being made away from home base. Strange city, where's the best restaurant, we've worked hard, let's relax a little, we deserve it, great little jazz place just outside of town. Trouble. Little sleep. Pounding head and furry mouth. Not the way you want to be as you step to the podium for any kind of meeting.

Do save the celebrating (or commiserating) for the night after the presentation.

Don't smoke during the presentation unless you know the habits of those to whom you're speaking. Especially don't smoke if it's a small room. Too much controversy over this right now to risk offending someone you're trying to win over to your side.

Don't be worried about being nervous. Often a good sign. It's the body getting ready for the big moment. It often precedes the beginning of the surge of adrenaline. As a matter of fact, on the few occasions when I've not been nervous, I've found that my part has come out flat.

Don't build challenges into your presentation. This is a strange malady that sometimes is affected by people who are quite experienced. If they have to make a presentation a number of times, they build in obstacles to keep from being bored. And they do this unconsciously. Perhaps they forget some of the visual material they're using. Or even the notes to their talk. The most common challenge, as I said earlier, is to give the presentation without rehearsing or reading it through beforehand. They think it will keep things looser and fresher. But sometimes it comes out slower and less effective.

Do give credit to those who've worked with you. And this means avoiding the personal pronoun wherever possible. Try to make it "we," not "I."

Do know when to stop. And that's when you've made the sale, or can do no more. When the sellee says: "Terrific. I agree with you. Let's work out a schedule as soon as possible and get going," leave as soon as possible. Don't unsell what you've done by overselling. And if you come to that point where you can do no more, where the sellee is not sold, where you've done everything you can, don't belabor it. Pack up your marbles and go home and regroup to figure out the next steps. There's always another and, it is to be hoped, a brighter day.

THE BUYING OF AN IDEA

As you can see, the beginning of this chapter almost exclusively centers on the selling of an idea, because this is a most important part of managing the creative mystique. But those who have this sometimes unenviable and certainly rather complex task are often on the receiving end. They are the sellees, the buyers, the ones to whom presentations are being made. And the way they listen and react can have a lot to do with how the creative process develops and is directed. Let's look then at some of the subjects already covered—only from the sellees' point of view.

What Are They Talking About?

If the idea being presented has to do with a specific subject, know everything there is to know about the subject (obviously not the idea) that you can. If it's for a product advertising campaign, bring yourself up to date on the latest developments about the product, its market, competition sales history, and so forth. You want to be able to help them with the communication of their idea by knowing the facts. Before the presentation, ask for a briefing on the subject to be covered, on any problems that may have arisen, on anything that you should be aware of or think about before the presentation starts.

Whom Do You Want at the Presentation?

The answer here is probably everyone who's concerned with, responsible for, or affected by the subject to be covered. However, there are those times when circumstances dictate a small, intimate meeting with just the principals of the selling team. What circumstances? When the subject is so confidential that great numbers of people being exposed to the idea may offer a security risk. Or when it's politically unwise (although we don't like to admit the existence of office politics, they are a fact—and sometimes can damage ideas and presentations).

Or you may want a smaller meeting to keep it workable. Or for the very simple reason that you have more important things for some of your people to do. Whatever the reasons, make sure that you review the number of people that are needed before each meeting and adjust the size accordingly. And tell the sellers so that they'll know whom and what to expect.

Of course, the danger in eliminating some of the participants is that you must be sharper and wiser than ever because you'll have to compensate for their thinking. Don't jeopardize a good idea by not having the right people available to receive and critique it. And if, in the middle of the meeting, you find that a missing person's expertise is needed, call him in. If he's not available, ask for another meeting and make sure he's there. Better this than: "Gee, I wish I'd brought Steve in. His thinking might have saved the whole thing."

How Many Presentations Will There Be?

This is the presenting-to-different-levels syndrome. Sometimes you can control it. Without miffing your cohorts, underlings, or associates, you may be able to combine a number of them in one meeting rather than having three separate affairs. If you can, do it. The sellers would much rather gear up for one big show rather than three little ones.

What Is the Seller's Team Like?

Are they thorough people? Based on past experience, will they have done their homework? Are they loquacious? Do they tend to overtalk? Overexplain? Are they too dramatic? Knowing their habits and proclivities can help in the way you prepare yourself to receive the idea—or even guide (not direct!) them in the way they present it.

How Can You Help Them?

Try and make the conditions for the meeting as hospitable as possible. After all, the sellers are bringing you something that may help you, your career, your company, your way of life, your future. Don't make it tough on them. Treat them as partners, not suppliers. Ask what they need, from equipment to time. Make sure that your people are available for the meeting. Try to schedule it at a time that's conducive to receptivity. Then try to make the whole meeting work as well as possible. And this can be influenced by as small a thing as a brief but warm and sincere welcoming speech—not just an, "OK, it's your meeting, guys. Let's get going."

Should You Be Receptive to the Presell?

I think that wise people are, because they're constantly looking for more information and opinions to help them in the final decision. But the good ones know how to control the presell. They will stop the enthusiastic seller from going too far, too fast. ("Don't you want to save the presentation until the presentation, Sam?"), or from disrupting the chain of command ("I'm glad you've given me this background, Sam. But I really don't want to go any farther until my people have seen it.") And they may even be able to help with the idea, without having to know what it is. In the advertising campaign for Life Savers: "Life Savers—a part of livin' " it was a presell conversation with the then vice president of marketing, William Mack Morris, that gave us specific thoughts for this campaign. We were preselling the concept of people being involved, at various phases of their lives, with Life Savers. Without ever seeing the actual campaign, Mack encouraged us to try to go farther by urging us to position Life Savers as a part of each situation, not the focal point. Keep it warm and natural with the emphasis on the people involved with each other. "That," he said, "is what I think you mean by 'part of livin.' " We agreed and adjusted our presentation accordingly.

Should You Be a Part of the Planning?

Not if you're the final decision maker. The people selling you should be in charge of how they do it. But if you're one of the chain of selling command, if the presentation has been made to you and must now go on to your superior, you could play an important part in the presentation by constructively critiquing it. After all, if you accept the premise that's been presented, you become one of the sellers, even if only behind the scenes. Your advice and help can be invaluable.

How Should You Criticize the Seller's Idea?

In Nancy L. Salz's book, *How to Get the Best from Your Agency,* the author suggests the following guidelines, among others (the parenthetic comments are mine):

Make general comments first, specific comments second. (In other words, don't go directly to the periphery of the problem.)

Be honest. (One of the first things a creative person must learn is to listen to criticism—because one never knows when the critic may be right. And it's hard to be right if you're not honest.)

Give reasons for your comments. (And make the reasons as specific as possible.)

State your problem, not the solution. (Then if you have what you feel is an interesting solution, suggest—don't dictate—it. Solutions are the creative people's business. But it's a foolish person who doesn't at least listen to suggestions.)

Be appreciative. (This goes with being polite. No matter how bad something is, someone has undoubtedly put a good bit of work into it. Acknowledge it, even if you have to give the project thumbs down.)

Don't hesitate to ask for more work, if it's needed. (To put it another way, don't settle for less.)

These general guidelines should be incorporated with the material from Chapter 4, "How to Be a Creative Judge," which as you may recall, give some fairly specific suggestions on the subject.

Keeping these guidelines in mind seems obvious. To my amazement, I've found that some organizations actually preach the opposite. They advocate showing no emotion and making no comments at the meeting. Just receive the idea as noncommittally as possible, then think it over for a few days, talk it over with your colleagues, and forward your comments to the sellers. And when you do, make sure it's to the business people, not the creative. Because you know those creative types. Unpredictable. Can't tell how they'll take criticism. Besides, I feel uncomfortable talking to them. Get the feeling that they don't particularly like us.

Right.

If your organization acts that way, a lot of nice people won't like or respect you. And life in the business world won't be as pleasant or as much fun as it might be.

What Should You Say after the Presentation?

Thank you. And then, having listened carefully to the recommendation, you agree or disagree. If the sellers are vague on what the next steps should be, you must ask for them or outline them yourself. The efficient conclusion to any presentation is the reaching of a decision. Do everything possible to make it happen. If, however, it's impossible, explain why and the steps and timetable needed to reach the final decision. The most frustrating words to hear after any presentation are: "I don't know how it went, what we accomplished, or what we're going to do next."

IN SUMMARY

For the seller:

1. Before attempting to present or sell anything, know everything there is to know about what you're selling.

2. Be familiar with your audience. Know to whom your selling, how many there'll be, how many times you'll have to make the presentation. Watch out for presentation fatigue. Know how they've reacted in the past.

3. Try to control the size of your audience according to what you want to accomplish. Informational meetings can be large, decision-making meetings small.

4. Develop the art of preselling and remember its objective: not to sell but to get the sellee in a receptive frame of mind. But beware of using the presell to jump the chain of command.

Presentation planning:

1. Start with what you want to accomplish—the objectives.

2. Find out how much time you've been allotted.

3. Work out the structure of presentation and assign roles. Be aware of and careful of egos, but don't let them influence the effectiveness of the presentation. Go with the best you've got.

Presentation techniques:

1. Use whatever visual aids you need and can afford. And allow yourself time to plan around these aids. Make sure you have somone who can operate them and, if you're presenting in strange territory, make sure equipment is available. Check it out.

2. Allow time for rehearsal. If everyone cannot attend at once, make sure that everyone knows what everyone else is saying and doing.

3. Make sure that the structure contains an introduction, a main section for the presentation of the subject, and a conclusion or summary.

4. The introduction, like the presell, should set the stage for the main course.

5. The presentation section should be the culmination of your efforts. Make sure that the presell and/or the introduction do not overshadow it.

6. The summary should be given directly after the presentation and probably before the rebuttal or question period. If at all possible, it should be handled by someone other than the person making the main presentation.

7. To anticipate reactions, a role-playing rehearsal, using members of your organization not involved in the project being presented, can often uncover overlooked obstacles as well as prepare the selling team for a variety of eventualities.

8. After all the preparation and rehearsal, sit back and analyze what you've done—and what action you'd like taken. Make sure that it's logical, practical, and salable.

9. Develop the techniques of presentation, with particular attention to being flexible and able to improvise.

10. Pay attention to the basic do's and don'ts, which are often over-

looked, even though they're nothing more than applying common sense.

The buying of an idea:

1. Know what the presenters are talking about, what they're trying to sell you.
2. Know whom you want at the presentation.
3. Know, and try and control, the number of times the presentation must be made. Obviously, the fewer the better.
4. Knowing what the seller's team is like can help you prepare yourself to receive the idea, or even guide the way it's presented.
5. Try to make the conditions for the meeting as hospitable as possible.
6. Be receptive to the presell.
7. If, after you've received the presentation, it must be presented again to others, be helpful in your critique. Lend your expertise to the cause.
8. Make a tactful, wise, honest, thoughtful, and intelligent critique of the idea presented.

This has been a long and perhaps more detailed chapter than either of us expected. But it's been that way because I feel that the art of selling and buying an idea is often the culmination of the creative process. It's the mandatory step in bringing what's been proposed to life. Without it, you have a good idea that never gets beyond the bottom drawer of the desk. It would be like working for years composing a symphony, recording it with the New York Philharmonic in Lincoln Center, setting up an exquisite sound system, and playing it full blast on an uninhabited atoll in the Pacific. It's not so hot if it's not heard.

6

RESEARCH:
HOW IT CAN
HELP—AND
HOW IT CAN'T

Mention the word research in front of creative people and watch what happens. Eyes will begin to dart nervously; cheeks will flush; voices will get thin and hard; strange twitches will develop. In general, creative people are uncomfortable, at best, in the presence of research projects. But the fact is that as long as money is being paid for ideas, people will be looking for ways to minimize risk. And that means trying to find ways to predict the success or failure of the idea before the money is spent. Enter research. Not white coats and test tubes and rats in labs, but market research that attempts to measure people's reaction to a variety of stimuli. The conclusion: research is not going away, so wise creative people should learn how to let it help them and what its real (not emotional) limitations are. This chapter will concern itself with how the manager of the creative process can help unify the creative and research forces.

There is an obvious and a not-so-obvious reason for the nervousness, insecurity, and even hate on the part of the creative people toward the research function. The obvious: research may be a roadblock to their eventual success. The not-so-obvious: research may usurp an important part of the creative process: the ability to predict how people will react to certain stimuli. The author who writes a mystery novel featuring killer computers knows it will be a success because she's capitalizing on the public's interest in this new technology. The copywriter knows that a commercial based on the MTV format will be a success because this dubious art form is currently the rage of both cable and network television. The lyricist knows that the public is waiting for another song of unrequited love set to a funky bluegrass beat. Now, if market research shows them to be wrong—if computer technology has been overdone, if the public is sated with MTV, if funky-bluegrass-lost-love is past its prime—their egos will be hurt, their confidence in their judgment shaken, their livelihood endangered, and their workload increased because they may have to start over. Not a happy situation.

"PRE" RESEARCH THAT SHOULD BE WELCOMED

This, then, is the reason for creative people's uneasiness, to put it mildly, when their work becomes involved in the market research function. But it's not all bad. There are really two types of research that most marketing people are involved in: research that helps find out what motivates people to act the way they do (it's often referred to as "pre" because it usually takes place before an idea is developed) and research that attempts to measure public reaction to an idea ("post" because it is used after the idea is developed). It's the "post" that causes the majority of the creative-research flare-ups. Most people welcome "pre." Through focused groups, idea stimulation sessions, and in-depth, one-on-one individual interview sessions, the creative person can watch and listen and learn. I personally have never failed to come up with an idea, or direction, or some kind of revelation after participating in or reviewing this type of research.

In the example of the Life Savers advertising that I've alluded to some pages back, the whole basis for the "Life Savers—a part of livin' " approach grew out of some answers from simple interviews with people. We were looking for a "handle," a reason why people liked Life Savers candy beyond the usual "tastes good" reason. We were trying to find out what the taste really meant to them. What a Life Saver was like when it first went into their mouths. What their tongues did. The tactile sensation of the candy. How soon the flavor came through. How long it lasted. Whether they could remember the taste when they weren't having a Life Saver.

After loosening the respondents with some general questions, the interviewer started the probing by asking them if they had ever tried Life Savers and, if so, how and why they liked them. The answers kept coming out like:

"Sure I've tried them, who hasn't?"

"I like them because . . . well . . . because they're Life Savers."

"Yeah, I've had them. I've been eating Life Savers for a long time. My Gramp used to carry Pep-O-Mint in his shirt pocket and give me one when I was little."

"Life Savers? Yeah, they're good. I can't remember when I first had one. They've always been around."

Now these answers were supposedly the opening ones that would lead us into the specific taste questions that we were trying to find out about. But as we looked at these warm-up comments and others like them, a concept began to take shape. Life Savers had one thing that no other candy had: a long history, a tradition. They seemed to have been a part of everyone's growing up. Of course, in this was the implicit thought that they couldn't have lasted as long as they had if they weren't good. And out of this came the concept of building a campaign around what the people had told us. Life Savers have been, are, and will always be "a part of livin'."

Some creative people seem to have two problems with "pre" research. The first is time. They feel they really don't have enough time to get involved, to listen to people, to read tapes of answers, to look for reactions. They reason that the time this takes could be better used crouched over a typewriter or drawing board creating. What they really fear is that if they go through this exercise and come up with nothing, they'll really be in a time bind. True. But it's a risk that must be taken because the potential for success, or for keeping from going in the wrong direction, or even for confirming basic ideas is greater with the research than without. Try to avoid the problem by building in time for research in the creative development timetable. Much better to spend a week on the research and a week on the creative idea than two weeks on the creative heading the wrong way. If the assignment is too tight to allow enough time, talk to the research people and get their thoughts and opinions based on past experience and other research results. Remember, at this point you're looking for insights to feed the creative mind.

The second inhibitor of "pre" research to creative people is the strong one I talked about in the section on developing strategies. Some of the people feel that they don't want to clutter their minds with extraneous thoughts. They think that a clear head better allows for the free association of ideas. If they get lots of information, their minds may be cluttered with minutiae and the direction they're waiting for to appear like magic will be obfuscated with irrelevance. Again, if you're in charge of creative people, convince them that this type of research can help. If you're working closely with them, you can help organize the research thoughts and conclusions in their minds.

A FORMAT FOR FINDING OUT

For example, supposing that we have a strategy that states that the main point that we wish people to take away from advertising for the Pegasus 4 is that it's a quality car. Now, before going ahead and asking the creative people to develop a campaign, it would seem prudent to find out what the public's perception of the Pegasus 4 actually is. Do they already think of the cars as quality automobiles? If so, the advertising would be designed to reinforce that feeling. But perhaps quality is a completely new thought in context of this car. Then we'd have to find a way to introduce quality into their thinking. And shouldn't we find out what quality means in regard to cars? The answers to all of these questions could be listed under the heading "Pertinent Consumer Perceptions," which, as you remember, was described in Chapter 2. And here's a simple four-step process to help get these answers.

1.   Before spending money on your own research, review all existing research. In our example, automotive publications are a very good source for this kind of thing. They would probably show that European cars receive the highest ranking for quality, Japanese cars running a closer second than some years ago, and U.S. cars are last—but improving. They might even give some kind of ranking of different makes in regard to quality perceptions. In this we see that our car, the Pegasus 4, ranks near the norm—not high or low. But it's certainly not perceived as a top quality car.

2.   If need be, augment the existing research with your own. Here we might want to find out what "quality" means to our audience. The answer comes out "reliable and dependable." And this turns out to be the general feeling about "quality" no matter what the demographics.

3.   If you feel it's needed, do some quantitative research to probe your audience's feelings. We might use this to find out what image the Pegasus 4 actually projects. And we discover that because this car started out some years ago as an inexpensive import designed to give good gas mileage and practical transportation, it's still viewed as a no-nonsense, no-frills vehicle that provides the bare basics—but does it well. In the parlance of the trade it's "El Strippo." This is somewhat surprising and discouraging because the most recent Pegasus 4's are indeed much more than basic transportation. They are moderately priced (not low) fairly sophisticated sporty cars providing great value for the money spent. And yet the public relates their image to the earlier models.

The results also tell us that it's the older segment that looks upon the car as basic transportation and, in fact, the younger people are more inclined to think of it as it is: a sporty car that provides value. The quality image also improves with the younger people.

4.   Draw some conclusions. It's nice to do this with both the research and creative people together. It might go something like this.

a. *Pertinent consumer perception.* In general the Pegasus 4 is seen as inexpensive, basic transportation. However, with the younger age group (18 to 35), which is our target audience, the image seems to be moving up the scale to good value in a sporty car. The quality perception is growing, especially among car buffs who appreciate the mechanical and engineering aspects. And this relates to the reliability-dependability definition of quality.

b. *Strategy.* To reinforce, with our target audience, the quality image.

c. *Executional directions.* Because of what we've discovered (our younger target audience already believes the Pegasus 4 is a quality car), we do not necessarily have to develop advertising that proves quality, as Volvo did in a recent campaign (testimonial advertising based on the thousands of miles that various delirious owners have driven. "I love my wife—but oh you Volvo"). We can, therefore, concentrate on advertising that emotionally suggests quality but does not necessarily have to substantiate it.

Again, the reason for this simplified exercise is to give a suggested format that might help those of us entrusted with the guidance of the creative process in our daily rounds. It's a format that I've found good in helping sort things out at the beginning of a creative task. And, more than anything else, it utilizes market research in a useful way that can make believers of even the most obdurate copywriters. Finally, I think the thinking behind the format can be applied to any creative project. And if research help is not at hand do some digging, as was mentioned, much of what we would like to know is often available in libraries and newspaper and magazine files. And sometimes even in our own heads, if we just use them.

"POST"—THE HEART OF THE PROBLEM

Waiting for the results of research testing that purports to tell how the public reacts to a specific creative effort is like sitting in Sardi's waiting for the first edition of *The New York Times* to find out how the critic reacts to a Broadway show. Put yourself in the creative person's shoes (or sneakers, as the case may be). You've wrestled with a creative strategy for an advertising campaign for a new sugarless gum that contains an ingredient that helps foster healthy gums (you named it "Gum's Gum"). You prepared four different approaches and used "pre" research to find out how people would react. You narrowed it down to two approaches: one attention getting and humorous, the other much more factual. The client believes in the factual approach. Time is now too short to test them against each other. The decision is made to go with the factual approach.

You work furiously to add humanity to it to keep it from being too sterile and clinical. And you feel you've succeeded. The commercial is produced and costs more than estimated (trouble getting the giant mock-up of teeth and gums to snap at the right time). The music isn't quite right, so you bring out the bassoons to give the feeling of the gum working on the gums. And finally it's right. You like it. The client likes it. The sales force likes it. And then the research comes in. And you never find out whether or not the public likes it—because apparently no one has noticed it. Now the dilemma. Is the research valid? Is there anything in the research that can give a clue as to what the problem is? Are there mitigating circumstances that may have influenced the research? A judgment has been made by a number of experts in the business (advertising agency creative, marketing, research people, client brand managers, marketing experts, top management) that the advertising is presenting the new product in a way that should get attention and initiate trial. Is all of this experience and judgment wrong? The answer: not necessarily, but perhaps.

Now, before going any farther, for those involved with the creative process who have never been concerned with "post" research (and there are many, because this type of measurement doesn't seem to be involved in the writing of books or plays or movies or songs or even annual reports), here is a brief review of what I'm talking about. A description of the most popular methods used, condensed from a useful handbook put out by the Dancer Fitzgerald Sample research department.

1. *ARS*. Uses an in-theater procedure to measure the ability of a commercial to be recalled and be persuasive in a forced viewing situation. Participants are prerecruited randomly by mail to attend a preview of two half-hour shows. Interspersed throughout each program, shown

on closed circuit TV, are commercial breaks, which include the test commercial among others. Before and after the viewing, brand preference data are obtained to determine the persuasiveness of the commercial. (If a participant indicates after viewing the show that she would feel more favorably toward brand A than she did before the show, we can assume that something persuaded her to make that switch. And that something probably was the commercial.) Three days later each participant is called and asked questions that indicate whether or not she remembered the commercial. This is called "recall." It was the lack of recall that harpooned the Gum's Gum effort.

2. *ASI (Audience Studies Inc.) In-Television Test.* Somewhat similar to the ARS method in that it represents what is known as "forced exposure." Participants are recruited in shopping centers in the Los Angeles area and invited to a preview of new TV shows at an ASI theater. At the theater, participants are asked their brand preferences in each of four product categories. Then they are shown a pilot TV program followed by a sequence of five commercials. The first is a control, and the other four represent the product categories for which participants' preferences were obtained. While the majority of the respondents see a second TV program, a small group is probed in a second room for its reactions to the test commercials. Afterwards, the other participants are rejoined and once again asked for brand preferences. Any change represents the test commercial's persuasive power. This is followed by a short cartoon, after which unaided recall of the test commercial is obtained.

Throughout the entire preview half the participants use an electronic device to continuously record their level of interest in the program and the commercial content that follows. Also, after viewing each commercial, each participant is asked to rate it using an adjective checklist. To assess the overall response to the test commercial, participants are asked, using a five point rating scale, to what degree their interest in the product has increased or decreased as a result of the ad. Any specific questions or objectives can also be probed through this method.

3. *ASI Print Test.* This method measures 24-hour recall, persuasiveness, and involvement in the advertising and is used for magazine advertisements. Through the use of a random door-to-door sample, 200 to 250 readers are selected. They are given an advance copy of a magazine in which the test ad has been placed and asked to read the ad on the day it's received. They also indicate brand preference for specific prod-

ucts, one of which, of course, is the test brand. The next day the participants are interviewed for recall of the test ad, ideas about the product,
level of involvement with the test ad, and brand preferences as compared to those of the previous day.

4. *ASI Recall Plus*. A day-after-recall test. Commercials are run on
a controlled "family type" cable TV program. Participants are recruited
the day before and questioned about the program (and recall of the commercial) the day after. The "plus" part allows for gathering of additional
information from the participants that may be of interest to the future of
the campaign or product.

5. *Burke Standard Television Day-After Recall Test (DAR)*. A test
commercial is run as a cut-in to a regular TV program (a regularly sched-
uled commercial is replaced on a certain show) in 3 of 25 test cities. The
audience is not prerecruited and so, unlike the in-theater or ASI cable
test, it is not forced exposure. Twenty-four hours later, telephone calls
are made at random to find people who watched the show. From this it
is ascertained how many saw the specific commercial (Recall Score) and
what, specifically, they remembered about the commercial (Copy/
Visual Playback). The interviews are conducted among a base of 200
people who remembered the show. The percentage of people remembering the commercial is the recall.

6. *Communicus Post-Testing*. A target group of 400 participants is
shown instantaneous (0.1 to 0.6 second) flashes of slides of test ads and
then asked to play back brand identification and communications of the
ad. (Shades of World War II aircraft identification.) Obviously, this type
of research can be used only after the ad has appeared regularly in publications. The theory is that the quick flash will trigger a picture of the ad
from past normal exposures, and the ad's effectiveness may be judged
by the amount of information volunteered.

7. *Competitive Environment Test*. Measures the relative persuasiveness of advertising (TV and print) against major competition. Participants are given a list of competitive brands and the test brand. They are
asked to express the relative purchase preferences by dividing 10 points
among them. Then they are shown the test advertising and the current
advertising for each brand and asked to divide the 10 points again. The
before and after shift indicates the persuasive power of the advertising
in comparison to that of the competition.

8.   *Gallup & Robinson In-View Service (G & R Test).*   A mild form of forced exposure to determine day-after recall. On the day of telecast, viewers in the Philadelphia area are asked to view a UHF prime-time program that contains the test commercial. Then, 24 hours later, telephone interviews are conducted with 150 viewers. From this recall of the commercial, idea communication of the commercial and favorable buying attitude toward the product are determined.

9.   *Gallup & Robinson Magazine Impact Research Service.*   Similar in method to ASI and Burke print tests. Measures percent of people who claim to remember an ad and the advertiser, the ideas communicated, and favorable buying attitude.

10.   *Mapes & Ross Invited Viewing Technique.*   Again viewers are recruited on the day of a particular show, this time a prime-time movie on UHF. They are asked brand preferences as well as to view the movie. The day after, they are again contacted and asked if they recalled the commercial (situational points in the commercial must be given as proof), their brand preferences (again a measure of persuasion), and other diagnostic data.

11.   *Mapes & Ross Normal Viewing Technique.*   Similar to Burke Day-After Recall. It does not use forced exposure.

12.   *Mapes & Ross Print Test.*   Similar to the others.

13.   *McCollum/Spielman Advertising Control Theater Test.*   More forced exposure. Here 300 to 350 participants are invited to see a preview of a TV program in 4 of 12 widely dispersed facilities. Brand preferences are determined. Participants are exposed to the test commercial twice during the program. After the first exposure of the test commercial, recall and main idea are tabulated. After the second exposure, diagnostic data and brand preference are collected.

14.   *McCollum/Spielman Advertising Control Magazine Test.*   This is a bit different from the other magazine tests. Participants are prerecruited randomly by mail and asked to attend a theater preview of a new TV show. In the theater they are given a special theater playbill, called "Preview Studio Review," in which is tipped the test ad. Again, brand preferences are ascertained. Respondents are asked to look through the program. After viewing the TV show they are asked to reread the program. After the second viewing, brand awareness, main idea, copy recall, and post-brand-preference information are gathered.

15. *Starch Readership Test.* Measures recognition and readership of print ads. Interviews are conducted at home or place of business. The sample consists of 100 to 150 people who have glanced through or read a specific issue of a magazine. Each page is shown to the participants, at which time it is determined whether or not the participant remembers that particular page. If the participant remembers an ad, she is then asked which parts of the ad she remembers seeing. From this comes scores for Noted (percentage who remember seeing the ad), Associated (percentage who have read enough of the ad to associate it with the brand), Read Most (percentage who have read 50 percent or more of the ad's copy).

16. *Westgate On-Air Lab.* Participants are contacted two days before and invited to watch a test program on a regular TV channel. As an incentive, they are given a chance at a $25 cash drawing. One day following broadcast, participants are recontacted by phone. Recall of commercial and product, plus sales points and visual elements, are tabulated.

Testing of radio commercials is done in a similar way using day-after recall. In most instances, the participants are given something else to do (fill out a form or questionnaire) while a radio is playing in the background. Naturally, they are not told that they are involved in radio research. Some tests ask them to listen to a specific program and be prepared to give comments on the program. The commercial, of course, is buried in the program. All of this is done to try to stimulate normal nonfocused listening habits.

Now, back to Gum's Gum and the problem of whether or not the combined experience of marketing and creative experts is wrong. If we listen to the research results, we must say yes. But again, we must ask ourselves if the research results are infallible. And the answer must be no. They aren't infallible. There have been too many times when something has gone wrong, when something just doesn't add up. In a recall study in three different cities, the score in one city is 30, the second 26, the third 6. As you can see, the average is 20. Now, if we just look at the average, we may say that the score (20) indicates a problem commercial because the norm for the category is 24. The commercial is below normal in its ability to attract brand awareness. Panic and back to the midnight and weekend oil to create a new approach.

But what about the score that ruined the average? That 6? Does it seem logical that a commercial that scored above average in two cities would do so drastically, abysmally, poorly in a third? Hmmmm. What was the third city? Philadelphia. Was there any special happening in Philadelphia on the test night? What's that? Violent thunderstorms? Power shortages? Blackouts? When? Around the time the commercial with our show was appearing. But could that affect the score? The research company says no, because the viewer has to verify that she was looking at that specific program before she's considered a participant in the test. And if the power was out and the show went off, she wouldn't be a participant. But what if the power didn't go off but the storm raged during the show? Did she get up to check the windows? Was her attention diverted by the thunder, lightning, and slashing rain? Did the power flicker and the show go off for a few seconds and then return—halfway through the commercial?

Very few new commercials can register in any viewer's mind if they only see a part of it. It's hard enough to break through the clutter of thousands and thousands of impressions being emitted from the TV screen every day without having external forces pulling at the viewers' attention. This thunderstorm example actually happened. It was through the diligence of a conscientious research project director that we uncovered the problem. We retested the commercial in another city; it scored well, and the research person responsible had made a friend for life.

THE CASE OF THE FICKLE AUDIENCE

Sometimes the unexplainable remains unexplainable. But if everyone's judgment questions the research, it should be rechecked and perhaps redone. Good ideas are too rare to lose. To me, one of the most tragic things that can happen in the business is to be off and running—and then stumble and eventually fall because of questionable figures that are looked upon as the ultimate decision makers.

A few years ago we were wrestling with the problem of a new campaign for Olympia beer (a beer born and brewed in Tumwater, Washington) to help reverse its sliding sales curve. After a number of forays in different directions, we came up with what I felt was a good concept—directly relating the beer to the things that the people who drink it like. As I've mentioned before, beer is sold mainly through image. We felt if we could personalize that image, if we could relate the image of Olympia to the likes of some role model people of the northwest, if we could get the viewer to say, "Yeah, that guy's my kind of guy. He likes what I like," we might have something. So we made a commercial that went something like this.

> Open on a closeup of the face of an interesting looking man, about 28. He has long hair, a trim beard, and is wearing a lumberjack shirt. He looks directly at the camera and says "Know what I like? I like . . .
> (Cut to shot of 1956 Corvette winding through the California redwoods) driving through the redwoods early in the morning . . .
> (Cut to stock cars roaring into a turn during a race) seeing them scream into that first turn . . .
> (Cut to shot of glass of Olympia beer) and the taste of Oly beer.
> (Cut to shot of our hero looking through a transit while two other men about the same age and dressed in outdoor working clothes stand next to him talking and looking at blueprints) I like working with guys who know what they're doing . . .
> (Cut to our hero and woman walking away from the camera on beach at sunset) walking on the beach with Marny, . . .
> (Cut to slow beer pouring shot) and the taste of Olympia beer."
> (Dissolve to shot of our hero and Marny entering warm, friendly bar near the beach. People greet them naturally with smiles and waves.)
> Music and singers: "The great fresh taste of Olympia beer."
> (Cut to closeup of hero) "That's what I like."
> (Super: "Olympia beer. That's what I like.")

I think you get the idea. Part of the beauty of the campaign was that we could, in a way, portray a profile of the Olympia drinker. And we could localize the campaign. As you see, the commercial just described was set in the San Francisco area. We did one with a crane operator who liked raising roses in Seattle, a computer operator in Chicago, and a free spirited motorcycle rider who cooked great Mexican food in Tucson.

About three months after the campaign appeared on TV, the people at Olympia decided to see if research could give them an indication of the effectiveness of the advertising. They selected a research organization that claimed that measurable results could be obtained by increasing the number of commercials in a selected test city over a given period of time and then comparing the results with the rest of the marketing area, which would run at the normal rate, and a second test city, which would receive no advertising. Presumably, if the advertising was working, attitudes would change in the "heavy-up" city.

Our research department agreed that this could be a viable test for advertising of products that had a perceivable point of difference (greater viscosity, fewer calories, no salt, more horsepower, and so forth), but they questioned whether it would be a fair test for image advertising. And most beer advertising is pure image because people do not buy beer for its physical properties (taste, number of calories, color) but rather for what they feel the beer stands for. This was discussed in some detail in Chapter 5 in the Hamm's beer example. It takes advertising weight and time to establish or reestablish an image. History shows that in the case of beer advertising, this can be as long as three years. For this reason, we advised against this particular research test. Not enough time for the image to take effect. Unfortunately, at that time there were few knowledgeable marketing people in top management at Olympia. They were financially oriented and wanted some indication of what return they could expect for their money. They went ahead with the test.

The sales curve, which was plummeting at the beginning of the test, continued its downward spiral. The advertising had no apparent effect. In fact, in a rather devastating comment, the research company opined that it would be better, from a cost standpoint, to run no advertising at all. We again pointed out that the time element was the key to image advertising, that a swing in advertising awareness could not be expected after only three months of advertising, no matter what the weight.

No soap. The campaign was doomed. An immediate search for a replacement was instituted. Another of Olympia's agencies was asked to join the fray (not a welcome sign!), and they eventually came up with a very bright humorous approach, which was accepted with alacrity (an even worse sign). Meanwhile, our "You know what I like . . . " campaign continued to run while the new approach was being produced. Three months later an updated research report arrived. Raised eyebrows. Gasps of surprise. In the heavy-up test market the awareness curve was reversing itself. The head of the research company said that he'd never seen such a dramatic change in such a short time. There was light at the end of the tunnel.

But alas, the decision had been made. We lost the account and the new humorous campaign went on the air. Sales continued to plunge at an even dizzier rate. A year and a half later, with no improvement in sight, the brewery was swallowed in a takeover, the top executives left, the humorous campaign was withdrawn, and the new advertising agency dismissed. Olympia ceased to be an important factor in the beer market.

Of course there were other things that influenced the downfall. A lack of understanding of the advertising-marketing functions by Olympia's management. An inability, on our part, to convince that management that our recommendations were the right ones without hard figures to back our arguments. A belief on the client's part that a "quick fix" could reverse the sales picture. But the key, I believe, was the misuse and misinterpretation of research. Or to put it another way, if there had been no research, it's possible that a good number of people would still be saying," . . . and I like the taste of Olympia beer."

MORE NAGGING WORRIES ABOUT "POST" RESEARCH

And there are other reasons why creative people ponder over the fallibility of "post" research. Does a prerecruited audience, which many of the testing systems depend on, represent an unbiased opinion? Even though they are not supposed to know they're judging the effectiveness of advertising, are they in a completely normal viewing mode when they're in a theater or screening room rather than at home in front of their TV set? Does reading superfluous material with a radio playing in the background accurately replicate radio listening situations? What about a car radio, where more attention may be paid to the commercials? When people are asked to glance through a magazine, will they be more attentive to the material than normal? And how do you measure the unmeasurable—the deep, unconscious feelings, moods, and desires that may be released by something in the advertising. The research fraternity is constantly hard at work to find ways to uncover these inner feelings and what motivates them. If your job in working with, directing, or managing the creative process deals with the kind of creativity that uses research as an aid, do everything you can—including spending money—to continue trying to find out (and quantify) what makes people act the way they do.

But, obviously, the biggest worry for all creative people, without exception, is that their efforts will be judged as a success or failure exclusively by a quantitative score measuring "recall" (i.e., the percentage of viewers that actually recalled the advertising 24 hours after seeing or hearing it). The critical word here is "exclusively." Some advertisers will allow no advertising to appear before the public unless it obtains a certain score in recall testing. The "must" score is usually four or five points above the norm. Obviously, this is putting all the money on the line. Everything depends on the score. Now, what does this beget? It seems to me, that if the success or failure of an idea depends on score, we have an unwritten change in the objective. The creative person's goal is no longer to produce great or unusual or "breakthrough" ideas that will move product sales, or a company image, or a thoughtful concept to great new heights. The objective becomes: get a high recall score.

Thus, subtly the approach to the creative challenge begins to take on a new look. Watch out for music—it tends to weaken the score. Don't open on a mood-setting long shot of a Vermont farmhouse in the early morning mist. Soft. Mood openings usually don't score. Stay away from animation. Doesn't score. Put the product in the first five seconds. If you don't, low score. And on and on and on, until we get to the final creative dictate.

WRITER: (bursting into account person's office, bubbling with unrestrained creativity) Hey, hey Sambo. Got a minute, because I've got an answer. I mean this is it. The big idea. The Holy Grail. Sit tight and listen because I don't think anyone's ever done this before.

ACCOUNT PERSON: Oh, oh.

WRITER: This is still rough of course, but you'll get—whadya mean "Oh, oh?"

ACCOUNT PERSON: Ahh . . . no one's ever done it before, you say?

WRITER: Nope. I guarantee it.

ACCOUNT PERSON: Listen, Suzanne. I know you have a great background as a nurse and psychologist before becoming a copywriter. You know people. You know what makes them tick. I've never met anyone who had a better feeling for the inner workings of emotions. But one of your greatest strengths is that you're also practical in this business.

WRITER: Yeah . . . yeah. Whaddya getting at?

ACCOUNT PERSON: You know the rules. We've got to get a good test score. We're down to the last go-around on this one. We're in the quicksand grabbing for the vine. If we don't get a good score it's bye-bye. Not the time or place for something that's never been done before.

WRITER: But . . . but . . . how do you know that this won't get a score that'll crack the ceiling?

ACCOUNT PERSON: I don't. But we can't take the chance that it won't. So give me something that I know will score. A good slice of life or a startling demo. Something involving. Something different—but in the same format.

WRITER: I can't. Because what you'll get is more of the same.

ACCOUNT PERSON: Who cares . . . if it scores?

WRITER: You mean you want the same thing that everyone else is doing, but done differently?

ACCOUNT PERSON: Now you're gettin it.

WRITER: But if you do the same differently it won't be the same, and if you do the same the same it won't be different.

ACCOUNT PERSON: You think too much. Just do it.

Exaggerated? Not much. Of course this doesn't mean that a bland so-called safe commercial will necessarily be high scoring. Or that a break-through concept won't get a good score. It just means that when the objective changes to "get a score," the safe ground rules are suddenly applied and often required. During the recession of the late 1970s and early 1980s, the inclination of many advertisers to not take chances became more and more popular, with the resultant dependence on "post" testing. In my opinion, this is one of the principal causes of the wave of very ordinary advertising that swept over us in that time period. As a comparison, much of the rest of the world was producing bright and inventive advertising—but then much of the rest of the world had not discovered our testing methods.

And this doesn't mean that a high scoring commercial will not be effective in its impact on a product's success. It often is, but not necessarily. As I mentioned earlier, many high scoring commercials register the brand name or the idea (thus the score) but do not motivate any action.

In conclusion, the complete dependence on score does tend to put walls around the scope of creative imagination and ingenuity. So, in helping to manage the creative process, do everything you can to convince your clients, customers, superiors, researchers—whomever you have to—not to use "post" research or testing as the sole arbiter of the worth of an idea.

WHAT'S GOOD ABOUT "POST" RESEARCH

I've come down hard on the testing system, but there are some things that creative people should like about it, namely anything that helps them develop ideas or gives them insights into what they may be doing wrong. Most of this comes from the question section of the various testing techniques: the part where the interviewer asks for a description of what the advertising was about. These are known in the business as "internals" or "verbatims." In one of our Toyota commercials we used Scrooge to personify the money-saving attributes of the inexpensive Corolla. The announcer identified him at the beginning of the commercial. But the internals showed us that few people recognized him as Scrooge, and thus the pecuniary aspects of the Dickens character were not coming through. The impact of the dramatization of the main point of the commercial was weakened. So we corrected the problem by simply adding a title along the bottom of the screen: "Ebeneezer Scrooge, well-known pinch-penny."

The internals can also point up certain strengths in the commercial. An ocarina and bass were once used in a commercial playing "When You're Smilin' " for Bayer aspirin. The internals from the research kept referring to the unusual light-hearted approach. And so we made the music the key part of the radio campaign, and within six months when this particular arrangement of "Smilin' " was played, it was identified with the Bayer product by, as I recall, over 80 percent of the people who heard it in a "blind" test. The positive comments on a silver Celica in a Toyota advertisement alerted the company to a run on silver cars and caused us to adopt silver as theme color for all Celica print ads. These illustrations point out the advantages to the creative forces of learning from the internals. As in the aforementioned cases, the comments can give direction for improving communication. Or they can even save some advertising from never appearing.

Astute analyzers of these "post" test results give us insights into another way to look at them. First, they carefully go over the internals to see if there are things that would work against the objectives of the advertising. Objectionable commercials can get a high recall and kill sales. Then they look at the internals to see if they are indicating that the message is motivating. Again, advertising with high awareness can get a good score but not necessarily motivate sales. Remember the "Get a Lark, get a Lark, get a Lark, get a Lark" campaign (sung to the tune of the "William Tell Overture") back when cigarettes were OK on television? Candid shots of people holding up their Lark packs. Very clever. Nicely done. And I'll bet it got high recall. I know it built awareness for Lark. But sales? I doubt it, because cigarettes are sold on image (as I mentioned before) and, in my opinion, it would take a long time for people holding up packs of cigarettes to create an image. Camel Filters, on the other hand, created a campaign in the 1960s that depicted the oddballs of life buying exaggerated spoofs of the competition: extra-extra longs, filtered cigarettes with two-inch filters, perfumed smokes, and so forth. Then Mr. Right stepped up and asked for the real smoke, Camel Filters, as the slogan "Camel Filters, they're not for everyone" was intoned. Later, in print, a companion campaign was created ("Can you spot the Camel Filter smoker?"). Both of them were recalled very well. But, unlike the Lark campaign, they were creating an image for the product. Not for everyone, but probably for you if you're a good guy—square jawed, wise, sympathetic, tough, understanding, decisive, tolerant, etc., etc. And who isn't, or doesn't think he is?

SOMETIMES IT'S NOT "HOW MANY" BUT "WHO" THAT COUNTS

And this brings us to another point. The Camel people were segmenting their audience. They were playing to the already established image of the brand. (Strong. Tough. The gutsy smoke for the blue collar worker.) They directed their efforts toward the more conservative "real American" during the turbulent 1960s and early 1970s. They said "we're not for everyone," and they didn't care if they didn't get everyone, because they knew they wouldn't. Similarly, when Toyota wished to establish a performance image when they introduced the Supra, they believed that an effective way to do it would be to first gain the acceptance of car aficionados. To do this they used the famous former race car driver and current engineer-builder-owner, Dan Gurney, as a spokesperson. They didn't care that a good bit of America had never heard of him. They knew that the audience they wanted to impress—the car buffs—was both familiar with and impressed by Dan. They were segmenting their audience. Once they got the car buffs enthused, they knew that the performance image would have a foothold and begin spreading to the general public.

The point is that this segmentation can affect the way "post" testing is analyzed. The recall score may be modest because you're aiming at a smaller audience, and, therefore, fewer people are paying attention to the commercial. But look at the internals. If they're long and detailed, the indications are that the people who did notice the commercial really got involved. And there's a very good chance that this is exactly the audience that you want. There are those who feel that gaining the interest of a comparatively small audience that may take action as a result of their efforts is better than getting awareness from a larger, much broader audience with little interest in what they're talking about. Of course, the temptation is always to go for everyone. And with broadly applicable packaged goods products like aspirin or cereal or tooth paste, this is a practical objective. If you're dealing with a specialized product with a narrower audience, consider directing the attack specifically to that audience. But judge your research results accordingly.

FIND OUT THE DISEASE BEFORE YOU GIVE THE MEDICINE

A final positive bit of advice on the analysis of "post" testing results. If the recall score indicates that few people are noticing the commercial, try to ferret out the possible reasons why before throwing the whole thing out. And involve the creative people in this analysis right along with the research experts. Have them feel they're part of the process so that they'll understand the problem less emotionally and gain insights into what to do next. And what to do next obviously depends on what you find out. Now, here we must assume that the idea had enough merit, in everyone's judgment, to have a chance to be effective. Therefore, we must also assume that something blocked the message. While the research and programming people look for the variables I discussed earlier, the creative/research team should dissect the work. Here's a checklist that I've used as a guide.

1. Is the brand mentioned and visually identified enough? People may be noticing and remembering the commercial without remembering the product or sponsor.

2. If this is the case, is there something that can be done to add a memory trigger to the brand name? Music? An audio or visual mnemonic device?

3. Is the commercial confusing? Is the writing getting in the way of the message? Are there too many scenes jumping back and forth? Is the pace too rapid?

4. Are the visual scenes interesting enough to hold the viewers' attention? Are the opening three or four seconds arresting?

5. Is the audio track completely clear? Can I understand the announcer and/or the actors? Are the music and/or sound effects too loud or too soft? (Soft music or effects can be a disturbing irritant under the voice track because the ear strains to hear what the sound is and can miss the message.)

6. Is the commercial overly complicated in its plotting? If so, perhaps the judicious elimination of a scene or two in the editing can simplify the flow.

This checklist has one main objective: to save a good idea. I think another of the tragedies in the creative process is to lose months of energy and work and the resultant effort because no one used research, or their heads, to help solve the problem and save the project.

TESTING—BEFORE THE MONEY IS SPENT

Can we save some money by finding out how a commercial will perform before the commercial is actually produced? Again, yes and no. A number of advertisers make rough versions of their advertising for testing, thus avoiding the expense (and time) of producing a finished commercial before making a final decision. There are three basic forms that these rough executions take:

1. *Animatics.* These are essentially a series of drawings that appear on the screen more or less as slides, or with some very limited movement, against a sound track and a simple version of music, if required. This is the least expensive of the processes.

2. *Photomatics.* Similar to an animatic, but photographs are used instead of drawings. Again, there is little motion, and while the photomatic can give a truer representation of the finished product, it is more expensive and takes more time because sets, casting, and lighting are often involved.

3. *Rough production.* The commercial is produced very inexpensively on 16mm film or videotape. While it is more expensive than the other two methods, it is still less expensive than full production. The advantage is that it allows for the nuances of casting, acting, and movement. The disadvantages are time, money, and certain limitations. For example, it's hard to project complicated scenes or large scale extravaganzas in rough production.

Research organizations have enough statistics to prove that this pre-testing is valid: that the basic impact of the commercial, in most cases, will coincide with the score of a finished commercial. That's fine—but how can you be sure that you are one of the "most cases"? And there, of course, is the problem. Do drawings do justice to a mood approach that involves the viewer with beautiful photography? Can drawings represent a star performer whose live personality is important to the campaign? Do drawings indicate a cartoon approach to the public? (Remember, animatics can appear on the air for testing one time only with no explanation as to just what they are.) Does still photography give a true feeling of fast action? Can inexpensive production represent the production values that may be important to the impact of a concept?

All of these are valid questions and worries. But they do not mean that pretesting using any of these methods should be abandoned. What should be done is that each individual-proposed approach should be carefully considered, and decisions as to which form of testing and what problems should be acted on accordingly. The objective is to find out how the public will react to the advertising, not how efficiently and inexpensively you can put together a pretest. And perhaps you may find that your approach is so unusual, so different, that there is no way to pretest it. Then don't. Roll the dice and reach for the stars if you and your cohorts are convinced that you have a big idea.

HOW RELIABLE IS THE TESTING OF ROUGH IDEAS?

Many knowledgeable experts are confident enough in the system to make "go" or "no go" decisions on it. It seemingly is the answer that they've been looking for. However, in a recent issue of their house organ, the BBDO advertising agency reports that three research firms had reservations about this testing. They do not believe that rough executions of commercials can consistently predict a finished commercial's performance. One firm, ARS, found that animatic and photomatic scores differed significantly from finished commercial scores three to four times more often than could be accounted for by sampling variance alone. Strong stuff. Such results could indicate that if this type of quantitative pretesting is used exclusively as the final arbiter of the effectiveness of a commercial, a good number of interesting creative ideas may be doomed to oblivion.

My feeling, and the feelings of a growing number of people— creative, research, and managerial—involved in this complex problem is that the pretesting of rough commercials and the eventual posttesting of finished advertising should be used more as a disaster check and creative guide. Again, BBDO says: "In short, pre-finished testing can give some guidance in deciding whether certain commercials are worth producing. But it should never be used as the sole basis for such a decision." I would modify and broaden that thought and repeat once more for emphasis that until an infallible method of testing creative ideas and executions is developed, no research testing of any kind should be used as the sole basis for a creative decision.

THE ROLE OF THE RESEARCHER AND THE CREATIVE PROCESS

The role is simple: to be as helpful as possible. To try to understand the creative person's views and frustrations. To become a partner in the creative process. To worry and sweat right along with him. To be creative in a research way, first trying to open the door to new thinking and then trying to discover different ways to measure or prove the advertising's effectiveness.

And, in the case of advertising agency researchers, to remember for whom you're working. An agency's job is to produce effective advertising for its clients. And this has to be the ultimate objective of all the agency employees. In the case of the researchers, a part of this process has to be objectivity and honesty. If this is not true, the only people being hurt are the people that are supposed to be helped—the agency and the client. But a good research department does not sequester its people in an ivory tower, calling upon them to drift down to the mortals from time to time to favor them with erudite opinions. A researcher should be a part of the working team. And that includes help in selling an idea. Here are two examples: one where a researcher helped and the second where he hindered the presentation process.

When we, at Dancer Fitzgerald Sample, were involved in the presentation to win the Toyota account, we were in a final competition with two other agencies. Each of us had been asked to develop advertising that could be used for the coming year. (The losing agencies would be paid for their efforts. The winning agency, obviously, walked off with the marbles.) We developed four different approaches. We wanted to do some qualitative research with focused groups to find out if there were any hidden problems in these approaches.

To dramatize our capabilities and speed, our research director came up with an inspired piece of theater. As we finished the presentation of the creative material, a map of the United States appeared on the screen. The research director stood up and pointed to New York, Kansas City, El Paso, and Los Angeles and said something like: "At this moment in these cities we have focused groups standing by with animatics of these commercials." She then picked up the phone. "Hello, Los Angeles." A light on the map blinked on. "Standing by in Los Angeles," came back over the amplified phone. She did this with each city and then turned to the audience. "We're ready to go the minute you assign us the account. This research will be done today and tonight. The answers will be telexed to us and collated. We will analyze them and have a recommendation as to which campaign to go with in 48 hours." It was impressive. And it had been conceived and worked out by the research director. She knew for whom she was working.

On the other hand, once we were doing some research for a dog food account. We were using an experimental technique to find out which of three different proposed campaigns could be most effective in the current competitive environment. In the test we compared each of the three proposed pieces of advertising against the competitors. We knew that our new advertising for a little known product would not outscore the competitors in a one-time viewing. That wasn't the point. We wanted to compare our three approaches to each other to find out which one scored the highest. The competition merely represented an environment for the testing. The research project director brought the results in. Campaign "B" was by far the winner among the three. However, he pointed out that the competition had scored higher than campaign "B." And he showed us this on a chart. We asked him if this had any bearing on the comparative scores. He said no, but that he thought it was interesting. We again asked him if he felt that it was realistic for any advertising, on a one-time viewing, to outscore competitive advertising for established brands that had been running for years. He said no. And so we thanked him and asked him not to include anything about the competition in the presentation because it wasn't relevant, would cause client uneasiness, and could cloud the issue and jeopardize the campaign. The researcher nodded and then presented our scores and, in a monumental case of bad judgment, compared them with the competitive scores. In spite of the fact that he kept insisting that the test was not designed to compare the advertising with the competition, the damage had been done. The client became uneasy, the issue was clouded, and we lost the campaign. The researcher now peddles his wares elsewhere.

IN SUMMARY

1. Market research is a fact of life, so the person involved with the creative process should learn its advantages and limitations—and then let it help.

2. "Pre" research is usually welcomed because it can give fuel to the creative process by uncovering insights into how people think, act, and respond to stimuli.

3. Some creative people object to any kind of "pre" research help because they feel that it's too time consuming and may clutter their minds with unnecessary information. A bad theory.

4. A format for uncovering pertinent consumer perceptions of a product, institution, or existing idea should consist of the following steps:

   a. Review existing research,

   b. Augment existing research with new research, if necessary. Qualitative research to probe audiences' feelings is sometimes most welcome, and

   c. Draw some conclusions, which would include the arrived at present consumer perception, a restatement of the creative strategy, and some suggested executional directions based on the perceptions and strategy.

5. "Post" research is often suspect in the creative person's mind because it can crush ego, challenge creative instincts, cause more work, and imperil livelihood.

6. All advertising people should be aware of the problems in the various testing techniques that could affect the test results.

7. Dependence on "post" testing tends to put restrictions on the creative effort when the objectives become getting a high score rather than producing effective advertising.

8. However, the internals from "post" testing can be most beneficial to creative people. They should be looked at carefully because

the comments may give clues as to how the advertising might be changed to better communicate the idea.

9. A checklist to help find out why a particular commercial is not communicating should include examination of the brand name awareness, the complexity of the execution, the interest factor of the idea, and the quality of the audio track, including music and sound effects.

10. Testing of rough versions of commercials prior to actual finished production has become more and more popular. There are three basic rough testing forms: (1) animatics, (2) photomatics, and (3) rough film or tape production.

11. Unfortunately, there are also a number of built-in drawbacks to this type of production and testing. One research firm has found that animatic and photomatic scores differed from finished commercial scores three to four times more often than could be accounted for.

12. In the final analysis, until an infallible system is developed, no form of market research testing should be used as the sole judge as to whether or not the advertising should or should not run.

13. The role of the researcher in the creative process is to be as helpful as possible by trying to understand the creative person's point of view, to become a partner in the creative process, to try and open the door to new thinking, to try to discover more reliable ways to prove the advertising's effectiveness, and to help sell the advertising idea.

The overview is, as I said, that research is still looking for ways to help the creative process. Good creative leaders will do anything they can to aid that search.

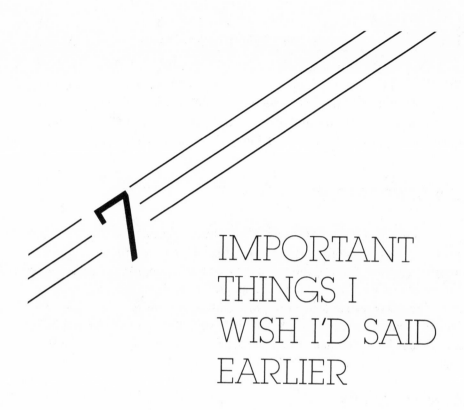

IMPORTANT
THINGS I
WISH I'D SAID
EARLIER

I must say, this being my first attempt at writing a book like this (or like anything, for that matter), I find that I've written copious notes to myself on the backs of magazines, cash register tapes, parking lot tickets—anything handy at the time—reminding me of points that I should make. Unfortunately, now that I'm up to the last chapter, I find that I haven't yet made them. And so the next few pages will be a compilation of random thoughts collected from the backs of magazines, receipts, and so forth. My mother, who delights in this sort of stuff, refers to hers as "gems of wisdom." I hope some of these are too.

ON LEADERSHIP

Throughout the book I've touched on the subject and flirted with the idea of leadership and its relationship to the creative process. But what are the qualities that are the requisites for those people who are going to be working with, looking over the shoulder of, directing, encouraging, stimulating, censoring, listening to, cajoling, administering, chastising, and rewarding creative people? Well, I suppose there are lots of them that would be welcomed. But I think that there are four that are necessary, with a few caveats.

Creative Ability

Should the person in charge of the creative entourage (or person) be able to do it himself? In some cases it's obviously both desirable and practical. I've been in situations, usually late at night on foreign soil (that's any soil away from the home typewriter), where a client decision or set of circumstances dictates revisions or even a new creative approach overnight. And there's no one available but the creative leader. At that point it's very nice indeed to have a leader who can sit down at the machine, dig into his bag of tricks, and use his facile mind and fast fingers to solve the problem.

So it's great for moments of crisis. But there are other times when it's not so great. In many cases the creative abilities of the leader, when used unwisely, can lead to unfair competition, as I reviewed in former chapters. The leader can't resist giving out an assignment and then getting into the act himself. ("What the hell, I've got a few ideas here. I'll just work them up in case the troops don't produce.") The trouble, of course, is not adding an extra creative mind (his) to the project but rather leaning too heavily toward his own efforts when decision time arrives. It's hard to be impartial at this point.

Another problem is that unless creative leaders practice their art constantly (and most of them can't because leadership has its own demands on time), their work can become dated. They can lose fluidity, the supple creative flow that comes from writing or designing or painting or composing or directing more or less regularly. They lose the cumulative dexterity that builds up. And this makes it much harder for them to rule against their own work. They're forced to admit that they used to be better.

Of course, there are certain fields where the creative areas are so specialized that it's ridiculous to think that leaders or managers have to be specialists in the fields they're overseeing. You don't need a photographer to direct a photographer, or a songwriter to supervise a lyricist, or an interior decorator to manage an interior decorator. Obviously, it helps immensely if the managers know something about what they're managing. But it does not have to be their vocation or even intense avocation.

The conclusion, I guess, would be that the creative ability desired in any type of leadership position would be dependent on the requirements of the job and how involved the leaders must be in the creative process. If they're managing and overseeing, a creative flair and understanding will probably suffice. But if they're going to be involved in doing it, they'd better know what they're doing.

Time and Desire to Learn

This is a follow-up of the above. If the creative project involves areas that are alien to the person in charge, she should certainly develop the time and desire to learn something—at least the rudiments—of the subject. Our vice president in charge of sales should have some familiarity with the requirements and limitations of the theatrical extravaganza she's responsible for to introduce her new lingerie line. An account supervisor should know something about the basics of print production before he makes promises and commitments to a client. And an advertising or brand manager should know how to read a rough cut, optical indications, a rough mix, and an answer print before passing judgment on a TV execution.

Objectivity

A must, particularly when a number of different creative ideas are being presented as an answer to a creative challenge. Emotion often plays a part in the creative process, but the leader has got to be able to step back and know when emotion is furthering the cause or when it's furthering more emotion. Objectivity also generates a sense of fairness. And this is indispensable. Without it, leaders lose the respect of their followers. Leadership suffers. The work suffers. And often some good creative people say the hell with it and go elsewhere.

The Ability to Inspire

The value of stimulation varies with the creative demands. But no matter what the leader's role, it can't hurt. (Remember, we're talking about inspiring people, not telling them how to do it.) Show me the chairman of the board who comes out in his shirt sleeves, throws his arm around the shoulder of a young writer, and says, "Hang in there. I know you can do it, kiddo. It may take some time, but I'm with you all the way," and I'll show you a company with great esprit de corps—and a writer who'll walk through fire to get the job done. Compare this with the organization whose chairman sends a note to the executive vice president: "Pursuant to the special writing job being handled in your department, I would appreciate it if your writer would bend every effort to getting it to me as soon as possible. If this is difficult, I suggest you add some other people to the project."

For those directly involved with being creative day after day—the creative directors, theatrical directors, advertising managers, producers, and so forth—the ability to stimulate and inspire is perhaps the most important quality they can have. They can be brilliant creative people themselves, but if they can't inspire the people working for them, they probably shouldn't be leaders.

ON BEING A CHEERLEADER

Sometimes the art of inspiration is the result of the mood in which people create. I've always felt that the mood should be upbeat, optimistic, smiling. And that usually calls for a leader who can set that tone. Of course, it's not an absolute must. There are plenty of leaders and editors and managers who do it quietly, conservatively, reservedly, even shyly. If that's your nature, fine. But then be prepared to have someone else in the group as the alter ego. Someone who says: "Hey, looka that. The glass is already half full. Let's see what we can do to get it to overflow." Not: "Oh, oh. The glass is half empty. We're going to have to work like hell to keep it from going down any farther." I knew a creative director who came into his office one Monday morning excitedly and asked his secretary to get everyone together for a very important meeting in the conference room in exactly 30 minutes. Unprecedented. Never been done before. What's up? Must be something big. Buzzes of conjecture as 40 writers and artists and producers and assistants and secretaries gathered. The creative director was waiting. On the conference table in front of him was a small paper chicken sitting on a nest. "Watch," he said, and then lit a fuse at the chicken's tail. It sizzled quietly for a second, and then flame shot from the chicken's rear, and four small eggs blasted across the table. The smoke curled contentedly from the chicken. The reaction was spontaneous. Awed expressions. Grins. Giggles. Laughter. They looked at the creative director. He stood up. "That's all," he said. "I found this at a flea market in Vermont yesterday. Isn't it something. I couldn't wait to get back here and show you. Now *that* is excitement." And he left. No moral. No analogies. He just wanted to share his delight with everyone. People went off to their tasks shaking their heads and grinning. And the mood of the day had changed.

ON STAGNATION

A dreadful word. Argh. Mud and slime and mosquitoes. Swamp gas bubbling in murky pools. When this happens to one of your creative people, what do you do? And I'm not saying that he produces bad work. He just reaches a plateau. The same old thing. OK, but nothing new. Well, first look for the reason. It's like one of the theories of holistic medicine. If disease strikes, look to the activities of the patient in the immediate past for a clue that may have opened the body to accept disease. Stagnation or plateauing is a creative disease. It can be caused by unhappiness or even happiness, anything that diverts the attention or concentration of the individual. Or it can be caused by new interests or an inclination to become involved in a number of different things that waters down the principal creative thrust. One of the best writers I know eventually left the advertising agency business because his interests and attention kept being consumed by other creative challenges. He would be working on a TV campaign and suddenly have a chance to do a free-lance book on furniture refinishing, and then a children's TV program, and then. . . . But it made little difference. The TV campaign suffered. The extracurricular writing didn't. We had a long discussion about this, and he finally decided that his mind loved new and quick challenges and that he was happy (and good enough) to take these on one after another without the day-to-day responsibilities of an advertising copywriter. And so he did. We lost a good copywriter. And he solved the problem of stagnation.

Obviously, it doesn't always have to end this way. Much of the time you can solve the hidden pressure that's leading to creative plateauing. But not always. Because sometimes the problem does not grow out of other pressures. Sometimes it comes from working too long or too many times on the same assignment, project, or problem. It may be that after the sixth straight year doing the annual lingerie buyers' show the creative team handling this should be changed. Or it may be that the team working on the problem has been together for so long that they're beginning to take each other for granted, and the synergistic effect that this often begets is suddenly begotten. A change in the team personnel might help. I recently heard of an account leaving one advertising agency for another because the client just got tired of the same old faces, the same meetings, the same approaches, the same sameness. Plateauing. If the agency had been more alert they might have saved the business by reassigning some people and adding a big dose of freshness to the project.

Another solution to this dread malady could be the diversification of projects the creative people are assigned to. One theory is to keep creative people full time on a given account as long as they keep producing and then, after a given period of time, rotate them. I've had a fair amount of success taking the opposite tack. I assign the people to a number of accounts so that there's a variety in their day, minds, and creative meanderings. It helps the back burner theory. It provides orderly relief. It gives the client more people attacking the problem. And it has made for a minimum of stagnation—and a good bit of longevity.

Every now and then, in spite of all of these cures, things don't seem to improve. It may be that the person has been in the business too long without a break. Perhaps she's a workaholic or worrier who keeps skipping vacations. The cumulative effect of coming up with something new and different can be more than a burnout. It can be a bonfire. Then is the time to consider a leave of absence. Let the person take off for six months or a year. Often it will refresh, rejuvenate, restoke the furnace, rekindle the fires. And if it doesn't, neither of you has lost. If she'd stayed, you'd eventually have had to suggest that she try another job elsewhere. Messy. Particularly with someone who has given her all over a long period of time. The leave allows her to step back and survey her life and then make her own decision. If she decides to come back and still is plateauing, it's much easier to discuss the inevitable because presumably you'd already covered that subject. And 9 out of 10 times you won't have to ask her to call it quits. She'll do it herself, usually with a touch of resigned relief.

ON GETTING THE WHEELS TURNING

These might be called tricks of the trade. Devices that I've used and read or heard or talked about that get the creative person's mind and imagination into gear.

1.   Urge them to look at other examples that have been done in their field. A songwriter might listen to lyrics of people he admires. An artist should browse through books and galleries. She might try and imagine what went though great artists' minds as they crafted their master-pieces. If you're dealing with a copywriter, have him look through books of winning ads. The object here is not to practice the unconscious art of plagiarism, but to step into another mode. To inspire people to think like some of the greats. To push creativity to a new and perhaps different level.

2.   Urge your people to learn to look at things differently. Have them look at a rose, for example, as though they were bees. Circle it and come in close. Crawl inside the petal with their eyes. Let them feel the velvety texture, the airy bounciness, as though they were walking on it. Then they might lie on the ground and look up through the leaves to the underside of the petals. When they begin to look at things differently, they could begin to think differently—and this could open new creative channels.

3.   Following up on this theory, when working with a writer you might urge her to put down what she has in mind as simply and directly as possible. Then to take that piece of work and redo it using different words, a different structure, or a completely different approach. In my first job, I was given an assignment to rewrite a headline. I did, four different ways. My boss said fine and sent me back to my desk and asked for 20 more. I was stunned. "What you've done is the obvious," he said. "Now what you're going to do is push yourself into the unusual. You're going to begin to be creative. And as you do, you'll find more than 20 ways. And you'll probably discover a whole new approach to the ad. And I'd like that."

ON BUILDING LOYALTY

A prime ingredient in managing the creative process. How do you do it? By being fair, honest, tactful, supportive (even when your troops may be wrong—but choose this position carefully). By being willing to work directly with them if the need arises, including doing grunt work. And by not asking them to do anything you wouldn't do or haven't done. By listening and giving in sometimes, even when you're right. And when you're wrong, by admitting it. This builds ego, humanness, and a feeling for fair play. It can result in a most rewarding loyalty. And the loyalty of your people can help pull you through the squeeze play more often than you might imagine.

ON EMPATHY

We know that good writers, if not all creative people, have a certain degree of empathy for the world. It's what makes them relate to and emulate the emotions, feelings, hopes, and dark wonderings of the characters they invent and write about. But the people who are running the show also need empathy. They need to try to put themselves in place of the creative people they're working with. And to do this, it's good if they can get inside the creative person's head. To feel the challenges, worries, pressures, distractions he's up against. It's like the flight surgeon who flies five missions so that he can get an idea of what the people he's trying to treat are up against. Editors who have been writers (a not uncommon occurrence) are other examples.

In the advertising agency business a number of agencies have training programs for account people to help them better understand the creative process. At DFS, the culmination of this program is an actual creative assignment where the account people are given a strategy and asked to solve it, individually and then in teams, with their own advertising campaign. To help them in the presentation phase, they are assigned art directors who act as their "wrists," drawing and designing as the "students" tell them. The campaign is carried right through to the final presentation process, usually before a board of creative directors and management supervisors, so that they can participate in all phases of the creative adventure. The results have been delightful in building empathy for the creative people. And this understanding manifests itself in many ways—including budding friendships, which purists in the business may call unnatural, between creative and account teams.

The question arises at this point, "Would it help to reverse the roles, to have the creative person participate in some kind of management training program?" Mixed emotions on this one. Sounds logical, but I don't think that creative people should get involved in this type of activity for the following reasons:

1. It may start to inhibit their creative exploring. Remember, a part of the creative psyche is the unconscious desire to keep from starting. The open door to the complicated field of management can offer a whole new universe of excesses. ("Wait a minute. I can't start writing until we're sure our market penetration is secure enough." Or: "The cost per unit is too high for the strategic approach we're using. Why don't you see what you can do to get the cost down before I start spinning my wheels.") The creative imagination is a marvelous sight to behold. And it's at best when working up reasons not to create.

2. It takes time away from creating.

3. It's easier to give a creative patina to MBA's than to turn an art director into a pseudo business manager. The creative curiosity tends to go too far. Often the inquisitive mind keeps probing, to

the frustration of the businesspeople, and challenging well established theories. Now this may sound healthy and productive, but most of the time it isn't. Time and patience are wasted because the creative people want to reinvent the wheel. And by learning a little bit about a lot of things, they become confused. The imagination of the brain's right side, when applied to the theories of the cool, more practical left side, may even lead to creative panic. ("Have you seen the profit objectives this product has to produce? Impossible. I don't think any campaign can help. I don't know where to start or what to do. I think I'll ask for a reassignment. I think I'll shoot myself!")

On the other hand, the creative person should spend time with the people on the other side. She should try to relate to the problems the businessperson has daily, striving to accomplish what has to be accomplished. Empathy. The creative person should put herself in the other person's cordovans. Even a surface understanding of the other side will help.

ON LISTENING

Too many people in all phases of the creative process (and perhaps in life, for that matter) jump before they know where or why they're jumping. The problem begins with the subconscious, which often starts to work before all of the information or facts are received. And this diversion certainly lowers attention and eventually blocks listening. Other people stop listening so they can talk—and perhaps even sound as though they know what they're talking about. Still others have preconceived ideas about the subject and therefore don't listen at all. If you're running an information meeting and suspect that some of this is going on, spice your talk with questions. ("The plot line seems to call for a musical theme here. I think we might consider a 12 bar blues. What do you think, Fred?") It's amazing how many people don't like to look stupid in a meeting. If you know and have worked with the people a long time (and it's a small meeting, where the dynamics of embarrassment may not be important) force them to listen by saying "Listen!!!"

ON GETTING ALONG WITH PEOPLE

It's usually easier and more rewarding to do this than not. Or don't make enemies with anybody. Or friends are mostly better. All those things we all know. But we're still human and react the wrong way to some people and situations. The real problem is that creative people, because of the temperaments, insecurities, and worries that have been discussed earlier, tend to have more fragile interpersonal relationships. And creative leaders or managers, therefore, must keep theirs on an even keel to compensate for and help smooth over the turbulence that too often erupts in the ranks. Remember, the leader's job is to produce good work, and that usually means keeping people reasonably contented or, at the least, just slightly militant.

A brief word here on politics. People often use politics as an excuse to "get along with people." I think the difference is the final objective. Getting along with people is done so that a better atmosphere for good work can be maintained. Politics seems to have as its objective the personal gain of the individual who's being political. To be realistic, all of us practice politics from time to time—often under the guise of tact. But when politics becomes a way of business life, disharmony, distrust, and divisiveness enter the scene. I once had the misfortune of working with a man who was so obviously political and at the same time so smooth at the art of talking his way in and out of situations that he was known as "The Wizard of Ooze." We marveled and laughed at his ingenious ploys. But we didn't trust him. The sad part is that if he'd directed his mind and talents to the challenges and projects at hand, rather than his own political gain, he could have been a most successful leader. But he didn't. And that did him in. He lost his job, and as his reputation grew as "The Wizard," his career slowly continued down the yellow brick road—away from the Emerald City.

If you find yourself worrying about how you'll look if you support a certain thesis or if what you're about to propose will offend an executive vice president, even though you believe in it, then politics may be overshadowing performance and judgment. Be aware. And be wary. Concentrate on the actual, not political, benefits of your work. This doesn't mean that you should hide your stars behind a cloud. When your people do something good, make sure your superiors know about it. But that's not politics. That's just common sense.

ON LIVING WITH A CREATIVE PERSON

If you're a husband, wife, lover, or some other category living with someone involved regularly in the creative process, life may be exhilarating, surprising, imaginative, and seldom dull. But it won't be easy. Because the atmosphere can be depressing, argumentative, hostile, and certainly emotional. This means that for some degree of ambient stability, the partner of the creative force must be aware of and try to add balance to the wildly gyrating moods. Those couples that seem successful in getting along together are the ones where each gives some kind of support to the other. In the case of the creative person and the partner who's (how can I put this?) ordinary (no), noncreative (no), less volatile (not bad), it's the latter whose job it is to act as the ego booster, critic, disciplinarian, appreciative audience, often organizer, and always general helpmate. Here are some practical pointers from conversations I've had with those who have cast their lots with creative breadwinners.

1.   When he reads you his latest aloud and asks you what you think, be like the ideal client. Always start with the positive. Then later, ease into the more critical comments, of course preceded by "These are just my thoughts, and I probably don't know what I'm talking about," or some such other tribute to self-deprecation. Your job is to walk the tightrope between boosterism and honesty. The objective is to keep his spirits up and at the same time give him helpful criticism, if at all possible. If it's good, pour on the praise. If it needs work or you don't understand it, ask him to explain why he did it the way he did. Try to get him to reexamine what he's done. Be wary of saying, "I don't know, dear, I just don't like it."

On the other hand, you might want to say, "Terrific, you've done it again," when he hasn't. I know the wife of a very insecure and moody but very good copywriter who always tells him that everything is wonderful, no matter how unwonderful it actually is, just to keep things mellow and upbeat throughout the weekend. Her feeling is that he'll find out on Monday if it isn't great. Meanwhile, she can avoid hours of dark depression, ranting, and general antisocial conduct. And maybe she's right. She has worked out a system to keep their life together on a somewhat even keel. And as far as I can see the copywriter's work hasn't suffered from it.

2.   Work around her work habits. If she has to work at home, respect her working hours. Don't interrupt with minor crisis and/or telephone calls. And when she's caught in a creative crunch, be especially alert to make everything as easy as you can. But when things are less than frantic, assert yourself. Don't spoil her. Creative people can be very creative in working out ways to get their way. Remind her that a partnership works both ways and that you have your life as well.

3.   It seems to me that the toughest situation is where both parties are engaged in creative activities or even the same creative field. Two writers. Two art directors. Two architects. It's obviously easier if they're in business together working on the same challenges. But if they're not, they have to be especially aware of each other's moods and habits. And they have to work much harder at the dance of life. But even in these situations, one of the people probably has to sublimate his ego. To bend more. To accommodate quicker. I have admiration for and delight in these people. To me they represent a true partnership.

ON COLLABORATION

In any phase of creative development, it can do nothing but help if the collaborators can collaborate. And the world is full of collaborative successes. Rogers and Hart. Williams and Kazan. Masters and Johnson. But their accomplishments, which they usually say come from a major dose of synergism, seem to be the result of creative specialists in different but related fields working together. A composer and lyricist. An author and director. A writer and a researcher. A copywriter and an art director. They don't compete. They augment each other's creative needs. Because they are not really specialists in the same fields, they can be somewhat objective about each other's ideas and approaches. They can act as sounding boards, and because they presumably have respect for each other's abilities, they can build on the ideas. In the series "The Creative Man," appearing from time to time in *The New York Times Magazine*, Samuel G. Friedman quotes Stephen Sondheim as saying: "Collaboration is the very essence of creativity in the theater" ("The Worlds and Music of Stephen Sondheim," by Samuel G. Friedman, *The New York Times Magazine*, April 1, 1984).

Another and probably inevitable result of any kind of good creative collaboration is the temperamental clash. Good collaborators know how to take advantage of this. They fight for their points of view. They may stalk and scream and sulk. But after awhile, they think and try it another way. If they don't, they don't collaborate anymore.

If you're in a position of managing creative collaborators or teams, be aware of the possibilities of these tensions. When you're assigning two people, who may never have worked together, to a project, give each one privately a position buildup of the other, concentrating on accomplishments. The objective, of course, is to inject mutual respect before the collaboration starts. Then when and if tensions rise, the cooler part of the brain might say: "Hold on, this woman that's trying to develop something that's absolutely ridiculous is the same person that won three Clios and was named Art Director of the Year two years ago. She can't be all bad. Listen, right side, listen."

Of course there is a danger, and that's when the participants are not of equal talent. The less talented may use his collaborator as a creative crutch. He leaches on. He agrees to everything. ("Gee, that's swell, Steve. You've done it again. I wouldn't change a word.") And Steve likes it because he can do what he wants and have his ego stroked at the same time. No-talent, meanwhile, has found a hiding place as a partner, and, as such, he receives credit for working with Steve.

To make sure that this doesn't happen, you obviously have to know your people. And if you don't, find out. Give out individual assignments. No collaboration. See what they can do on their own. If they're what you think they are, they should be able to produce. If they don't, or can't or come to you and say, "I really need an art director to help work something out," be wary. It might be the beginning of the coattail caper.

Of course, there are those who don't want to collaborate, who are much more comfortable doing it alone. Fine. Let them do it. Unlike the theater, there are a good number of creative areas where collaboration is not a must. At least for a while. But there comes a time in most creative projects where collaboration is necessary. When it's time to turn the manuscript over to the editor. Or the script to the film crew. Or lyrics to a composer. Unfortunately, some of the "lone wolves" resist collaboration even then. The playwright who believes she can direct better than the director. The copywriter who does his own layouts and wants an art director to do just as he says. The composer who thinks she's also a lyricist and accepts a partner only to smooth over the rough edges. These situations call for all of the skills of the creative manager. Suggesting. Wheedling. Pleading. Even threatening. In the advertising area, I've even had to take the work away from a writer when he'd finished, send him off on another task, and then work as his surrogate with the art director. But luckily, when the right collaborators get together, we have a chance for creative magic. And isn't that what we're all striving for?

ON BEING CURIOUS

Bill Moyers, the journalist, in an article in *ADWEEK* (January 25, 1982) calls curiosity "the seed-power of creativity." Something I wish that I'd said or at least thought of back in that section in Chapter 3 on "What to Look for in Creative People." Look for the curious mind. Of course, all curious people are not necessarily good creative people. But every single good creative person I've ever met has been curious (sometimes in more ways than one). They take clocks apart to see how they work. They wonder how Hopper achieved the feeling of dazzling sunlight on a Victorian house. And they try and find out what makes a baby suddenly cry, or an audience react enthusiastically to a scene or even a line one night and then sit on their hands the next. They wonder and they cogitate and they worry and they explore. How can anyone explore the unknown, the different, without this curiosity?

ON THE BIG IDEA

In almost any creative venture, the big idea is what we're looking for. It's the core of the plot line in the theater. In *You Can't Take it With You* it's the refreshing relief of a nonconformist family making it in the very straight world of the 1930s, an escapism that unleashed the hidden frustrations everyone had in those somewhat depressing Depression years. In *La Cage aux Folles* it's the dynamics of a poignant alternative life style colliding in delightful comic relief with the ultrastraight society. In current mystery-adventure stories, it's the formula for the complicated, unexpected plot switches, exemplified in the popular works of writers like Robert Ludlum. In advertising, as defined by some of the bright management people I work with, it's very simply a strategic benefit of a product, service, or company transformed into provocative consumer terms. And big ideas are hard to come by. There aren't a lot of them in evidence today. Oh, there are ideas and good ideas and better ideas. But big ideas? Ideas that make you say, "Wow"? Ideas that stick in your mind and get talked about the next day? Not so many. Keep your eye on the word provocative. If it's not provocative, it probably is not a big idea.

Again, if I had a formula for coming up with the big idea every time, I probably would not be pouring my mind, heart, and experience into this book. I would be too busy rushing to the drive-in deposit window at the bank. But the people in charge of managing creativity have responsibilities to keep their wards constantly searching for the big one. And this striving to go beyond demands prodding, pushing, stimulating, and inspiring. One of the toughest creative jobs is to have to do this by yourself. (Good editors seem to manage this.) Just you and the people you've got to inspire. This is where understanding the creative mystique can be invaluable. And where the creative manager who doesn't quite understand ("Creative people baffle me. They're a different breed, so I find it easier to leave them alone to do their thing.") may be running the risk of being doomed to accepting the ordinary. Of course, there are creative people who have built-in motivation and will push themselves to always try and do something better. But the understanding, prodding, pushing, stimulating, inspiring editor or creative director or producer or chairman of the board can make the difference between good and "Oh boy!"

Obviously, every assignment doesn't call for the big idea. In fact, many times the sellees are wary of it because of the associated risk that usually is present in anything that's new, different, never-been-done-before. Stretch for the big one anyway. It's much easier to make the unusual usual than vice versa. A very bright and understanding account person I once worked with had an interesting approach. He felt that his client was wary of the unusual, so when we came up with a big idea, he'd say, "Dull it up a little and we'll sell it. Then when they get used to it, we slowly hype it back to what you want." It was called selling by degrees.

ON THE ACCEPTANCE OF AN IDEA

Great ideas can come from anywhere. Sometimes they spring full-blown from one mind. Or the spark starts developing between two people and is added to, developed, embellished, honed, and refined by a number of creative people. But once it's ready to go wherever it's going (most ideas aren't built to stay hidden in the dark crevices of someone's drawer, closet, steamer trunk, garage, attic, or brain), the fragile testimonial to individual or group creativity must have everyone involved in the acceptance process attuned to the value (and possible rewards) of the unusual. Of taking a chance. If any of these decision-making people lean too far away from risk taking, the ordinary will be their reward. "But," you say, "are you asking me to risk all on what may be an unproven and thus unproductive approach to a problem? You have to accept the possibility of failure when you venture into uncharted waters," you say. "But not with my money, Buster!"

What you really mean is not with my company's or stockholders' money. If it were your money alone, you might risk it—as many people do when investing in plays or movies or paintings or new inventions. But risking the establishment money may mean the loss of credibility and job, not only for the idea's conceiver, but for the people that authorized the risk of seeing it through as well. And so what do you do? In the advertising world, we advocate, when necessary, appropriate, and practical, the double approach. Recommend the "safe" approach (and it doesn't have to be bad to be safe!) and then recommend the new, unusual, the perceived riskier concept for special test markets. Find out something about it, without taking the chance on all the marbles going down the drain.

Of course, we can adjust and test and rationalize all we want, but there will always come the time when someone has got to say go or stay home. The "goers" take the chance. And the goers sometimes see such successes as Federal Express, Yoplait, L'eggs, or Volkswagen blossom from risk taking that comes from doing it differently.

ON KEEPING AN IDEA PURE

An author has an unusual device for her novel. The entire book will be done in two columns on each page. The left hand column will describe the action, the right hand the thoughts in the hero's mind during the action. The editor likes the idea but worries that the two columns will not be balanced. "Fine," says the author, "that's the way it is. The action may be simple, but what's going on in the mind is voluminous and often complex. I want to convey this feeling. Sometimes the action will trigger the thoughts. Other times the mind will wander into areas that have nothing to do with the action." The problem is that the editor really wonders if the whole structure is wrong. He suggests that the two-column format be abandoned and the book be written with a continuous flow, with the thought process done in italics. The author almost knocks her glass of white wine onto an adjoining table at Le Cheval Blanc in exasperation. The unusual structure is a part of the concept. It offers three different ways to read the book: the complete left-hand column first, the complete right-hand column first, or back and forth from action to thought. It invites reader involvement.

A tough decision. Both points of view may be valid. The art of compromise may be invoked. (Make the action more descriptive, without obvious padding, to help the narrative balance.) But to change the format would indeed be affecting the purity of the original idea. And if any idea is looked upon as novel and interesting—and has some redeeming merit—it should be given a chance. Too many are watered down by layers of people who want to make improvements. Unfortunately, some of the time the improvements are devices to allow the improver to participate in and gain some degree of authorship of the idea, even subconsciously. It's a difficult role for those empowered with passing on the merits of creative work. And it's one reason why so many advertising agencies, for example, make sure that the person who came up with the original concept—no matter who they are or what position they hold—stays with the project from start to finish. There's no passing the idea from one stage to another without someone looking over everyone's shoulder to make sure it stays pure to the original concept. And that someone should be the person who came up with the idea in the first place.

ON FAILURE

Be prepared to accept it, but never be content with it. As I discussed in the first chapter, failure often means the lack of acceptance of an idea, and in the business of creating and presenting ideas, some failure is inevitable. And sometimes it may mean that the project is really not as good as you thought. It might even deserve to fail. Accept it. And try to learn from it. Make your people aware of this philosophy. Often when they conceive an idea, they're tentative and unsure of it, particularly in the early stages. It would be easier for them to take rejection at that point. But as the idea is nurtured and grows, their confidence in it also grows. And the turndown becomes proportionately harder to take.

So if, at the start, you sense that the sale will be unduly hard, for whatever reasons, be frank and practical. Not pessimistic but realistic. Then when you go in for the big, well-rehearsed presentation and you've tried to anticipate and step around all of the roadblocks that may be thrown in front of you, remind your people once more that they've done a terrific job and that you're going to push it with everything you've got but that the acceptance of the idea may still be a long shot. Mention again what you said at the beginning so that the defeat won't be as unexpected and traumatic. The nice thing, of course, is that if you're successful it becomes all the sweeter.

One of the greatest challenges to any creative leader is to be able to regroup her people and rebolster their morale after a disaster. This is particularly rough because she's human, too. Her spirits have also suffered a sharp blow. Her prestige and credibility may be a bit tattered. She doesn't feel so hot. But she must mask these feelings and think of her people. They must come out of the experience looking forward, not back. Ready to go at it again. Ready to give their all for the company, the U.S. of A., God, the Harvard backfield, and their leader, who isn't so bad after all.

One of the ways to alleviate the ego crush of failure among your people is to refer to the number of times you've suffered through it. Remember, they look at you differently. You're probably older, have had more varied experiences, and, if you're doing your job right, are somewhat admired. They may have put you on a pedestal. Therefore, finding out that you've faced the dismal depths of failure makes you human, brings you to their level, offers hope that there may be a tomorrow. My Uncle Boyd, of bridge-playing, milk wagon fame (see Introduction), once helped me through a disastrous love affair by taking me step-by-step through a similar experience he had had with, believe it or not, a girl named Edna Onion. Just the name made me feel better.

ON STRESS

Stress seems to be one of the most popular subjects in the United States at the moment. Books, articles, seminars, clinics, retreats, entire philosophies have been dedicated to the problem and how to cope with it. Everything from meditation to medication has been advocated and, if practiced or ingested correctly, seems to work in varying degrees, even though we all know that a touch of stress is purportedly good. Life without it would be dull. However, we're talking about abnormal stress. The creative person and manager are probably as prone to this as any people in any occupation. Aside from the usually stress-related pressures of deadlines, creative blocks, presentations, fear of failure, personality clashes, constant travel (in many cases), creative people seem to have more than the normal amount of stress in their private lives—much of it undoubtedly brought on by the above. I think that anyone involved in managing the creative process must be aware of this and prepare to deal with it accordingly. And that means to do some practical research on the subject. Know where to turn if necessary, including professional help. Over the years, I've worked out a few devices and habits that help me reduce the sweaty palms, the clenching stomach, the hyperventilating lungs, and the thumping heart in myself and in others.

1.   I believe in exercise. No matter how tight or pressured or troubled I am, I feel better after a workout. And so I run in the morning and try and play tennis three times a week, once at least at lunchtime. This is an important relief valve in a pressured day. The challenge here is to set up some kind of schedule and then to discipline yourself to follow the schedule. But once you get in the routine, it's not hard. The running, as we've all read, actually does become somewhat addictive.

2.   I consciously try to relax and step into another mode when I feel the pressure building. A few deep breaths help. A sense of humor is

indispensable. A brisk walk to get away from the pandemonium and smell the roses is not bad. In the cases where stress is brought about by a personality clash, I try to listen and put myself in the other person's position, to understand his thinking and frustrations. This pulls me away from my own inflammatory reactions, cools things down, returns the pulse to something like normal.

3.   When I'm dealing with stressful situations with my creative charges, I try to present a soothing, understanding facade. I listen. I cluck sympathetically. I look for the stress signs building. Wild eyes. Twitching. Inability to sit still. Irritation over little things. I invite them to talk about it before the explosion. Then I promise some kind of relief. In my business, much of the pressure comes from overwork. I promise help. I'll put more people on the job or reduce the workload. If the stress comes from not being able to produce, I use the devices mentioned earlier to try to get the wheels moving. If the stress is from a personality clash, I'll see if it can be faced and worked out. If it can't, I promise changes. But if the stress is brought about by something more deep-seated or if it doesn't respond to any of the kindly creative leader's gentle ministrations, I recommend professional help. As was mentioned earlier, though the temptation is great, we are not psychiatrists, psychologists, or social workers.

ON TELLING THE TRUTH

For years the creative practitioners of advertising have been accused of warping the truth, of misleading the public, and sometimes of downright lying in order to gain a competitive advantage in peddling their client's wares. Recently, we see that bending the facts for effect is not the exclusive province of the advertising fraternity. In a somewhat celebrated instance, the respected writer Alastair Reid has admitted modifying facts in nonfiction articles. I believe it was apparently done for journalistic clarity, simplicity, and drama. No matter. It was done. And, I suspect that it's a more widespread practice than any editor or publisher cares to know about. Again, the purpose seems to be not to create different impressions than the truth warrants, but to make the piece more readable. Obviously, it's a practice to be avoided because, as *Time*

Magazine comments, "Any departure from fact is the first step on a slippery slope toward unbelievability."

But in the advertising field, much more rests on the interpretation of facts than readability. Products can make millions for their companies by exploiting a real or perceived advantage. The temptation to shade the truth is always present. It's the duty, therefore, of creative leaders to be the conscience of their people and, in some sad instances, of their clients. They must fight the practice assiduously. Now, the hard part comes in distinguishing between persuasion and slight fabrication. If advertising is perceived as another form of salesmanship, then the creative forces should be allowed to use any form of persuasion, as long as it's legal. Is it wrong to claim that Miller Lite beer is less filling? Less filling than what? Less filling than Miller High Life? Probably not.

But if we were to qualify every statement, we would be bordering on the ridiculous. Even so, those of us in the business are constantly frustrated with the disclaimers that we are forced to insert in our advertising when we make certain statements. Take the mileage for cars, for example. Every time mileage, as estimated by the Environmental Protection Agency, is given the following must accompany it: "Remember, use this estimate for comparisons. Your mileage may be different, depending on your speed, trip length, and weather. Actual highway mileage will probably be less than the EPA 'Highway Estimate.' " And if you wish to inform the public of the suggested price of the car (something quite a few people would like to know), you have to include this disclaimer: "Manufacturer's suggested retail price. Dealer's actual retail price may vary. Price does not include tax, license, transportation, optional or regionally required equipment." You've probably seen these in mice type along the bottom of your television screens under the mileage and price figures. In radio, it's worse. The disclaimers must also be given. And they take so much time that if you were to do a simple 30-second radio commercial it would have to go something like this:

> Presenting the all new Pegasus 6 with amazing gas mileage. 32 EPA in the city and 58 EPA on the highway. Remember, use this estimate for comparisons. Your mileage may be different, depending on your speed, trip length, and weather. Actual highway mileage will probably be less than the EPA "Highway Estimate." And the suggested list price is only $7,250. Manufacturer's suggested retail price. Dealer's actual retail price may vary. Price does not include tax, license, transportation, optional or

regionally required equipment. That's the all new Pegasus 6. Get down to your dealer and see one today.

OK, there's the bare bones commercial. Not much persuasion or information about what you get for this price. Now read the commercial at a normal speed and time it. It should come in at about 35 seconds. The problem is that you only have 30. Oh sure, you can get some machine-gun mouthed announcer to blast through it in time. But to what effect? Think about this. We've loaded our life with so many disclaimers that we can't even tell the public two facts about our car in one 30-second commercial. We have to use two commercials to do this, thus doubling the costs, just to accommodate those legalisms.

I think that we should begin using our heads and more common sense. We can safely assume that the reading and viewing public has, by this time, a certain built-in sophistication that realizes when it's bombarded with persuasive puffery and when it's told to consider hard facts. The various networks, the National Advertising Division of the Better Business Bureau, and the FTC all have apparatus designed to make sure that the claims are true claims. When Cheerios states that it's the number one selling cereal for children, General Mills had better be able to prove it. When Bayer aspirin states that more doctors recommend aspirin for pain relief than any other product, they must substantiate it. If they can't, their advertising will not be allowed on the airwaves. And if somehow it gets through and is detected later, they can be fined and forced to run corrective advertising.

But ultimately, it's still up to the creative people and therefore the creative leader to see that shaded truths don't get a foothold in their advertising. In the public's mind, advertising has already "slid down the slippery slope toward unbelievability." It's up to us to keep it from sliding any farther.

ON LETTING GO

Most of the time we equate this with the gentle, white-haired gaff who's headed for retirement. He has to learn to turn his work, his responsibilities, his knowledge over to the next in line. Some do it graciously, some don't. But they all do it because they have to. Unless they own the place, their departure from the organization is inevitable. (And if they are the owners, they should also realize this fact. Too many companies have drifted into red ink or oblivion because the owner has drifted into senility, or at least recalcitrance, while refusing to hand over the reins.)

But the problem that affects the creative process is that of the bright creative person being rightfully promoted to a leadership position. And in doing this, they must cut down on the job or line creativity and start assuming the mantle of creative inspiration, direction, and leadership. But they don't want to let go. And so they try to do both, full time. They'll fail. Oh, they can do a bit of each, but something always suffers. If you're in a position to promote one of your people into management, and she's been very good as a line creative person, try and make the change gradual. Let her continue with some specific line responsibilities. But ease her into the management function, at the same time. Let her take over slowly. Give her time to get her people in place so that she can feel wistfully confident that they can do the job she was doing. Meantime, convince her that you're there to look over her shoulder and to guide her in the beginning and to support her at all times. And as she grows, you let go. After a while, you'll find that it's really not so bad.

ON THREE INGREDIENTS THAT LEAD TO CREATIVE SUCCESS

In various places in this book I've discussed different aspects of these ingredients. Because I think they're so essential, another look may be worthwhile. They don't guarantee success, but without them the creative process and resultant product can fall apart.

Ingredient Number One: Time

Scene: Creative director's office, late July afternoon. He stares morosely at a blank sheet of yellow paper in his typewriter. Friendly account man enters.

ACCOUNT: Hey, hey babes. Good news.
CREATIVE: (Suspiciously) Ummmmm.

ACCOUNT: Got you three months to work on the new airline campaign.

CREATIVE: Three months? Wow! Great!

ACCOUNT: Yep. Air date mid-October. Meet tomorrow with the new strategy. Bring your people and shoot the questions to us. We'll fill you in.

Scene: Creative director's office, one week later. Same friendly account man enters.

ACCOUNT: Hey, hey babes. How's it going on the new campaign?

CREATIVE: (Warily) Workin' on it, Georgie.

ACCOUNT: Super. When do you think we can look at something?

CREATIVE: Jeez, George, I dunno. We don't have air date until mid-October and it's only the twenty-second of July.

ACCOUNT: Yeah, but remember, we've got the travel agents' convention in September, and the client wants to show them finished commercials.

CREATIVE: Hold it. Back up the truck. What travel agents' meeting? You said we have three months.

ACCOUNT: C'mon babes, you know we always have these meetings to pump up the travel agents.

CREATIVE: (Note of growing despair creeping into voice) But you promised three months. That means we've got to be in production second week in August.

ACCOUNT: Hold the phone. I said three months to work on the new campaign. I figure that means everything that goes with it. Dealer meeting, research. . . .

CREATIVE: (Voice beoming fainter) Research?

ACCOUNT: Yeah. We've got to do animatics on the different approaches, at least three of them, so we can run some quantitative research.

CREATIVE: (Still fainter) How long's that take?

ACCOUNT: Get top line in three weeks. Diagnostics in five.

CREATIVE: (Practically whispering) Two weeks for three animatics,

five weeks for research before we can actually shoot. That means
I've got to have three campaigns ready to go . . . tomorrow.

ACCOUNT: Like I said, what time can we see something?

CREATIVE: (Fill in suggested response here).

Anyone who has ever been involved with any kind of creative project
is familiar with the problem. In one form or another, it always seems to
appear at the inappropriate moment. Oh, accommodations are always
made, because they have to be. The research time gets cut down, production is speeded up, and the creative people work nights and the one
weekend left and, of course, come up with something. Perhaps it will
even be good. It certainly will be professional. But the chances of its
being   "my-gawd-I've-never-seen-anything-as-good-as-this-in-my-life"
advertising are somewhat slim. Because the creative forces do not have
the time to do all of the important things I've urged them to do in the
previous chapters: to learn, to think, to explore, to reject, to start over,
to take it beyond good to great. So make time the essence of your creative people's lives. Plan assiduously. Be tough. Insist on the amount of
time needed. Change the schedule if necessary. Meeting a schedule is
useless if you meet the deadlines with the wrong stuff. Remember, after
the fact, no one remembers that you didn't have enough time to do the
job right. All they see is what they got—probably a rather ordinary
piece of work.

Ingredient Number Two: Talent

I've talked about the hiring and working with and evaluating of talent.
But perhaps I haven't put enough emphasis on the searching out and
developing of new talent. And I say develop because proven talent—I
mean real talent, not just practitioners of the creative art—is hard to
find. In many fields, there is just not enough to go around. And so organizations are turning more and more to young people to fill their
needs. The film departments of leading universities are providing fresh
talent for all phases of the industry. Wise publishers are nurturing
bright writers in their twenties. At Dancer Fitzgerald Sample we've recently instituted a creative intern training program that utilizes the best
people we can find from various colleges and universities. We intend to

grow our own. We're dedicated to making these people the best copy-writers and art directors that we can.

To do this, the organization doing the hiring must put in some time seeing that the trainees are indeed trained. It can be a strain on your senior people who will be doing the training. But time must be given to do the job properly, or the results can be less than satisfactory. This is most important because, in the end, talent is perhaps the most precious of the three ingredients.

Ingredient Number Three: Courage

Sometimes referred to as guts. The courage to pursue the unusual. The courage to take risks. The courage to fail. The courage to keep going when the prospects look the blackest. Because, without this courage, everything you've worked for can fall short. The only way we can hit the homerun is to have the courage to take a swing at the ball. Time, talent, courage. Make them prerequisites in your search for creative excellence.

ON SAYING "SO LONG"

The title of this book did not really come into being until the book was finished. Much like the "Introduction." As I was winding down this last chapter, the editor, Steve Kippur, said, "When you're finished, write the introduction." "But I've already written it," I whined. "Ah, but that was what the book was supposed to be about. Now rewrite it again about what the book is really about." And so I did. And as I wended my way through these 80,000 and some odd words, I found that there is nothing really usual about anything connected with the creative mystique. And that's what has made it so different, exciting, challenging, and re-warding for me and, I know, for many others. I hope that in reading this you've soaked up some ways to help creative people do their jobs better. Just remember, do it with care and sagacity. Don't try to make the un-usual usual. Because if you do, a lot of the magic can disappear.

In Chapter 5, on presentations, I said that the time to end is when you've made the sale, can do no more, or have nothing more to say. Which is right now.

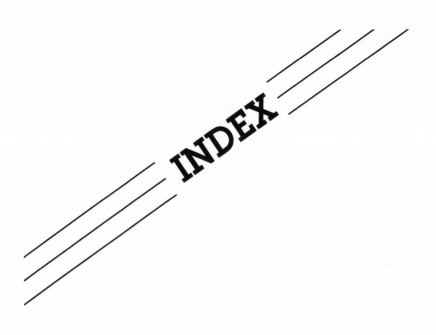